ONETTI
AND
OTHERS

SUNY series in Latin American and Iberian Thought and Culture
Jorge J. E. Gracia, editor

ONETTI AND OTHERS

Comparative Essays on a Major Figure in Latin American Literature

edited by

GUSTAVO SAN ROMÁN

State University
of New York
Press

Published by
State University of New York Press, Albany

© 1999 State University of New York

Production by Susan Geraghty
Marketing by Fran Keneston

Printed in the United States of America

For information, address State University of New York
Press, State University Plaza, Albany, N.Y., 12246

Library of Congress Cataloging-in-Publication Data

Onetti and others : comparative essays on a major figure in Latin
    American literature / edited by Gustavo San Román.
        p.   cm. — (SUNY series in Latin American and Iberian thought
    and culture)
    Includes bibliographical references and index.
    ISBN 0-7914-4235-7 (alk. paper). — ISBN 0-7914-4236-5 (pbk. :
    alk. paper)
    1. Onetti, Juan Carlos, 1909–1994—Criticism and interpretation.
    2. Latin American literature—20th century—History and criticism.
    I. San Román, Gustavo, 1956–   . II. Series.
    PQ8519.O59Z793 1999
    863—dc21   98-42362
                                                          CIP

10 9 8 7 6 5 4 3 2 1

For Glauco

CONTENTS

NOTES ON
CONTRIBUTORS

Steven Boldy is Lecturer in Latin American literature at the University of Cambridge. He has published on a range of Spanish American authors, including Carpentier, Rulfo, and Borges and is the author of *The novels of Julio Cortázar* (1980). His main research in recent years has been on Carlos Fuentes; apart from several articles on this author, he has published a critical edition of *Agua quemada* (1995).

Peter Bush works as a freelance literary translator and is Director of the British Centre for Literary Translation at the University of East Anglia, England. His recent translations include *The Marx Family Saga* (1996) by Juan Goytisolo and *The Voice of The Turtle: An Anthology of Cuban Short Stories* (1997). In 1995 he won a Best Translation of the Year Award from the American Literary Translators Association. He is currently directing a project on The Translator as Reader and Writer funded by the Ariane program of the European Union.

Linda Craig is Senior Lecturer in Spanish at the University of East London. Her main research interest is in the issues of marginality and gender in the works of Onetti, Manuel Puig, and Luisa Valenzuela. She is currently researching similar areas in the work of Rosario Ferré.

Sabine Giersberg is finishing a doctorate on "Sadness as an Existential and Aesthetic Category in the Work of J. C. Onetti" at the University of Mainz, where she teaches in the Department of Romance languages. She has published articles on Onetti and Clarice Lispector.

Paul Jordan lectures in the Department of Hispanic Studies at the University of Sheffield. His main research interest is in twentieth-century Argentinian literature and has published articles on Arlt, Cortázar, and Onetti.

Mark I. Millington holds the Chair of Latin American Studies at Nottingham University. His research is in the fields of twentieth-century

Spanish American narrative and cultural difference, with particular interest in the application of critical theories. He is author of *Reading Onetti: Language, Narrative, and the Subject* (1985) and *An Analysis of the Short Stories of J. C. Onetti: Fictions of Desire* (1993). He has published articles on García Márquez, Borges, Monterroso, Donoso, Gallegos, Carpentier, and Vargas Llosa.

María Rosa Olivera-Williams is Associate Professor at the Department of Romance Languages and Literatures of Notre Dame University. She is the author of *La poesía gauchesca: de Bartolomé Hidalgo a José Hernández* (1986) and has contributed to collective studies on Armonía Somers, Cristina Peri Rossi, José Emilio Pacheco, Juan Gelman, Mario Benedetti, and feminist criticism.

Hilary Owen is Lecturer in Portuguese at the University of Manchester. She has published several articles on women's writing in postrevolutionary Portugal and in modern and contemporary Brazil. She is the editor of *Gender, Ethnicity, and Class in Modern Portuguese-Speaking Culture* (1996).

Gustavo San Román lectures in the Department of Spanish at the University of St. Andrews, Scotland. His publications include articles on Horacio Quiroga and Cristina Peri Rossi, *Amor y nación. Ensayos sobre literatura uruguaya* (1997) and *"Paja Brava" de El Viejo Pancho e outras obras de José A. y Trelles* (1998).

Donald L. Shaw has taught at the Universities of Glasgow and Edinburgh, and is now Brown-Forman Professor of Spanish American Literature at the University of Virginia. His range of publications in modern Spanish and Spanish American literature is extensive, including, in the Spanish American area, books on Gallegos, Borges, Carpentier, and Skármeta, as well as his highly influential *Nueva narrativa hispanoamericana* (1981). His last book, *The Post-Boom in Spanish American Fiction* (1998), is in the present SUNY series.

Philip Swanson has taught at universities in Ireland, the United Kingdom, and the United States. He is now Professor of Hispanic Studies and Chairman of Department at the University of Aberdeen. He has published widely in the Latin American field, including books on Donoso and García Márquez, as well as the edited volume *Landmarks in Latin American Fiction* (1990). His latest book is *The New Novel in Latin America: Politics and Popular Culture after the Boom* (1995).

Peter Turton was until recently Senior Lecturer in the School of Languages and European Studies at the University of North London. He is the author of a book on José Martí (1986) as well as several articles on Onetti and a critical edition of *"Esbjerg en la costa" y otros cuentos* (1994).

BIBLIOGRAPHICAL NOTE

Whenever possible all references to Onetti's works in this volume are to his *Obras completas* ["Complete Works"] (Mexico: Aguilar, 1970), indicated as OC after the first quotation in each article. Otherwise they are to his *Cuentos completos* ["Complete Short Stories"] (Madrid: Alfaguara, 1993), indicated as CC on first occurrence, or to the following individual works not included in either of these collections: *Tiempo de abrazar* ["Time to Embrace"], ed. Jorge Ruffinelli (Montevideo: Arca, 1974); *Réquiem por Faulkner y otros artículos* ["Requiem for Faulkner and Other Articles"], ed. Jorge Ruffinelli (Buenos Aires: Calicanto, 1976); *Dejemos hablar al viento* [*Let the Wind Speak*] (Barcelona: Bruguera, 1985); *Cuando ja no imparte* [*Past Caring?*] (Madrid: Alfaguara, 1993). Within each chapter, all unambiguous page references are incorporated in the main text, and full bibliographical information is included in the Works Cited section at the end.

All Spanish or Portuguese titles of works by Onetti and other literary figures are followed in the first citation by a translation in square brackets. If a published English version exists, the title appears in italics (regardless of whether it is a short story or a longer work); for easier reference, the list of recent English translations of Onetti is included below. If there is no English version available, the title appears in inverted commas. In the case of works by authors being compared with Onetti, full details of the English version, if available, are given in the Works Cited in the relevant chapter; in the case of other works mentioned in passing for which a translation exists, the reader is directed to Jason Wilson, *An A to Z of Modern Latin American Literature in English Translation* (London: Institute of Latin American Studies, 1989) for full details. Unless otherwise indicated, all translations from the Spanish or Portuguese are by the author of the essay that contains them.

All quotations from Onetti are printed here with the kind permission of the estate of Juan Carlos Onetti. Copyright Juan Carlos Onetti and the Estate of Juan Carlos Onetti, 1970, 1974, 1976, 1985, 1993. Quotations from Cedric Watts' *A Preface to Conrad* (Longman, 1982) are reprinted by permission of Addison Wesley Longman, Ltd.

ENGLISH TRANSLATIONS OF ONETTI'S WORKS

Body Snatcher [*Juntacadáveres*]. Trans. Alfred MacAdam. London: Quartet, 1991.

A Brief Life [*La vida breve*]. Trans. Hortense Carpentier. New York: Grossman, 1976. London: Serpent's Tail, 1993.

Farewells and *A Grave with No Name* [*Los adioses* and *Para una tumba sin nombre*]. Trans. Peter Bush. London: Quartet, 1992.

Goodbyes and Stories. Trans. Daniel Balderston. Austin: Texas University Press, 1990. Contains *Los adioses* and the following stories: "A Dream Come True" ["Un sueño realizado"], "Esbjerg by the Sea" ["Esbjerg, en la costa"], "The House on the Sand" ["La casa en la arena"], "The Photograph Album" ["El álbum"], "Hell Most Feared" ["El infierno tan temido"], "The Image of Misfortune" ["La cara de la desgracia"], "Sad as She" ["Tan triste como ella"], "New Year's Eve" ["Justo el treintaiuno"], "The Stolen Bride" ["La novia robada"].

Let the Wind Speak [*Dejemos hablar al viento*]. Trans. Helen Lane. London: Serpent's Tail, 1996.

No Man's Land [*Tierra de nadie*]. Trans. Peter Bush. London: Quartet, 1994.

Past Caring? [*Cuando ya no importe*]. Trans. Peter Bush. London: Quartet, 1995.

The Pit and *Tonight* [*El pozo* and *Para esta noche*]. Trans. Peter Bush. London: Quartet, 1991.

The Shipyard [*El astillero*]. Trans. Rachel Caffyn. New York: Scribner's, 1968. Trans. Nick Caistor. London: Serpent's Tail, 1992.

"Welcome, Bob" ["Bienvenido, Bob"]. Trans. Donald L. Shaw. In *Spanish Short Stories 1*. Hardmonsworth, U.K.: Penguin, 1966: 83–101.

Introduction

Gustavo San Román

Juan Carlos Onetti was born in Montevideo in July 1909 and died in May 1994 in Madrid, where he had settled in 1975 after falling foul of the military regime that had taken over power in Uruguay two years previously. For many critics and fellow writers Onetti, like Jorge Luis Borges and Juan Rulfo, was one of the foundational figures upon whom Latin American fiction was to build the 1960s "Boom." This literary phenomenon made the world aware of magical realism and exciting new narrative techniques through now-established names such as Gabriel García Márquez, Carlos Fuentes, Julio Cortázar, and Mario Vargas Llosa. Onetti is widely perceived as a writer of difficult but strangely alluring prose, more for the initiated than for the many, which in the words of an acute English commentator exemplifies "something like a Conrad who had soaked himself in Beckett, or a Dashiel Hammett who had been reading Camus and Ionesco" (Wood, 20). This evaluation rightly points to the potential benefits of a comparative study of Onetti's work, a task undertaken in the present volume by a number of academics from British, German, and American universities.

Onetti's international reputation was slow to come, but it began to consolidate after the publication of the Italian translation of his best-known novel *El astillero* [*The Shipyard*] (1961), which won a prestigious prize in 1974. His fame was crowned in the Spanish-speaking world in 1980 when he received the Cervantes prize from the king of Spain, after two older fellow Latin Americans, Alejo Carpentier (1977) and Borges (1979), and before younger writers such as Octavio Paz (1981), Ernesto Sábato (1984), and Carlos Fuentes (1987). Like Borges, but unlike Paz, however—or García Márquez and the Spaniard Camilo José Cela, winner of the 1995 Cervantes Prize—Onetti was overlooked by the Swedish Academy, who thereby missed the opportunity of making his small country the target of the egalitarian impulse that seems to have influenced their choices over the past few years. In some ways, this comparative volume is a tribute in compensation for that relative lack of international recognition during Onetti's lifetime.

This last statement needs some qualification, however, since Onetti has in fact recently received a good deal of attention. The 1990s have seen a strong wave of interest in Onetti by publishers, academics, and the media. His books have been reissued in Spain or the River Plate and his last novel, *Cuando ya no importe* [*Past Caring?*], published in March 1993, went out of print within two weeks and by the end of 1996 was running in its fifth issue, having sold fourteen thousand copies; a similar fate has befallen his complete short stories, *Cuentos completos* (1994). A collection of Onetti's newspaper articles (*Confesiones de un lector* ["Confessions of a Reader"]) and a homage volume that contains paintings by Uruguayan artists (*Miradas sobre Onetti*) came out in 1995. A volume of Onetti's shorter fiction for the international Colección Archivos of critical editions is under way. English translations of most of his works have recently been produced or reissued (see list under bibliographical note). Television and film have also become involved, with two interviews of the writer in his bed carried out in 1989, one by Uruguayans (*Onetti, retrato de un escritor*) and a second, lasting three hours, by a Spanish team led by Ramón Chao for French television (published in book form in French in 1990 and in Spanish in 1994). Onetti plays an important mythical role in the film *El dirigible* (1994), whose footage includes images of him, while his story "Bienvenido, Bob" [*Welcome, Bob*] was the basis for an experimental video (*Las trampas de Onetti*, 1994). An illuminating early interview on film, which for reasons of political uncertainty could not be shown at the time, *Juan Carlos Onetti, un escritor* (1972–73), was released in Uruguay in 1996 (see Manuel Martínez Carril, "Onetti y el cine," in *Miradas sobre Onetti*, 22–23); the first biography of Onetti, by María Esther Gilio and Carlos María Domínguez, came out in 1993; also that year, a special issue of the Montevideo *El País Cultural* was devoted to him. Academic studies in the last few years include two collections of essays in Spanish (*Onetti: papeles críticos*, 1989; *La obra de Juan Carlos Onetti*, 1990), Mattalia's monograph (1990) and her critical edition of *La vida breve* [*A Brief Life*] (1994), books by Elena M. Martínez (1992) and by Maryse Renaud (1993–94), the proceedings of the international conference that took place in Montevideo in April 1994, shortly before Onetti's death (1997) and, in English, Mark Millington's second book on Onetti (1993), Peter Turton's critical edition of four short stories (1994), and Judy Maloof's feminist study (1995).

The present volume appears therefore in a context of heightened interest in the work and personality of Onetti. Most of the articles are a selection of revised papers from a conference held at St. Andrews University, Scotland, in July 1995, the first international gathering since the author's death and the first to take place in an English-speaking setting. The goal of *Onetti and Others* is the placing of Onetti's work on the map of twentieth-century literature by examining its relations with a number of other authors in Latin America and beyond. Unlike fellow writers such as Donoso (*Historia personal del "boom"* [*The Boom in Spanish American Literature: A Personal History*], 1972) or Fuentes (*Myself with Others*, 1988), who wrote their literary memoirs, Onetti, though often outspoken about writers he admired, only expressed his opinions on his peers rather playfully in interviews or in a number of short pieces for newspapers (gathered in *Réquiem por Faulkner y otros artículos* ["Requiem for Faulkner and Other Articles"] and in *Confesiones de un lector*). The very relevant task of searching for his intertextual links in any depth he left for others to do, and hence this volume.

Although inevitably not all obvious areas of comparison had takers (notably, there are no pieces on Faulkner or Céline), the essays reflect current interests and a range of critical perspectives. They also explore a wide sample of Onetti's production. Most of the studies represent synchronic comparisons, that is, ones between Onetti and a roughly contemporary figure; the aim in these cases is to explore Onetti's views on issues also facing other writers. These essays tend to highlight differences rather than similarities, and this is most evident in the case of the three contributions that compare Onetti with a woman writer. The main areas of contrast in this case are found to be in the characterization of males and females, including notions and ideals of sexuality, and in certain rhetorical features. Gender is also a significant arena of comparison in some of the essays on Onetti and another male writer, which reflect current interest in masculinity studies. Other pieces move more explicitly along the diachronic axis of comparative literature and by referring to earlier texts touch on a traditional concern in the discipline, namely influence. The articles have been arranged along geographical lines, starting with Latin America in general (the literature of the 1940s, Donoso, Fuentes), then moving toward Onetti's home territory of the River Plate (Borges, Roberto Arlt, Felisberto Hernández, Armonía Somers, Luisa Valenzuela) and taking one writer from Brazil (Clarice Lispector), and eventually opening up onto Western culture more generally in comparisons with Conrad and Ecclesiastes and in a discussion of the task of translating Onetti into English.

The first essay, by Donald L. Shaw, places Onetti in the context of the progress of Latin American fiction in the twentieth century, where he played a crucial part in the innovations that led to the Boom. Shaw suggests that the importance of Onetti in relation to the 1940s is not connected to the rise of the "urban" novel, as has been claimed, since that phenomenon had already begun by then; he proposes, moreover, that the time scale of the Boom must be adjusted to show that the movement began in the 1950s, with its gestation involving the previous decade. The 1930s and 1940s were completely different in their contribution to the onward development of Spanish American fiction. Failure to perceive this difference, in terms of a radical shift of outlook from one decade to the other, argues Shaw, is what makes a writer such as Mario Benedetti, for example, a contemporary of Onetti's and a fellow Montevidean, an essentially less important novelist. Despite the unwillingness of some early commentators, recent critics have recognized that the 1940s brought a radical change in the relationship of fiction to reality. In this light it is possible to see Onetti's *La vida breve* [*A Brief Life*] (1950) as the inaugural novel of the Boom.

There follow two essays that compare Onetti with established figures from the Boom. Steven Boldy's essay focuses on the first full-length fiction by Onetti, *Tierra de nadie* [*No Man's Land*] (1941) and the first novel of the Mexican Carlos Fuentes, *La región más transparente* [*Where the Air Is Clear*] (1958), which, he finds, share some basic thematic concerns but differ in style and scope. Both are landmark narratives on a capital city and a country, and each displays the influence of John Dos Passos and especially his 1925 novel *Manhattan Transfer*. In both works there is a deep interest in questions of national identity, which reflects the contemporary debates in each country at the time of their conception. But whereas Onetti's novel tends toward timelessness, meaningless dispersal, a uniform drabness of human nature, and a bracketing off of any transcendence, that of Fuentes works by building up layers, confronting different voices, and outlining significant historical patterns from generation to generation. The characters Diego Aránzuru and Ixca Cienfuegos represent the authors' different attitudes toward narration and meaning. Boldy finds Onetti's novel, though dialogic and ambiguous, uninterested in history in the way that Fuentes' texts are, which makes the two writers complex in different ways.

Philip Swanson's "Onetti and Donoso: Heroes and Whores in *Juntacadáveres* and *El lugar sin límites*" considers two novels that center around brothels and brothel owners seen in relation to the power structures of small-town rural communities. Linking up with the general phenomenon of the Latin American "new novel," both works can be perceived as deconstructing the classic motifs of traditional realist fiction: the family as social nucleus, the family home, and the vocational hero give way to unconventional relationships, the brothel, and the inversion of the ideal of personal growth. Within this general scheme, the pattern of correspondences is nevertheless subtle and ambiguous. Effectively, Onetti and Donoso highlight some of the differences and points of contact between a modernist consciousness and a postmodern consciousness. The relationship of the male hero to whores is particularly revealing. There is, in Onetti, something of a sense of male identity, the existence of a species of vocational (even, at times, utopian) ideal, a clear sense of social hierarchy and, behind the apparent multiplicity of voices, a spirit of disinterested observation and possibly a cohesive and unitary narrative viewpoint. In Donoso, on the other hand, the question of masculine identity, the vocational ideal, and the notion of society is much more fundamentally problematic and the narrative focus more displaced. Swanson concludes that *Juntacadáveres* [*Body Snatcher*] (1964) illustrates a moment of transition between the modernist and postmodern sense of self, the latter being firmly represented in Donoso's 1966 novel [*Hell Has No Limits*].

Moving toward Onetti's own home territory and beginning with his first adoptive land, Argentina, the study by Mark Millington compares a story by the Uruguayan, "Jacob y el otro" ["Jacob and the Other"] (1961) with one by Borges, "La casa de Asterión" [*The House of Asterion*] (1949). "Otherwise, or Reading Onetti with Borges" studies how the male subject relates to others: how his own identity is shaped by confrontation, submission, or negotiation in relation to an other. The argument builds on an account of an unsuccessful meeting between Onetti and Borges in a Buenos Aires bar in the summer of 1948–49, as related by Emir Rodríguez Monegal. The account makes use of fighting metaphors that are significant for the discussion of the texts chosen for analysis, which are both about hostile encounters. A crucial element in both stories is space, the house in Borges' text and the wrestling ring in Onetti's, both of which function as borders of the self. It turns out that neither space is impervious to outside influence, as both locations are regularly visited by others who challenge the status of the protagonists but on whose arrival the subject's own identity depends. The interaction between self and other is fundamental to the status of each; thus, Theseus gains an identity as the killer of Asterión, who in turn becomes the Minotaur by being destroyed. Similarly, Jacob's ever-fragile self depends on the availability of others who are willing to challenge him, as well as on his defeating them. In returning to the encounter between the two writers, it is noted that although their skirmish did not end in open confrontation, it served to consolidate each writer's status at the time: Onetti stands for the challenger who is isolated as his taunt is not taken up by Borges, a superior figure in the contemporary literary world of Buenos Aires.

Rodríguez Monegal concludes his account of the meeting between

Onetti and Borges by suggesting that on that occasion Onetti was impersonating Roberto Arlt, the aggressive writer of the urban underworld of Buenos Aires, whose semblance was so different from the aristocratic intellectual image that was often attached to Borges, and that made the two writers paradigmatic representatives of the Boedo-Florida polarity in contemporary Argentinian literature. It is fitting, therefore, that the next essay should explore the relations between Onetti and one of his self-confessed mentors. In one of the three diachronic studies of Onetti and a predecessor in this collection, Paul Jordan's study brings in Arlt. In what is partly (and appropriately, given Onetti's interest in the genre) detective work, Jordan proposes and explores a connection between Arlt's last novel, *El amor brujo* ["Love the Magician"] (1932) and Onetti's first, *Tiempo de abrazar* ["Time to Embrace"], which was written in 1933, but was then lost, a reconstructed and incomplete version finally being published in 1974. The essay takes as a starting point a prologue written by Onetti for a 1971 Italian edition of Arlt's best-known novel, *Los siete locos* ["The Seven Madmen"]. In the prologue Onetti mentions most of Arlt's major works, yet, while the point that Arlt read *Tiempo de abrazar* in 1934 is put quite emphatically, there is, strangely, no reference to its near contemporary, *El amor brujo*. Jordan argues that *Tiempo de abrazar* represents a moment of escapism in Onetti's early development: it appears to be the product of a reaction against the extremely pessimistic social, sexual, and political vision expounded in this least known but most starkly coherent of Arlt's major narrative works. However, the adventure fails, and the end of the novel brings in a reconciliation with Arlt's vision, preparing the way for Onetti's first major work, *El pozo* [*The Pit*] (1939), where idealism is condemned by a disillusioned and pessimistic protagonist who is typical of Onettian fiction thereafter.

Crossing over the River Plate into Onetti's native land, the essay by Gustavo San Román explores the connection between the great Uruguayan writer and one of his most highly regarded literary contemporaries, Felisberto Hernández. The work of the two men has some common qualities, notably a dense and ambiguous prose, but the essay focuses on a difference in "the authority behind their narratives," and considers two texts written within a few months of each other, *Para una tumba sin nombre* [*A Grave with No Name*] (1959) and *La casa inundada* [*The Flooded House*] (1960). The argument builds on the different treatment that each author gives to characters on account of their body weight: Onetti likes thin figures while Hernández is partial to fat ones. Relatedly, Onetti twice makes rather intriguing reference to Hernández's own body size in a short piece he wrote from his Spanish exile. The two observations are used to explain differences in writing practice through consideration of the role of the narrative voice and the presence of food in each text. It is proposed that Onetti tends toward "thin" discourse, where there is a strong narrator and a fairly firm narrative line, while Hernández is inclined to "fat" writing, with a slack control over the plot that corresponds to the dependency of the narrative voice on other characters and circumstances beyond his control. These findings are related to the critical reception of the two writers in Uruguay, and to the image that each provided in terms of contemporary notions of masculinity.

In the first of three essays which compare Onetti with women writers, María Rosa Olivera-Williams introduces a close contemporary of Onetti, Armonía Somers. As in the case of other fellow Uruguayan female writers (such as Delmira Agustini, Juana de Ibarbourou, Idea Vilariño, and Sylvia Lago), behind the respectable figure of the real-life author there lies in the literary persona of Armonía Somers, a powerful subverter of bourgeois values. The area of interest in Olivera-Williams' study of two short stories, Onetti's "La cara de la desgracia" [*The Image of Misfortune*] (1960) and Somers' "El hombre del túnel" ["The Man in the Tunnel"] (1963) is the manner in which sexuality and writing create a more palatable world and a more fulfilled self. Each narrator posits an image of femininity and masculinity according to his or her own desires, and the implications in each case both reflect and amend social expectations. The outcome of the analysis is the confrontation of two closely gendered forms of writing: "we can say that the masculine rhetoric of Onetti inserts him into the cultural system, whereas the feminine rhetoric of Somers places her on its margins." Thus, in the case of Onetti, fiction allows him to create a story of lost love and innocence in the face of an unjust and godless world while remaining in the realm of realism; the route for Somers, on the other hand, is the fantastic.

The second study to bring in a woman to contrast Onetti's vision of sexuality is Linda Craig's comparison of *Juntacadáveres* and the Argentinian Luisa Valenzuela's *Hay que sonreír* [*Clara*] (1966). The theme, as in Swanson's essay, is prostitution, and this time the author draws both on the historical and cultural background behind the texts as well as on Luce Irigaray's ideas on *écriture féminine*. The essay points out the importance of Christian thought in the construction of gender roles and then traces the way in which Onetti's text is shaped by historical forces, while Valenzuela's seems to represent the beginnings of an alternative sensibility. *Juntacadáveres* contains a depiction of a hierarchy of the human race that places Larsen above the prostitutes, the corpses of the title. *Hay que sonreír*, by contrast, starts from the perspective of the prostitute as a protagonist who apparently rises in society from her humble beginnings to become the wife of a middle-class man. In spite of their similar themes, the novels differ in their conception of a hierarchy and in their perception of woman: Onetti's system is rigid while Valenzuela's is flexible, since her protagonist shifts within it. However, this versatility is of limited value to her since she actually remains trapped within the cultural interpretations of woman that surround her. While Onetti's text depicts the negative, Christian view of woman as given, Valenzuela's more ambiguous treatment brings to light the contradictions implicit in such a construct.

The third contribution to place Onetti against a woman author, by Hilary Owen, introduces a Brazilian perspective through the work of Clarice Lispector, whose "A partida do trem" ["The Departure of the Train"] (1974) is compared with "Bienvenido, Bob" (1940). The essay uses the French feminist theories of Hélène Cixous to compare the textual encoding of gender and sexuality in the two texts. Drawing on Cixous' concept of "bisexuality" in writing, Owen focuses on the two stories' references to music, sensation, sound, the body, and mortality, as well as on the tropes of negation, fragmentation, repetition, ellipsis, and nonlinearity. It is shown that while Lispector exemplifies the French critic's concept of écriture féminine in her challenge of logic and celebration of sensual variety, Onetti's textual practices conversely operate within Cixous' model of a masculine libidinal economy where differences are turned into sameness.

The intertextual focus then shifts to an English-language author whom Onetti highly respected: Joseph Conrad. In the clearest study of influence in this collection, Peter Turton is inspired by the coincidence of name and function between Conrad's Stein in Lord Jim (1900) and Onetti's Julio Stein in La vida breve (1950). The latter exercises the same role toward Brausen, La vida breve's protagonist, as does Conrad's Stein toward Jim, that is, he plays the role of a benevolent and skeptical worldly-wise father figure; but whereas Conrad displays great skill in handling his material to achieve an aesthetically satisfying work, Turton proposes that Onetti ends up by botching the last part of a very fine novel. This is because the solutions that Brausen hits upon for his salvation are not really credible in terms of what Brausen is, or at least have been presented too crudely to function as an integral part of the novel. Conrad saw Jim clearly from the start, while Onetti saw Brausen and then tried to turn him into an anti-Brausen. The true trajectory of the Onettian protagonist is in fact more Conradian, appears after La vida breve, in particular in El astillero [The Shipyard] (1961), and is more closely embraced by failure.

The final two essays open up the intertextual links of Onetti to the widest range in the collection: the first brings in a major source in Western culture that Onetti acknowledged as one of his most fundamental sources, Ecclesiastes; the second considers the problematic question of translation from other languages into English in general and focuses specifically on the case of Onetti. In her essay, Sabine Giersberg pursues the pessimism expressed both by Onetti and the various mouthpieces in his fiction and explores the connections with the Old Testament text. The links found are both thematic and formal. Thus, the extreme despair expressed in Onetti is traced back to that ancient source, and account is taken of existentialism in Heidegger's version. But the connections are also formal: the tendency in Onetti's characters toward depersonalization and failure to progress toward goals, which is an aspect of the exposition on the futility of life in Ecclesiastes, is linked to his plots' refusal to engage in linearity or mimesis, as illustrated in the circularity of "La casa en la arena" [*The House on the Sand*] (1949) or in Larsen's reflections on fate in *El astillero*. The most powerful link between Onetti and his most ancient source is an unwillingness to engage in a conceptualization of human experience, choosing instead a poetic path. Unlike Ecclesiastes, however, which also suggests that life should be used energetically while its powers remain, Onetti remains abjectly pessimistic.

Closing the volume is an iconoclastic and stylistically refreshing contribution: "Translating Onetti for Anglo-Saxon Others," by Peter Bush, who has so far rendered six of Onetti's texts into English. The essay begins by questioning the received wisdom on the status and function of translation, and does so by drawing both on recent debates and on Bush's own considerable experience in the area. Literary translation, it is proposed, challenges common-sense ideas about the status of English and is central to the formation of a canon that wishes to promote the hybridity of culture. New theorists have opted for the baroque and the oblique and focused on the foreignizing as opposed to the assimilationist potential within the practice of translation. Bearing in mind in particular the case of *Cuando ya no importe* [*Past Caring?*], translation is seen as a crucial stage in the creation of a new culture of reading and writing and the agency of the literary translator as one key element in a series of complex interactions, both human and cultural. The essay's last two sentences express a desideratum applicable to the new comparative studies, and the editor would like to make it part of the goal of this collection.

How does Onetti emerge from this volume? What traits has the interplay with others confirmed or discovered? It is fair to say that he has not been given an easy ride, since no essay engages in mere celebration. It is also clear, however, that Onetti's place as a distinguished figure in the development of Latin American writing appears confirmed by the studies that consider his work in the light of writers who followed:

according to Shaw, Onetti wrote the first novel of the Boom; in Swanson's view, his work marked the transition to postmodernism; for Boldy, his concentration on the visions and existences of small-time characters ranks in significance with the erudite and history-conscious *tours de force* of the younger Fuentes. The studies that consider Onetti and an admired predecessor, for their part, appear to point to what—adapting Harold Bloom's model for poetry according to which "weaker talents idealize; figures of capable imagination appropriate for themselves" (Bloom, 5)—we might call a "strong" Onetti, since he both let it be known who his masters were and refused simply to be a follower. Even though Turton concludes that Onetti's achievements in *La vida breve* do not quite live up to Conrad's in *Lord Jim*, this criticism is inspired only by that novel's ending, and the critic proposes that in later works Onetti masterfully adapts Conradian techniques. A parallel evaluation emerges from the comparison with Ecclesiastes, since Onetti seems to have "misread" that text for his own purposes, disregarding the optimistic side of the ancient source. As for Onetti's relationship with his admired Arlt, according to the case made by Jordan, it is similarly one of learning while distancing on the part of the younger writer.

A more guarded assessment can be perceived at first in the comparisons with women writers, both on the grounds of Onetti's representations of female characters and of what was seen by some early criticism as his depiction of universal human concerns. It is proposed instead that such a perspective should more properly be seen as shaped by the contingent specificities of history, culture, and a privileged gender. And yet, it is precisely in the process of placing Onetti in his circumstances that his worth as a writer also comes through. Owen suggests that his masculine discourse, though on the surface powerful and self-sufficient (a view consistent with San Román's findings in his own paper), can also be shown to display typical signs of repression when confronted with the semantic possibilities of Lispector's "bisexual" discourse. For her part and while critical of the culture that lay behind Onetti's view of men and women, Linda Craig considers Onetti's honest portrayal of prostitution and gender roles one of his strengths. Moreover, in the third essay on the interplay between a woman author and Onetti, Olivera-Williams notes that cultural pressures affect him as much as his contemporary fellow writer Armonía Somers, and although in some ways these pressures are more favorable to him as a man, "a strong current of social criticism" nevertheless occurs in his work. Onetti's historical location also helps relativize his position vis-à-vis fellow male writers, as becomes apparent when he is placed before an insecure compatriot of his, Felisberto Hernández, and a more senior and established figure in contemporary Buenos Aires, Borges.

The result of both the interplay with others and the variety of approaches taken by the essays in this collection, then, provides a complex and more refined picture of Onetti, albeit one inevitably tinged by current interests and expectations. The impression that Onetti comes through such a multifarious inspection as a worthy and enduring figure received a most pertinent signal of confirmation at the colloquium that originated these papers. Peter Bush asked in his paper whether a reader of *Cuando ya no importe* in Montevideo could not engage in meaningful discussion with a reader of its English translation, *Past Caring?*, in Edinburgh. An eloquent if indirect answer was given afterwards when at the launch of *Past Caring?* the young Scottish author Alan Warner spoke both of his upbringing in rural West Scotland, where he felt particularly isolated as a would-be writer, and of the profound effect and lasting influence that reading Onetti had had on his work (see Warner, "Reign in Spain"). (For a first attempt at a comparison between the two authors, see San Román, "Alan Warner, el Onetti escocés"). It is fitting that Warner—who has published his second and third novels to high acclaim since that speech—should be part of what has been described by Alan Taylor in a recent issue of *New Yorker* as the current "efflorescence" in Scottish literature, a situation that might one day be compared with the Latin American Boom.

The editor is grateful to all contributors for taking up so enthusiastically the idea of writing on *Onetti and Others* and for making the original conference a success. Thanks are also due to Dolly Muhr de Onetti for her communication to the colloquium (later published, although without an explanation of its original motivation, in *Miradas sobre Onetti*, 65–69) and for supplying a suitable photograph of Juan for the book's cover. Phil Swanson, Mark Millington, and Nigel Dennis provided editorial advice; Peter Beardsell supported an application for conference funds; Robert Crawford supplied a useful reference; Iain Stewart helped with the organization of the conference and the editing of the papers, and he translated two of the articles from Spanish. Support was also provided by the Research Committee of the School of Modern Languages from St Andrews University. Many thanks to them all.

WORKS CITED

Actas de las Jornadas de Homenaje a Juan Carlos Onetti. Ed. Sylvia Lago et al. Montevideo: Universidad de la República, 1997.
Bloom, Harold. *The Anxiety of Influence*. New York: Oxford UP, 1973.
Chao, Ramón. *Onetti*. Paris: Plon, 1990.
Chao, Ramón. *Un posible Onetti*. Barcelona: Ronsel, 1994.
El dirigible. Uruguay 1994. Film. Dir. Pablo Dotta.

Donoso, José. *Historia personal del boom*. Madrid: Anagrama, 1972. (*The Boom in Spanish American Literature: A Personal History*. Trans. Gregory Kolovakos. New York: Columbia UP, 1977.)

Fuentes, Carlos. *Myself with Others*. London: André Deutsch, 1988.

Gilio, Esther María and Carlos María Domínguez. *Construcción de la noche. Una biografía de Juan Carlos Onetti*. Buenos Aires: Planeta, 1993.

Juan Carlos Onetti, un escritor. Uruguay 1972–73. Film. Dir. Julio Jaimes.

Maloof, Judy. *Over Her Dead Body*. Bern: Peter Lang, 1995.

Martínez, Elena M. *Onetti: estrategias textuales y operaciones del lector*. Madrid: Verbum, 1992.

Mattalia, Sonia. *La figura en el tapiz*. London: Támesis, 1990.

Millington, Mark I. *An Analysis of the Short Stories of Juan Carlos Onetti: Fictions of Desire*. Lewiston, N.Y.: Edwin Mellen Press, 1993.

Miradas sobre Onetti. Ed. Omar Prego Gadea. Montevideo: Alfaguara, 1995.

La obra de Juan Carlos Onetti. Madrid: Fundamentos, 1990. (Proceedings of an international conference held at Poitiers University.)

Onetti, Juan Carlos. *Confesiones de un lector*. Madrid, Alfaguara: 1995.

Onetti, Juan Carlos. *Cuando ya no importe*. Madrid: Alfaguara, 1993.

Onetti, Juan Carlos. *Cuentos completos*. Madrid: Alfaguara, 1993.

Onetti, Juan Carlos. *"Esbjerg, en la costa" y otros cuentos*. Ed. Peter Turton. Manchester: Manchester UP, 1994.

Onetti, Juan Carlos. *Réquiem por Faulkner y otros artículos*. Ed. Jorge Ruffinelli. Buenos Aires: Calicanto, 1976.

Onetti, Juan Carlos. *La vida breve*. Ed. Sonia Mattalia. Madrid: Anaya and Mario Muchnick, 1994.

Onetti: papeles críticos. Ed. Rómulo Cosse. Montevideo: Linardi y Risso, 1989.

Onetti, retrato de un escritor. Uruguay 1990. Film. Dir. Juan José Mugni.

El País Cultural (Montevideo) 4.177 (26 March 1993). Special issue on Onetti.

Renaud, Maryse. *Hacia una búsqueda de la identidad*. 2 vols. Montevideo: Proyección, 1993, 1994.

San Román, Gustavo. "Alan Warner: El Onetti escocés." *Posdata* (Montevideo) 153 (22 August 1997): 73–82; shorter bilingual Internet version: *Barcelona Review* 5 (February/March 1998), http://www.web-show.com/Barcelona/Review.

Taylor, Alan. "Scottish Efflorescence." *New Yorker*, Special fiction issue, 25 December 1995 / 1 January 1996: 97.

Las trampas de Onetti. Uruguay 1994. Film. Dir. Hermes Millán Redin.

"Trois jours avec Onetti." Interview by Ramón Chao on French television program *Océanique*, FR3, 1989.

Warner, Alan. "Reign in Spain." (Review of *Past Caring?*) *The Scotsman* (Edinburgh), 29 July 1995: 16.

Wood, Michael. "A Faint Sound of Rust." *The London Review of Books*, 21 October 1993: 20–21.

1

Onetti and the 1940s

Donald L. Shaw

It is possible to argue that the principal dates in modern Spanish American fiction are 1926, 1950, and 1975. The year 1926 saw the peak of the regionalist novel, with Güiraldes's *Don Segundo Sombra* [*Don Segundo Sombra: Shadows on the Pampa*]; but it also saw the publication of Arlt's *El juguete rabioso* ["The Rabid Toy"], which heralded radical changes in the future Spanish American novel. Mention of Arlt is by no means irrelevant in a paper on Onetti, as we know from the many references to him in the latter's work and as we can see from the interview that he gave to Ruffinelli in the 1970s, reproduced in Reina Roffé's *Espejo de escritores*. In that interview Ruffinelli flatteringly attempted to suggest that *El pozo* [*The Pit*], which did not come out until 1939, "instaura o ayuda a instaurar una literatura urbana" ["establishes or helps to establish an urban literature"] (30). Sadly, despite his familiarity with the work of Arlt, Onetti accepted the flattery. But it is without foundation. The important inaugural writer of modern urban literature in the River Plate region is Arlt, not Onetti. To attempt to situate the latter vis-à-vis the 1940s by following Ruffinelli's suggestion would be to set off in the wrong direction. If we need additional proof, we need only recall that Dickman's *Madre América* ["Mother America"] came out in 1935, four years before *El pozo*, and that Mallea's *La ciudad junto al río inmóvil* ["The City by the Stationary River"] was published in the following year.

The second date, 1950, is that of Onetti's *La vida breve* [*A Brief Life*], which, in a recent article, I attempted to argue was the first full-fledged Boom novel. I do not wish to go into the argument afresh, but merely to reemphasize the central affirmation. The Boom novel may well have reached its apogee in the 1960s. But to suggest that the Boom *began* with the 1960s is, in my view, misguided. Not only does it overlook the watershed represented by *La vida breve*, but it propagates a periodization of the Boom that excludes major works that clearly belong to the movement, not only by Onetti, but also by Rulfo, Sábato, Marechal, and Carpentier. Not only for the sake of Onetti, but also in the interests of a sensible methodology, we should be wise to resist restrictive chronologies of the Boom. This is not to forget the fact, of course, that Onetti, on occasion, insisted that he had nothing to do with that movement.[1]

The third date, 1975, is the one sometimes thought to mark the approximate end of the Boom's real creative period and to indicate the time, give or take a year or two, when the Postboom begins to take shape. I have argued that a suitable choice for an inaugural novel of the Postboom is Skármeta's *Soñé que la nieve ardía* [*I Dreamt the Snow was Burning*] published in 1975 itself.[2]

Retracing our steps, we notice, of course, that 1926 did not mark the end of the regionalist novel, which scored a last major success in 1929 with Gallegos's *Doña Bárbara* [*Doña Bárbara*]. Two decades, in other words, separate the peak, and hence the subsequent decline, of regionalism, from the advent of the Boom. But they were two very different decades, so far as Spanish American fiction is concerned. The 1930s was a decade that is not likely to be reevaluated by future critics or historians of the novel in Spanish America. After the twenties, which saw Rivera's *La vorágine* [*The Vortex*] as well as *Don Segundo Sombra* and *Doña Bárbara*, it represents a trough in which the novel largely marked time, or moved in directions that with hindsight we can see as dead-ends. I refer, of course, to the old-style novel of protest, such as Gallegos's *Pobre negro* ["Poor Negro"] in 1937, the old-style indigenist novel, such as Icaza's *Huasipungo* [*Huasipungo*] in 1934 or Ciro Alegría's *Los perros hambrientos* ["The Hungry Dogs"] (1938) and the now almost forgotten anti-imperialist novel represented by works such as *Canal Zone* ["Canal Zone"] by Aguilera Malta (1935) or *Mancha de aceite* ["Oil Slick"] by Uribe Piedrahita, published in the same year.

To be sure, there were faint signs of regeneration in the 1930s, such as are visible in Asturias's *Leyendas de Guatemala* ["Guatemalan Legends"] in 1930 and Carpentier's *Ecué-Yamba-O* ["Ecué-Yamba-O"] (1933) as well as failed attempts which nonetheless have historical significance, such as Azuela's *La luciérnaga* [*The Firefly*] in 1932, with its premature attempt to illustrate the idea of the novel as an "hazaña verbal" ["a verbal exploit"]. There were a very small number of individual novels of real merit, such as Vallejo's *El tungsteno* [*Tungsten: A Novel*] in 1931 or María Luisa Bombal's *La última niebla* [*The House of Mist*] in 1935, but generally speaking the 1930s was a negative decade for fiction in Spanish America.

Not so the 1940s. This was the crucial decade of the century. It is astonishing that no one has written a book on Spanish American fiction in the 1940s. It is the great unwritten work in the field. For if fiction in the 1930s marked time, in the 1940s it underwent the change that was to give birth to the Boom. One way to see this rather clearly is to glance at the work of writers who failed to recognize or who rejected what was happening in the 1940s and as a consequence never became part of the Boom. An example is Onetti's fellow Uruguayan Mario Benedetti. Of him Elsa Dehennin writes: "Benedetti se sitúa en la corriente (*mainstream* dicen los ingleses) del realismo. No cuestiona la mimesis. . . . No hay experimentación ni juego discursivo" ["Benedetti situates himself in the current (*mainstream*, the English call it) of realism. He does not question mimesis. . . . There is no experimentation or discursive play"].[3] In his essay, "Subdesarrollo y letras de osadía" later included in *El escritor latinoamericano y la revolución posible* (1974) and more especially in a speech in Caracas in 1977,[4] Benedetti criticized certain unnamed Boom writers for what he called their "horror a la realidad circundante" ["horror of the surounding reality"] (7) and their total unrepresentativeness of average people in Spanish America. He went on to attack the idea of the novel as a verbal artifact, declaring that: "la palabra no existe, como quieren algunos ideólogos de la derecha, para ser el protagonista de la nueva narrativa latinoamericana. No, el protagonista sigue y seguirá siendo el hombre; la palabra su instrumento" ["the word does not exist, as some right-wing ideologues would have it, to be the protagonist of the new Latin American narrative. No, the protagonist remains and will remain man; the word his instrument"] (11). This is not to imply ignorance of the fact that Onetti himself makes a very similar remark in "La literatura: ida y vuelta" ["Literature: There and Back"] (see note 1 below) or that in the same essay he complained about the "absurdo abuso de las técnicas" ["the absurd abuse of techniques"] that he recognized in some Boom novels, and the danger that it could lead to lack of communication with the readers (202 and 199). But, apart from the fact that the notion of the novel as an "hazaña verbal" was coined by Miguel Ángel Asturias, and not by a right-wing ideologue, it is clear that Benedetti's stance is quite closely related to that of the regionalists in the 1920s and to that of the anti-imperialist novelists of the 1930s.

As we are all aware, especially after Carlos Alonso's *The Spanish American Regionalist Novel*, the writers in the '20s and '30s who belonged to these categories had a double imperative. On the one hand they sought a "cultural essence" in Spanish America, which they saw as being overtaken in the early twentieth century by a kind of crisis; on the other hand they tried to use fictional works as ideological weapons that at the least could raise the threshold of national and social consciousness in their readers, and at the most could actually speed up the process of social change. Plainly to embrace such civic and ethnocentric priorities is likely to involve, as was actually the case, a tendency to exploit the directly referential function of language. Conversely, when in the 1940s a quite different conception of the role of fiction began to prevail, with different priorities, any simple one-to-one vision of the relation of signifier to signified is called into question and language assumes a new importance. This shift in the conception of the novelist's task that took place in the 1940s is encapsulated between *El pozo* in 1939, which already revealed awareness of the obsolescence of the older pattern of fiction, and *La vida breve* in 1950, which consecrates the new direction. Ruffinelli reminds us that "En 1939 la narrativa uruguaya padecía aún las rémoras del nativismo" ["In 1939 Uruguayan narrative was still suffering from the drawback of nativism"].[5] There, as in the rest of Spanish America, the need to begin the modernization of the novel was already beginning to be apparent. Benedetti refused to acknowledge the change, regarding it as a sellout to cultural imperialism. To that extent, he and Onetti stand at opposite extremes. In other words, one of the best ways to see Onetti in relation to the 1940s is to contrast him with a contemporary novelist from his own country whose ideology prevented him from perceiving what was happening.

It is perhaps worth mentioning in passing that the misconception about what was actually taking place in the 1940s persisted for many years and is not wholly absent from contemporary criticism. In 1968, for example, those present at the Third Congress of the International Association of Hispanists heard Paul Verdevoye still insisting that the core element of Boom writings was "íntimamente relacionado con la búsqueda del ser nacional y la interpretación del individuo como miembro de la sociedad" ["intimately related to the search for the national soul and the interpretation of the individual as a member of society"], as if nothing had changed in the content of Spanish American fiction since the regionalist period. Rodríguez Monegal, on the other hand, put forward an approach, which is now almost universally accepted, according to which the fundamental contribution of the 1940s to fiction was precisely the notion of the novel as a verbal artifact, and in consequence that the most important thing about the new novel was "el lenguaje como la realidad única y final de la novela" ["language as the only and final reality of the novel"].[6]

In retrospect, writers like Benedetti and others of his persuasion, such as Viñas in Argentina, can be seen as fighting a lost rearguard action, in their fictional work and in their manifestos, against a series of fundamental changes that came over Spanish American fiction in the 1940s. Ángel Rama was correct in referring to Onetti's generation as

"esa promoción transformadora de la literatura nacional" ["this group which transformed our national literature"], which contributed to "la eclosión de una nueva literatura" ["the coming to birth of a new pattern of writing"] whose characteristic in the entire continent was "una nueva concepción del arte y de la vida" ["a new conception of art and life"] .[7]

For the sake of brevity and simplicity, let us focus simply on three of the changes abovementioned. The first and most important, which Viñas later correctly laid at the door of Borges, was a desire to "desacreditar la realidad concreta y de construir un producto que se le oponga" ["to discredit concrete reality and construct a product that would be opposed to it"].[8] It was this above all that emerged triumphantly in *La vida breve*, which, as Jacques Fressard was to write, illustrates "la incertidumbre de lo real, la inestabilidad de un universo en constante degradación" ["the uncertainty of the real, the instability of a universe that was in a constant process of degradation"].[9] The second has to do with the desire to replace the study of Latin American man—specifically—and his problems in dominating, controlling, and civilizing the so-called "barbarism" of the continent, by the study of the human situation in general, just as it happened to manifest itself in a Spanish American context. In other words, instead of describing the condition of Spanish American man, what writers now turned their attention to was the analysis of the universal human condition. In the third place, the predominantly optimistic metaphors underlying the earlier novels, would be replaced by much more disquieting ones.

Undoubtedly one of the most important single statements made by any writer during the 1940s was Asturias's remark in *El Señor Presidente* [*The President*] (1946), chapter 26: "Entre la realidad y el sueño la diferencia es puramente mecánica" ["Between reality and dreaming the difference is purely mechanical"] (178). What it tells us in a nutshell is that the reality of the imagination is just as real as what Viñas incautiously calls "concrete reality," since we are not necessarily equipped to be able to tell the difference. The figure who above all popularized this view, again essentially through his work in the 1940s, was Borges. In various essays published in that decade, collected in *Otras inquisiciones* [*Other Inquisitions*] (1952), he insists that reality is "inasible" ["ungraspable"] ("Nathaniel Hawthorne") and that "notoriamente no hay clasificación del universo que no sea arbitraria y conjetural. La razón es muy simple: no sabemos qué cosa es el universo . . . cabe sospechar que no hay universo en el sentido orgánico, unificador que tiene esa ambiciosa palabra. Si lo hay, falta conjeturar su propósito" ("El idioma analítico de John Wilkins" [*The Analytical Language of John Wilkins*]) (59 and 105). By adopting this stance, Borges was cutting the ground irreparably from under the feet of those earlier and contemporary writers like Benedetti and Viñas who still naively believed that the writer was somehow able to go out and observe, report, and interpret reality in a straightforward way.

To recognize this was to recognize that to foreground the here and now of Spanish America, to explore its presumed "reality" in search of cultural essences, or to protest against its economic dependency and multiform social injustices, was to render oneself obsolete. If we are not programmed to understand reality, there is little incentive to harness literature to the task of trying to change it. Rather, the objective is to propagate awareness of the presupposition that all attempts to describe reality in words are in fact fictions, and, bearing this in mind, to create works of imagination that illustrate the human condition as it appears when we cease to enjoy complete confidence in our understanding of the real either of ourselves or of the world around us. Thus it is that Asturias, in the mid-forties, in *El Señor Presidente* [*The President*], is able to undercut and render ambiguous the novel's apparent referentiality by introducing the inverted biblical myth-elements related to the fall of Lucifer. Thus it is that Sábato in *El túnel* [*The Tunnel*] can present reality through the eyes of an unbalanced narrator. Thus it is that Carpentier in "Viaje a la semilla" ["Journey to the Seed"], by inverting the time sequence of the plot, can question our comfortable worldview in which effects always follow causes. Thus it is finally that Brausen, at the end of the decade, can leave the "reality" of Buenos Aires for the Santa María which exists only inside his head. In each of these key works of the 1940s, that is, we suddenly see with extreme clarity, how in that decade fiction in Spanish America got away from what Borges has called "un alegato político, un pasatiempo folklórico o una descripción de las circunstancias económicas de tal o cual clase de población" ["a political plea, a folkloric pastime or a description of the economic circumstances of such and such a class of people"][10] and applied itself instead to what Carpentier was to call "el deber de 'revelar' realidades inéditas" ["the duty of 'revealing' hitherto unknown realities"].[11]

At the same time two other important developments were also taking place in fiction. One was a sharp turn away from love as part of any possible solution to, or attenuation of, man's accommodation to the human condition, now seen increasingly in negative terms. The other was an equally noteworthy tendency to express the writer's existential dissatisfaction by extending the use of inverted Christian myth, symbolism, and imagery that Asturias had pioneered in his parody of the story of Lucifer's fall and in the presentation of El Pelele as a parodic Christ in *El Señor Presidente*. Both of these developments are prominent in Onetti. He was among the first who undertook the task of deconstructing the "concrete" reality of the old-style realist novel. As Yvonne Perier Jones contends: "His techniques in imagery and narration are designed to undermine objective, external reality. . . . He dissects reality until it loses meaning and becomes amenable to multiple interpretation," while Djelal Kadir alludes to "a systematic doubting of reality" that thus becomes something "relative, fluid and elastic."[12] As for the role of love in Onetti's work, one need do no more than glance at the fourth chapter of Aínsa's *Las trampas de Onetti*, "La función del amor," to see how closely he aligns himself with the rest of the Boom writers. So far as the inversion of religious values is concerned, the figure of Larsen, who is an inverted saint totally dedicated, like Borges's Zur Linde, to an ideal that parodies Christian ones, is merely one example among many.

To conclude: during the 1940s fiction began to discredit humanly desirable myths of meaning by calling attention to the limitations governing our perspectives as individuals, our means of communication, and the cultural assumptions within which we operate. What emerged was the opposite of didactic writing. It began to tell us that our interpretations of reality are perhaps no more than security blankets, imaginary bulwarks against the imponderable. It began to challenge our mindsets with elegance, humor, and scrupulous absence of melodrama and outcry. The whole of Onetti's mature work is rooted in that crucial decade.

NOTES

1. J. C. Onetti, "La literatura: ida y vuelta," 202.
2. D.L. Shaw, *Antonio Skármeta and the Post-Boom*, 100.
3. Elsa Dehennin, "A propósito del realismo de Mario Benedetti," 1079 and 1084.
4. Mario Benedetti, "El escritor y la crítica en el contexto del desarrollo."
5. Jorge Ruffinelli, "Onetti antes de Onetti," 25.
6. Paul Verdevoye, "Socionarrativa hispanoamericana," 899; E. Rodríguez Monegal, "La nueva novela latinoamericana," 63.
7. Ángel Rama, "Origen de un novelista y de una generación literaria," 17–18.
8. David Viñas, *De Sarmiento a Cortázar*, 95.
9. Cit. Ángel Grenes, *Estructura y sentido en "El astillero" de Onetti*, 7.
10. Fernando Sorrentino, *Siete conversaciones con Jorge Luis Borges*, 120.
11. Fernando Arias, *Recopilación de textos sobre Alejo Carpentier*, 19.
12. Yvonne Perier Jones, *The Formal Expression of Meaning in J. C. Onetti's Narrative Art*, 7/1 and 7/8; Djelal Kadir, *Juan Carlos Onetti*, 143.

WORKS CITED

Aínsa, Fernando. *Las trampas de Onetti*. Montevideo: Alfa, 1970.
Alonso, Carlos J. *The Spanish American Regionalist Novel*. Cambridge: Cambridge UP, 1990.

Arias, Fernando. *Recopilación de textos sobre Alejo Carpentier.* Havana: Casa de las Américas, 1977.

Asturias, Miguel Ángel . *El Señor Presidente.* Buenos Aires: Losada, 1978.

Benedetti, Mario. "El escritor y la crítica en el contexto del desarrollo." *Casa de las Américas* 107 (1978): 3–21.

Borges, Jorge Luis. *Otras inquisiciones.* Madrid: Alianza, 1981.

Dehennin, Elsa. "A propósito del realismo de Mario Benedetti." *Revista Iberoamericana* 160–61 (1992): 1077–90.

Grenes, Ángel. *Estructura y sentido en "El astillero" de Onetti.* Montevideo: Casa del Estudiante, 1987.

Kadir, Djelal. *Juan Carlos Onetti.* Boston: Twayne, 1977.

Onetti, Juan Carlos. "La literatura: ida y vuelta." *Réquiem por Faulkner y otros artículos.* Ed. Jorge Ruffinelli. Buenos Aires: Calicanto, 1976. 193–204.

Perier Jones, Yvonne. *The Formal Expression of Meaning in J.C. Onetti's Narrative Art.* Cuernavaca: Centro Intercultural de Documentación, 1971.

Rama, Ángel. "Origen de un novelista y de una generación literaria." *Homenaje a J. C. Onetti.* Ed. F. Giacoman. Long Island City, N.Y.: Las Américas, 1974.

Rodríguez Monegal, Emir. "La nueva novela latinoamericana." *Actas del Tercer Congreso de la Asociación Internacional de Hispanistas.* Ed. C. H. Magis. Mexico: El Colegio de México, 1970. 47–63.

Roffé, Reina. *Espejo de escritores.* Hanover, N.H.: Ediciones del Norte, 1985.

Ruffinelli, Jorge. "Onetti antes de Onetti." *Juan Carlos Onetti.* Ed. Hugo J. Verani. Madrid: Taurus, 1987.

Shaw, Donald L. *Antonio Skármeta and the Post-Boom.* Hanover, N.H.: Ediciones del Norte, 1994.

Shaw, Donald L. "Which was the First Novel of the Boom?" *MLR* 89 (1994): 360–71.

Sorrentino, Fernando. *Siete conversaciones con Jorge Luis Borges.* Buenos Aires: Pardo, 1974.

Verdevoye, Paul. "Socionarrativa hispanoamericana." *Actas del Tercer Congreso de la Asociación Internacional de Hispanistas.* Ed. C. H. Magis. Mexico: El Colegio de México, 1970. 893–99.

Viñas, David. *De Sarmiento a Cortázar.* Buenos Aires: Siglo Veinte, 1971.

2

La tierra más transparente
or La región de nadie:
Onetti and Fuentes

Steven Boldy

The first full-length novel by Juan Carlos Onetti, *Tierra de nadie* [*No Man's Land*], from 1941, and Carlos Fuentes's first novel *La región más transparente* [*Where the Air is Clear*], from 1958, have as much in common as they are disparate in style and tone. Both are landmark novels about a city and a country: Buenos Aires and Argentina (and by extension the River Plate area) in the case of Onetti, and Mexico City and Mexico in the case of Fuentes. On each the influence of John Dos Passos and especially his 1925 novel *Manhattan Transfer* is decisive: its short chapters, which range from prose poems to fragments of conversations in parties, very loosely linked or juxtaposed, the large number of characters, all gradually building up an impression of the city. Both novels were written toward the end of a period in both countries of intense speculation about the question of national identity, and incorporate echoes of that debate into discussions among characters and into the more general symbolic development of the novel.

There is a seventeen-year difference between the publication dates of the novels, which makes for a significant gap in intertextual reference and political circumstance. The messianic Americanism of Neruda's "Alturas de Macchu Picchu" ["The Heights of Macchu Picchu"] from the 1950 *Canto general* [*Let the Rail-Splitter Awake and Other Poems*] taken up by Ixca Cienfuegos was not available to Aránzuru or Llarvi, but on the other hand Larsen in *El astillero* [*The Shipyard*] (1961) was certainly not tempted to take it up either. Much of the political disillusionment of the 1941 novel seems to relate to the German-Soviet pact, the defeat of the Spanish Republic, and the aftermath of the depression, while Fuentes's novel, written about the period of rapid capitalist expansion during the *sexenio* [six-year rule] of Miguel Alemán, 1946–52, might be seen to reflect that exuberance, for better or for worse. Nevertheless, the treatment of the Spanish Civil War in both novels seems directly to reflect the more general intentionality of each author. Onetti's Rolanda divests the period of its historical and ideological specificity as political struggle. For her its reality was simply poverty and the inevitability of prostitution and corruption: "Nada de guerra. Lo que había ahí era la miseria y todo se pudría . . . Están las niñas, siempre hay las niñas que tienen esa edad en cualquier guerra" ["Forget the war. What there was there was wretched poverty. . . . The girls are there, girls of that age are always there in any war"] (OC 245–46). Rolanda's suggested incursion into prostitution, probably promoted by her family, simply forms a series with that of Catalina-Katty, who works as a whore to support Aránzuru, and Labuk, who Llarvi speculates became a prostitute after he had beaten and rejected her. Rather than this uniformity, the corresponding example in *La región más transparente* (RMT) emphasizes opposition and reversal. The account by the militiaman to the widow with the "rostro catalán, de hachazos" ["chiseled Catalan face"] (RMT 302) of the heroism of her husband or partner in saving the lives of his comrades by giving the impression he was the only person escaping, serves as a reversal of the episode in the Mexican Revolution when Gervasio Pola chooses to give away the position of the companions who had escaped with him. The contrast between a uniform human nature in Onetti and an identity forged from alternatives and diversity in Fuentes's novel extends to most areas shared by the texts. Spain for Fuentes is both a real place and a symbolic alternative model of action or morality, whereas the alternative to Buenos Aires in *Tierra de nadie* is an invented zone, "la isla" ["the island"], insistently mocked and emptied of any meaning.

Despite the difference in dates between the two novels, the unequal development of the two cities means that in 1958 Mexico City was only just beginning to become the large, vibrant, cosmopolitan city that Buenos Aires had long been. Witness to this is the condescendence with which the Argentine intellectual Dardo Moratto treats his Mexican colleagues in Fuentes's novel: "Muy interesante, muy interesante ver las cosas cuando recién empiezan. Van bien, ustedes. Harán cosas" ["It's very interesting, very interesting to see things just when they are beginning. You are doing fine. You'll get somewhere"] (48). Though Onetti's work is a novel application of the techniques of Dos Passos to Buenos Aires, there already was in Argentina a tradition of modern urban novels, from Cambaceres to Gálvez and, more importantly, seminal novels by Roberto Arlt such as *El juguete rabioso* ["The Rabid Toy"] (1926) and *Los siete locos* [*The Seven Madmen*] (1929). Fuentes has no such well-established Mexican models to draw on, and the minute observation of Mariano Azuela and the satirical but affectionate tone of Salvador Novo's *Nueva grandeza mexicana* ["New Mexican Greatness"] are a long way from the outlandish, sordid, and despairing characters of Arlt.

The titles offer an interesting initial point of comparison. Both have clear geographical reference to "region" and "land," while Onetti's "no man's land" is apparently far bleaker than that of Fuentes. Fuentes's title moreover differs from Onetti's, which is a common metaphor with no specific reference to time or location, in that it clearly refers to Mexico's central region of Anáhuac and intertextually to a literary tradition, and a history. The well-known epigraph to Alfonso Reyes's 1915 essay in celebration of Mexico's central valley, *Visión de Anáhuac* ["Vision of Anáhuac"], is "Viajero: has llegado a la región más transparente del aire" ["Traveller: you have reached the region where the air is clearest"]. The description has been attributed to Baron von Humboldt, which provides a further level of reference. Fuentes uses the phrase with some irony, of course, of the noisy modern city, but also with nostalgia and affection: the effect is dialogue, ambiguity, certainly a cultural continuity not likely to be found in a "no man's land." Onetti's text has a dedication that aggressively separates him from a certain Argentinean tradition: "a Julio E. Payró con reiterado ensañamiento" ["To Julio E. Payró, with repeated cruelty"].

Some similar and important differences can be seen by a rapid glance at the opening lines of the two novels. *Tierra de nadie* begins:

> El taxi frenó en la esquina de la diagonal, empujando hacia el chófer el cuerpo de la mujer de pelo amarillo. La cabeza, doblada, quedó mirando la carta azul que le separaba los muslos. "Nos devolveremos el uno al otro como una pelota, un reflejo . . ."
>
> Mientras suspiraba, "nos devolveremos el uno al otro," sorprendió el nacimiento del gran letrero rojizo.
>
> Una mancha de sangre: *Bristol.* En seguida el cielo azuloso y otro golpe de luz: *Cigarrillos importados.* Nuevamente el cielo. En la cruz de las calles las enormes letras golpeaban el flanco del primer rascacielos, su torre escalonada. Bristol, el aire, cigarrillos, pequeñas nubes. Los golpes rojos se corrían por las azoteas desiertas, manchando fugazmente el gris hosco de los pretiles. (81)

> [The taxi braked at the street corner, thrusting the yellow-haired woman toward the driver. The head, bowed, stared at the blue letter that separated her thighs. "We will bounce one off the other like a ball, a reflection . . ."

While she was sighing, "we will bounce one off the other," she noticed the birth of the big reddish sign.

A blood stain: *Bristol*. Then quickly the bluish sky and another flash of light: *Imported cigarettes*. The sky again. At the crossroads the enormous letters struck the flank of the first skyscraper, its tiered tower. Bristol, the air, cigarettes, small clouds. The red flashes raced across the deserted roofs, fleetingly staining the sullen gray of the parapets.]

The novel opens in an anonymous city. The disjointed, noncommittal language, with four sentences without main verbs, is reminiscent of Dos Passos. There is a strange mixture of the depersonalized and the existentially vital: a message apparently important to a character, which the reader cannot understand. The character is nameless, and indeed is mainly alluded to as parts of her body are subjected to the movement of the automobile that precedes her in the narration, or seem to act autonomously from her: "La cabeza . . . quedó mirando la carta" ["The head . . . stared at the blue letter"]. The relationship between the characters is similarly described in mechanical terms independent of their volition, and that echo the movement imparted to the woman's body by the braking of the taxi. Both the intermittent movement and the notion of reflection are then taken up by another urban mechanical phenomenon: the flashing on and off of the cigarette advertisement and its fleeting illumination of the nearby buildings. At least a certain aesthetic continuity or wholeness of vision is suggested by the inseparability of taxi, woman, message, and advertisement. The autonomy of sounds and light, ("las enormes letras golpeaban el flanco del primer rascacielos," "los golpes rojos se corrían" ["the enormous letters struck the flank of the first skyscraper," "the red flashes raced"]), of mechanical movements and parts of bodies throughout the novel is striking: the noise of the telephone in Aránzuru's office, the eight hands playing cards under the light, the gyrating of a record in the room next to Llarvi's in Rosario. Such movements are described with a precision that would suggest a symbolic or allegorical import, but as Llarvi hints, such symmetry is tantalizingly meaningless: "El primer secreto consistía en que el disco giraba muy lentamente, despacio, despacio. El segundo secreto era que la vida no tenía sentido" ["The first secret was the fact that the record turned very slowly, slowly, slowly. The second secret was that life was meaningless"] (198). The cigarette advertisement, which is also present in the penultimate of the sixty-one chapters, in what is probably again a mocking, vacuous symmetry, offers two interesting features. It has the only proper name in the section, and is in a foreign language, imported into what we soon find is Argentina. Foreign capitalism is not much of an issue in the novel, though the bosses of the company against whom

Bidart strikes speak English, but, as we shall see, the foreign and specifically European perspective on Argentina is seen as falsifying and alienating its reality. One of the few other foreign or foreign-sounding products, the name of which is written in an ad "en el cielo con letras rojas"
["on the sky in red letters"] are the "medias Tax" ["Tax stockings"]
with which the woman from this section, "la mujer de pelo amarillo"
["the yellow-haired woman"], Mabel Madern as we eventually find out,
uses to hang herself (202).

La región más transparente opens thus:

> MI NOMBRE *es Ixca Cienfuegos. Nací y vivo en México, D.F. Esto no
> es grave. En México no hay tragedia: todo se vuelve afrenta. Afrenta,
> esta sangre que me punza como filo de maguey. Afrenta, mi parálisis
> desenfrenada que todas las auroras tiñe de coágulos. . . . Duende de
> Anáhuac que no machaca uvas—corazones; que no bebe licor, bálsamo
> de tierra. . . . Su danza (nuestro baile) suspendida de un asta de plumas,
> o de la defensa de un camión; muerto en la guerra florida, en la riña de
> cantina, a la hora de la verdad: la única hora puntual. Poeta sin con-
> miseración, artista del tormento, lépero cortés, ladino ingenuo, mi ple-
> garia desarticulada se pierde, albur, relajo.*

> [MY NAME is Ixca Cienfuegos. I was born and I live in Mexico City.
> This is not serious. In Mexico there is no tragedy: everything turns into
> an offense. Offense this blood that pricks me like a cactus thorn.
> Offense, my unleashed paralysis that tinges every dawn with clots. . . .
> Goblin of Anahuac who does not pound grapes—hearts; who does not
> drink liquor, earth balm. . . . His dance (our hop) dangling from a
> feathered spear, or from the bumper of a truck; killed in the ritual flow-
> ery war, in a barroom brawl, at the hour of truth, the only punctual
> hour. Merciless poet, artist of torment, courteous lecher, naive rogue,
> my dislocated prayer is lost, insult, bedlam.]

Instead of the Onettian anonymity the text immediately offers a name
and a specific location. The name (of the first-person narrator, poet,
or speaker) is strikingly dual: Aztec and Hispanic. The foreign element
is present from the beginning, but is a foreignness internal to Mexico,
not imported like Bristol cigarettes. It does not flash on and off alter-
nating with the sky of Buenos Aires, but is tensely juxtaposed.
Whereas the Onetti opening would seem to be free of any overt literary intertextuality that might mitigate or recuperate the starkness of
the scene, Fuentes's phrase about tragedy sets off a rich series of
echoes. The first line of *Lady Chatterley's Lover*, by D. H. Lawrence,
whose *The Plumed Serpent* is a clear presence in the novel, is "Ours is
essentially a tragic age, so we refuse to take it tragically." Ixca seems
to lament the loss of the tragic spirit in Mexican consciousness vis-à-
vis the troubled history of the country, and of the Nietzschean or

Lawrentian intensity, which characterizes his own poetic prose. Onetti's text and his characters explicitly mock such high seriousness. The other echo in Ixca's phrase "En México no hay tragedia: todo se vuelve afrenta" ["In Mexico there is no tragedy: everything turns into an offense"] is from Karl Marx: "Hegel remarks somewhere that all facts and personages in world history occur, as it were, twice. He forgot to add: the first time as tragedy, the second as farce."[1] In Marx the phrase refers to the mediocre replaying by Napoleon III of Napoleon Bonaparte's greatness. Fuentes's echo refers us to the theme of belatedness in the novel: that of the Manuel and Rodrigo who are unable to repeat the heroic actions of their fathers in the Mexican Revolution, and that of the Mexican bourgeoisie vis-à-vis its European model. Here we have at least three elements in the equation of identity that Onetti chooses to erase: history and the weight of the past, family and the struggle with the father, and Europe and others as a necessary component of one's personal or national self.

The main figure used in much of this passage is oxymoron. Ixca talks of his "unleashed paralysis," of an imbalance, perhaps, between stasis and movement, structure and plurality. The reference to the "Duende de Anáhuac" ["Goblin of Anáhuac"], probably Huitzilopochtli, the cruel Aztec sun deity, introduces two elements explicitly excluded from Onetti's world: the indigenous, and any sense of myth and transcendence. Talking of American tradition, for example, Llarvi immediately brackets off the autochthonous: "(prescindiendo de lo precolombino, una farsa ['apart from the pre-Columbian, a farce'])" (OC 142). Casal, similarly, talking about the lack of faith in Americans from the South of their continent to Mexico excludes the Indians from that category: "Separe los indios, claro; y los gringos" ["Leave aside the Indians, of course; and the gringos"] (207). Ixca laments the passing of the cosmic order represented by human sacrifice, but goes on to contrast two languages, urban and fallen, indigenous and transcendent: the feathered shaft and the bumper of the lorry, the Aztec flowery war and a brawl in a cantina bar. The reference is to the death of two characters in a road accident and in a fight, and to the question of whether their deaths make sense, indeed whether any sense, pattern, or transcendence can be attributed to what emerges as a chaotic and seemingly futile series of deaths. The desire for wholeness and meaning is essential to Onetti's text, but only rarely articulated: Aránzuru "hubiera deseado, antes de la partida de mañana, una gran vida, un pasado complejo y dramático para recordarlo de una sola mirada" ["would have liked, before his departure tomorrow, a great life, a complex and dramatic past to take in and remember at a single glance"] (228). Moreover it is immediately and categorically negated: "Todo hacia atrás era equívoco y no podía comprenderse" ["Looking back, everything was ambiguous and could not be understood"] (228–29). Ixca and Fuentes's reaction is not to exclude and negate, but to incorporate and contrast, as in the densely oxymoronic description that Ixca gives of himself as poet-narrator: he is a "courteous coarse-tongued, naive cunning character," while his language veers between or refuses to separate prayer or invocation, and obscene insult and buffoonery: "plegaria" ["prayer"] and "albur" ["insult"].

The discussion of national identity in the novels throws up a similar pattern. Whereas in *Tierra de nadie*, the views of Casal, Llarvi, and Mauricio are virtually indistinguishable, in *La región más transparente*, Manuel Zamacona, Ixca Cienfuegos, and Federico Robles represent widely divergent positions between which the text refuses to decide: socialism and a vaguely Christian sense of solidarity; capitalist expansion and emulation of the United States; renunciation of individuality and return to pre-Hispanic traditions. Both novels work against the background of a tradition of essays—in Onetti's case, works such as Scalabrini Ortiz, *El hombre que está solo y espera* ["The Man Who Is Alone and Waiting"] (1931), Martínez Estrada, *Radiografía de la pampa* [*X-Ray of the Pampa*] (1933), and Mallea's *Historia de una pasión argentina* [*History of an Argentine Passion*] (1935). Llarvi, indeed, institutionalizes the debate as he lectures on "La conciencia de América" ["The Conscience of America"] in Rosario, and struggles to put his ideas and readings into a book, but the importance he attributes to his own rhetoric is suggested by the following juxtaposition: "'América está en nosotros. . . . Aceptémosla como la tierra acoge a la semilla que habrá de romperla sin preguntarse el color del fruto.' ¿Dónde demonios quedaría el prostíbulo?" ["'America is in us. . . . Let us accept her like the earth accepts the seed which will break it without asking the color of the fruit.' Where the hell was the brothel?"] (189). More important to him than the striving after any definition of an inevitably spiritual nature is the recollection of the unspeakable, irreducible bodily presence of Labuk: "Era callada y sucia, simple. Sólo vivía, en realidad, en la cama, en su mundo ardiente y lúbrico" ["She was silent and dirty, simple. She only really lived in bed, in her passionate and lewd world"] (106). Fuentes takes up the fruit of a long Mexican tradition from Samuel Ramos, *Perfil del hombre y la cultura en México* ["Profile of Man and Culture in Mexico"] (1934), the works of Zea, Reyes, the Hyperión group, to Octavio Paz's *El laberinto de la soledad* [*The Labyrinth of Solitude*] (1951). Though individual statements from characters are often viewed with some irony, as with the writings of Zamacona, who like Llarvi tries to systematize his thoughts, key notions from the essays become essential parts in the conceptual structuring of the novel. This is the case with Paz's seminal work and the opposition and play between solitude and communion, "solo" ["alone"] and "juntos" ["together"], which is essential to *La región más transparente*.

If Fuentes in terms of national identity and in other areas tends to add layers and confront voices, Onetti subtracts and brackets off, in an almost mystical fashion. For Fuentes, the Mexican is asphyxiated and yet given meaning by his past:

> No podemos vivirnos y morirnos a ciegas . . . tratando de olvidarlo todo y de nacer de nuevo todos los días sabiendo que todo está vivo y presente y aplastándonos el diafragma, por más que queramos olvidarlo: Quetzalcoatls y Corteses e Iturbides y Juárez y Porfirios y Zapatas, todos hechos un nudo en la garganta. ¿Cuál es nuestra verdadera efigie? (RMT 278)

> [We cannot grope blindly through our life and death . . . trying to forget everything and to be born anew every day knowing that everything is alive and present and pressing down on our diaphragm, however much we might want to forget it: Quetzalcoatls and Cortéses and Iturbides and Juárezes and Porfirios and Zapatas, all of them a tangled knot in our throats. What is our true image?]

Hence the importance of memory in the novel if the past is an essential part of one's present identity. As the old joke goes, though, while Mexicans descend from the Aztecs, Argentinians descend from boats. In Onetti neither the country nor the city has a past, nor do individuals have memory. As Linacero in *El pozo* memorably puts it about Uruguay: "¿qué se puede hacer en este país? Nada, ni dejarse engañar. . . . Detrás de nosotros no hay nada. Un gaucho, dos gauchos, treinta y tres gauchos" ["What can you do in this country? Nothing, not even deceive ourselves. . . . Behind us there is nothing. One gaucho, two gauchos, thirty three gauchos"] (OC 71). Here and elsewhere, this at least saves the inhabitants of the River Plate from the German-style fascism of the "bestia rubia" ["blond beast"]. Buenos Aires is seen by Casal as the city of amnesia: "Una ciudad abierta, todo lo barre el viento, nada se guarda. No hay pasado" ["An open city, the wind sweeps everything away, nothing is retained. There is no past"] (208–9). Llarvi, soon before his death dismisses memory as "dirty literature": "Nunca comprendí ese cargamento de recuerdos que la gente se empeña en encontrar en cada nueva primavera. . . . Sucia literatura" ["I never understood that cargo of memories which people insist on finding every new spring. . . . Filthy literature"] (197). Indeed, literature, words, commentary, the attributing of meaning to being Argentinian is seen as a falsification and a European gesture. He almost seems to associate Europe with meaning and literature, America with meaninglessness:

Le deseo mucho éxito en las conferencias de Rosario. Hable de la
soledad del argentino y el hombre ensimismado. . . . Gran cuento litera-
rio la tristeza. El único que está triste es el europeo en Buenos Aires. Lo
grave es que el porteño está contento aunque no haga ruido; abandone
las nobles esperanzas de cambiarlo. Frío, un poco aburrido, antisenti-
mental. (166)

[I wish you much success in your lectures in Rosario. Talk about the
solitude of the Argentinean and the self-absorbed individual. . . . Sadness is a great literary invention. The only sad person is the European
in Buenos Aires. The most serious thing is that the Argentinean is
happy although he does not make a song and dance about it; forget
your noble hopes of changing him. Cold, a little bored, unsentimental.]

Various characters tend to associate the abandoning of humanistic
meaning, the European, the autochthonous, with a form of mystical qui-
etism:

No hay nada que hacer aquí. Cualquier cosa que uno se invente para
hacer es asunto europeo, no nuestro. . . . Todo es falso y lo autóctono
lo más falso de todo. . . . Algún día tendremos una mística, es seguro;
pero entre tanto somos felices. (163)

[There is nothing to do here. Anything you invent to do is a European
affair, not ours. . . . Everything is false and the native falser than anything. . . . Some day we will have a mystique, that's for certain; but in
the meanwhile we are happy.]

Later Casal takes the formulation even further. Again, renouncing faith
leads to a "cheerful American nihilism": "Un continente sin fe. . . . Aceptar la muerte como un fin, el fin, la liquidación, el no hay más. . . . Imagí-
nese un nihilismo alegre y en acción" ["A continent without faith. . . .
To accept death like an end, the end, the liquidation, the final cur-
tain. . . . Imagine a cheerful nihilism in action"] (210). The same process
of subtraction also works with personal identity and artistic expression.
Llarvi, in his search for self, imagines "sentirse despojado de todo lo
social" ["feeling himself stripped of all social attributes"], and then of
animality in so far as it is a shared human trait. The self is seen as a sort
of positive nothingness: "Queda entonces uno. ¿Qué hay? Sólo se puede
decir con una palabra: nada. Pero esta palabra, aquí, no es negativa. Sig-
nifica y afirma la existencia de miles de cosas. No se puede explicar ni
hay para qué" ["Then only oneself is left. What is there? It can only be
said with one word: nothing. But this word, here, is not negative. It
means and affirms thousands of things. It cannot be explained and there
is no reason to"] (198). There is an ethical side to the renunciation. To
search for a distinctive identity, necessarily outside the real is a dangerous form of romanticism, associated with the "resurrección pagana y las

procesiones y el famoso *Weltanschauung*" ["pagan revival and proces-
sions and the famous *Weltanschauung*"] of fascism: "La otra manera es
aceptar la realidad y tratar de hacerla mejor" ["The other way is to
accept reality and try to make it better"] (159).

In both novels, any sense of dynamism, change, or production of
meaning from the disorder of countless lives in the city is centered on
one main character, whose action is inseparable from the narrative process of the novel. These characters are Diego Aránzuru and Ixca Cienfuegos. Both are ubiquitous and sexually potent: Ixca seems to transform Norma Larragoiti's being and the outcome of the novel through
repeated sex, while Aránzuru has relations with most of the women in
the novel: Nené, whom he makes pregnant, the adolescent Nora,
Catalina-Katty who works as a whore for him, Violeta who also gives
him money, Rolanda, and two boys: "el niño de las botellas" ["the bottle kid"] and Lázaro, Ixca's role metamorphoses throughout the novel:
"Como Dios: en todas partes, nadie lo puede ver. Entrada libre a los
salones oficiales, a los de la high-life, a los de los magnates también. Que
si es el cerebro mágico de algún banquero, que si es un gigoló o un simple marihuano, que si viene, que si va" ["Like God: everywhere, nobody
can see him. Free access to the official salons, to those of the jet set and
of business leaders. People say he is the magical brain of some banker,
a gigolo or simply a junky, coming and going"] (41). Ixca is the double
of the novelist and at the same time of all the characters. While Ixca
manipulates the plot of the novel magically and is the memory of the
main characters, Aránzuru is an example to them of liberation, and
describes himself in mockingly Baudelairian terms, as the "señor
invitación al viaje" ["monsieur invitation au voyage"] (258). Perhaps
the crucial difference between them and their novels is that while
Aránzuru creates meaning or salvation by a rebellious artistic and existential transgression and invention set within but against reality, Ixca
seeks a deeper commitment to reality, past and present, personal and
transpersonal, in the mind and action of key characters, a revelation or
illumination of the given.

Aránzuru is linked to a series of zones and activities that stand in an
ambiguous relationship to the escape from the real into the potentially
fascist romanticism of unique national identities. The most notorious of
these is the island often referred to as Faruru, phonetically similar to his
own name. The paradisal island is as close as Onetti comes to a myth,
and though free from any contingency, it is provisionally situated in the
Pacific. Though it is clear from the beginning that it is an invention of
Num the taxidermist, Aránzuru is fascinated by the idea, and when he
acquires money, which is always necessary for fantasy or creation in
Onetti, he plans to go there. He is first to go with Violeta, but when he

sees her dressed in a grass skirt and beads, like the Hawaiian-style dancers at the beginning of the novel, reducing his utopia to a Thomas Cook holiday destination, he walks out on her and offers the trip instead to Rolanda, significantly a counterfeiter of passports. The island as an absolute but more and more ludicrous alternative to reality is mockingly reproduced in debased versions of itself, such as Aránzuru's country place known as the "molino de la alemana" ["the German woman's mill"], and the house provided for Violeta by Sam.

The counterfeit passports, however, which allow Larsen to become Emilio Landoni, again in exchange for money, link the island to other attitudes that hover tantalizingly between the simple acceptance of contingency and reality, its redemption through stylization, and the exaltation of counterworlds such as prostitution. This is symbolically the realm of literary creation. In *La vida breve* [*A Brief Life*] the counterworld of Queca and prostitution is the first step toward turning the escape to another place into the full literary reality of Santa María. By the time of *El astillero*, even the escapist myth of the island is tainted by the real. Gálvez dies in the River Plate when possibly trying to reach "la isla de Latorre" ["Latorre's island"] on the river, which contains a grim old house, the caretaker of which, we discover, is called Aránzuru. Foreshadowing Brausen in *La vida breve*, Aránzuru takes to inventing new identities for himself, and living them out in different spaces: from middle-class lawyer, he first becomes the pimp of Katty, and lives from her earnings in a provincial town. The falsity of his position becomes untenable when she discovers he is a lawyer and throws him out. He becomes an unsuccessful record-player salesman and a pederast, later the accomplice of Larsen's criminal activity, and at the end the "señor invitación al viaje."

When his metamorphoses run out of steam, he is left with no transcendental principle, that is, no island, as Num dies with the secret, and in total solitude: "Ya no había isla . . . , ni amigos ni mujeres para acompañarse" ["There was no longer an island . . . , nor friends to keep one company"] (261). Neither in his own psyche, nor through his influence on others has any sense of community or pattern emerged from the fragments of lives in the novel. Structurally in the novel, there are mirages of symmetry, which fail to develop into anything more than a drab uniformity of destiny: Larsen, Bidart, Aránzuru, and Casal, for example, are associated in one way or another with procuring, being "alcahuete" or "macró" ["pimp"] (121, 124, 260), a minor step in freedom beyond earning money by work, while on a more realist level there is a disagreeable insistence on violence done to women. Minor parallels are drawn between characters. Llarvi and Aránzuru drive Labuk and Catalina into prostitution, and are seen on trains with them (134, 136).

Llarvi suddenly believes Labuk has died, while the same happens to Aránzuru with Nora (198, 237). Mauricio and Aránzuru take to living in dirty, confined spaces. Such parallels initially seem to evoke some sort of pattern or continuity but have little more reality than the island of Faruru. A further absence of meaning is suggested as various major questions are left unanswered for the reader: Does Llarvi kill himself? Who is the father of Nora's child? Is Violeta actually shot by Semitern? Did Rolanda turn up at the appointment with Aránzuru?

   La región más transparente is a far more complex novel than Onetti's. In contrast to *Tierra de nadie*, where only the mother of Aránzuru is evoked in any detail (and with surprising tenderness), all Fuentes's main characters have a complex family past over various generations and covering key moments of Mexican history. The essential relationship between an individual and this past is often seen as being mediated by Ixca Cienfuegos. He first focuses on Rodrigo Pola somehow to force him to embody the Mexican identity and people. The paternal question Rodrigo must answer is the dilemma between solidarity and solitude: in an important episode in the Revolution, his father both denounced his companions and is seen to die in solidarity with them. Ixca struggles with Rodrigo's mother Rosenda over the memories of Rodrigo, his reading of his past, but Rosenda wins when Rodrigo takes as his model not his own father but the business tycoon Federico Robles. Ixca then turns his attention to this same Robles in whose past there is the same or a similar sort of dilemma. While his origins spoke of oppression as the son of a Michoacán Indian, while he had heard the lessons of syndicalist solidarity from his cousin Reyero, and had risen to power through the deaths of others such as the trade-unionist Feliciano Sánchez, whom he had killed in exchange for land and influence, Robles chooses to cancel or ignore this past. He would prefer to see his power as individual and self-sustaining. Symbolically, again, it is a woman and the mother of his child who manipulates his memory: Mercedes Zamacona, who as a witch had condemned him to a duality between day and night, to gain his force from the night, from her and the land and the community she represented, and squander it in a useless display of power during the day (424).

   In a sense this amnesia of the past and the others who have made Robles is equivalent to the meaningless dispersal at the end of *Tierra de nadie*. Throughout the novel there is a succession of deaths, which seem utterly futile and random: Gervasio Pola and his companions, Juan Morales, Feliciano Sánchez, Norma Larragoiti, Manuel Zamacona, Gabriel. Manuel wonders whether such suffering is the dark, meaningless homage demanded by a cruel land, or can be avenged, given a sense: "Lo espantoso, Cienfuegos, es que a veces no sabe uno si esta tierra, en vez de exigir venganza por tanta sangre que la ha manchado, exige esta sangre. Si esto fuera cierto, entonces sí acepto tus ideas: volcán anónimo, dispersión y muerte del hombre" ["The really terrible thing, Cienfuegos, is that sometimes one does not know whether this land, instead of demanding vengeance for all the blood which has stained it, demands this blood. If this were true, then I do accept your ideas: anonymous volcano, the break-up and death of man"] (397). That sense may be formal within the novel if a pattern emerges to link the deaths, or may emerge in the consciousness of a character. For Manuel the sense seems to be linked to a Christian idea of responsibility: "por cada mexicano que murió en vano, hay un mexicano responsable. Y regreso a mi tesis: para que esa muerte no haya sido en vano, alguien debe asumir la culpa" ["for each Mexican who died in vain, there is a responsible Mexican. And I come back to my thesis: in order that that death should not have been in vain, someone must assume the guilt"] (379). Ixca Cienfuegos, as the memory of the characters incarnate and engineer of the plot, manipulates the bankruptcy of Robles, the self-assertion and consequent death of his wife, and almost magically takes him to the wake of the migrant worker Gabriel, killed in a *cantina* brawl. Gabriel, because of the circumstances of his death, is the double of Robles's son Manuel, which seems to lead Robles both to recognize himself in the humble Gabriel and at the same time to remember and acknowledge the many dead on whom his own life was built: "Más allá de sus huesos y su sangre, en las vidas de otros que en ese minuto de humillación y carne rendida eran su propia vida, en las vidas mudas que lo habían alimentado, sintió la razón verdadera: y esas vidas mudas, cuyos nombres quizás no recordaba, se multiplicaban en una escena de pantomimas fatales, hasta abarcar toda la tierra de México, todas las derrotas y asesinatos y batallas, hasta regresar, reconociéndole, al cuerpo de Federico" ["Beyond his bones and his blood, in the lives of others who in that moment of humiliation and surrendered flesh were his own life, in the mute lives that had nourished him, he felt the true reason: and in those mute lives, whose names he perhaps did not remember, all the defeats and murders and battles multiplied in a scene of fatal pantomimes, spreading across the whole territory of Mexico, until they returned in recognition to the body of Federico"] (432).

Robles's recognition of his personal past and of the presence of others in his own identity, engineered by Ixca Cienfuegos, is one expression of the intention of Fuentes in this early but key novel. Robles's memories, contradictory, plural and painful, come to "abarcar toda la tierra de México" ["spread across the whole territory of Mexico"]. Onetti, in *Tierra de nadie* and subsequently, whether out of scruple, national circumstance, or personal disposition, was never willing to embrace such totalizing intention, however dialogic and ambiguous. To the somber splendor and *chiaroscuro* of the Escorial in *Terra Nostra*, he would always prefer the more perverse cat-and-mouse games with meaning and the crumbling skeleton of the shipyard in *El astillero*.

NOTE

1. *The Eighteenth Brumaire of Louis Bonaparte*, in Karl Marx, *Selected Writings*, 300.

WORKS CITED

Fuentes, Carlos. *La región más transparente*. Mexico City: Fondo de Cultura Económica, 1972. (*Where the Air is Clear, a Novel*. Trans. Sam Hileman. New York: Farrar, Straus and Giroux, 1960.)
Marx, Karl. *Selected Writings*. Ed. David McLellan. Oxford: Oxford UP, 1977.

3

Onetti and Donoso:
Heroes and Whores in Juntacadáveres *and* El lugar sin límites

Philip Swanson

The Chilean José Donoso has characterized Onetti as "uno de los grandes novelistas del continente" ["one of the great novelists of the continent"] and clearly regards the Uruguayan as one of the key influences in his own work and in the evolution of the "new novel" in Spanish America.[1] His eulogistic introduction to the Salvat edition of *El astillero* [*The Shipyard*] repeats as much, lamenting, here as elsewhere, the lack of recognition afforded the Montevidean's work.[2] The points of contact between the two seem obvious enough. Apart from certain similarities of background, their work, particularly their earlier work, appears to have an existential focus and offer a gloomy view of life concentrating on the sordid and on individual failure. This grotesque vision is often related to the sexual, nowhere more clearly than in *Juntacadáveres* [*Body Snatcher*] (1964) and *El lugar sin límites* [*Hell Has No Limits*] (1966). Both novels are set in small, isolated Spanish American communities, are centered around a brothel and brothel-owners and deal with monetary ambition and sexual nonfulfillment against a background of small-town social and political intrigue. More technically, both works, written in the mid-sixties at the margins of the so-called Boom, mark some kind of break with "tradition" in terms of an implied rejection of prevalent values and a form of narrative that is to some degree fragmented and elusive, suggesting a split with conventional realism and the assumptions underpinning it.

This creation of what Donoso himself calls, in the aforementioned essay on *El astillero*, "una literatura de ambigüedades inquietantes" ["a literature of disquieting ambiguities"] (12) is, of course, crucial to the notions of literary modernism and postmodernism. Yet it is the precise nature of this alleged "break with tradition" that illuminates some possible points of departure as well as points of contact between the two works. While distinctions between the modern and the postmodern remain notoriously porous—and appropriately so in the present case given the two texts' many shared characteristics—"postmodernism," in Smyth's summary of the debate, "differs from modernist aesthetics principally in its abandonment of subjectivity: the representation of consciousness is alleged to have been forsaken with the emphasis on the fragmentation of the subject."[3] As Smyth goes on to say, "that the self can no longer be considered a unified and stable entity has become axiomatic in the light of poststructuralism" (10). In essence then, modernism can be associated with epistemology and postmodernism with ontology. And, one might argue that, in their parallel "break with tradition," Onetti tends to display a fundamentally modernist consciousness while Donoso tends to display a postmodernist consciousness. In other words, though both explore a sense of disintegrating order and the loss of clear-cut values, Onetti's concern may seem to be the disorientation of the individual in the face of an increasingly absurd and meaningless world or environment, while Donoso's is more to do with the nature of identity itself as inherently unstable and arbitrarily constructed. Theories of critical reading should not always, of course, be confused with writing practice, and each of the categories mentioned might be seen ultimately to blend into the other. What one might discern, however, is the dramatization of a "moment," albeit incomplete and imprecisely articulated, in the development of twentieth-century consciousness, played out in the subtle and shifting pattern of correspondences and differences between the two novels under consideration.

One feature that *Juntacadáveres* and *El lugar sin límites* share is that the sense of "break with tradition" is brought out by the foregrounding of sexuality and desire, in particular so-called "unnatural" sexuality or desire. Western culture has traditionally naturalized and displaced desire so that sexual activity becomes associated with reproduction and the family, the useful and the functional—that is the "natural" and "necessary" social order. Catherine Belsey further comments that "the struggle to measure up, to establish a happy and wholesome sexual relation, to satisfy what might possibly be an insatiable desire, keeps us literally off the streets. Modern Western culture privileges private life and personal experience over every other kind of satisfaction."[4] Hence, of course, the centrality of the family home and the apprenticeship of the male hero in the nineteenth-century realist novel with its underlying assumptions of social (and even cosmic) order and coherence. In Onetti and Donoso the social nucleus of the family home is replaced with the brothel as the key social space. In *Juntacadáveres*, the brothel is presented as an outside threat to the precarious order of the local community. The demonization of the brothel is reflected in the carefully orchestrated campaign against it, inspired by religious institutions, which repeatedly associates it with "the work of the devil." Indeed one of the anonymous letters that form an important part of the antibrothel campaign reads, "Aliarse con el demonio . . . puede parecer un buen negocio. Pero la Divina Protección se aleja de nosotros" ["Joining sides with the devil . . . might seem like good business. But that takes Divine Protection away from us"], while another asks, "Para qué la iglesia si hay un lenocinio. Para qué un hogar si las mujeres se alquilan a diez pesos. Cuando un pueblo pierde el sentido de la decencia, es justo que pierda también la Divina Protección" ["Why bother with the church when you can have a bordello? Why bother with a family home when you can hire women for ten pesos? When a community loses its sense of decency, it's only fair that it should also lose Divine Protection"] (OC 865). In *El lugar sin límites*, meantime, reflecting the difference of emphasis alluded to earlier, the brothel does not so much form one of the binary poles in a conflict of inside-outside or order-chaos, because it has literally *become* the center of the community in so far as it is a major social arena for the leader of the community, the town's economic and political powerhouse, the landowner don Alejo (to the extent, in fact, that it becomes the headquarters for his electoral campaign and the site of celebration for the great and the good of the town following his victory). Moreover, the brothel does not so much function as a metaphorical demonized other, but represents an inverted world in itself where the binary order-chaos distinction has collapsed. Don Alejo's natural environment is the brothel as much as or even more than the family home or the church (where he is also, though only briefly, seen), but also the novel's pattern of inverted Christian imagery—discussed by me elsewhere[5]—presents him as both God and the Devil, suggesting the complete rupture of all binary divisions and the decomposition of all faith in external values. In Onetti's brothel, the gentlemen who use the facility are spied on and threatened with exposure because their antisocial behavior is in a state of tension with the supposed values of the institutional face of the local community. In Donoso's, such a tension does not really exist: the key moment of sexual activity there is the orgasm of the male homosexual transvestite Manuela who impregnates the female madam Japonesa Grande when their biological roles are overlaid by a performance in which the man acts out the part of the woman and the woman the part of a man.

These last remarks on Donoso also point up the problematization of the hero in the new novel. The institutional cohesion of the Church or the family home has its counterpart in the motif of the apprenticeship of the (usually male) hero. Again, both Onetti and Donoso break with the conventional pattern of the hero's preparation for his place in society. The linking of the hero to a brothel rather than to the family home or Church once more brings to the fore questions of sexuality and desire in an inevitable unsettling of fixed categories. As Belsey remarks, theorizing desire:

> Desire is in excess of the organism; conversely, it is what remains unspoken in the utterance. In consequence, it has no settled place to be. And moreover, at the level of the unconscious its objects are no more than a succession of substitutes for an imagined originary presence, a half-remembered "oceanic" pleasure in the lost real, a completeness which is desire's final, unattainable object. Perhaps, therefore, desire itself, the restlessness of it, and not our inadequacy, is the heart of the problem. (5)

The duality of desire and incompletion certainly characterizes the male heroes of Onetti and Donoso, though again in rather different ways. Both novels deal with men in relation to women, particularly whores. In a sense, both novels tend to reproduce what Bell, theorizing the prostitute body, has defined as "a process of othering [that] has produced the 'prostitute' as the other of the other: the other within the categorical other, 'woman'," the idea that "at the heart of the foundational metaphysics of Western thought [there] is the logocentric assumption of the binary opposition of masculine and feminine, the masculine being the privileged site and the feminine the disprivileged."[6] Masculine identity in Onetti certainly seems to have something to do with self-assertion over or, at least, othering of women. Junta Larsen seeks his elusive self-realization through the assembling of whores and the creation of a brothel. The young Jorge Malabia also appears to link the achievement of manhood with the possibility of using the brothel. Moreover, if one accepts, say, MacKinnon and Irigaray's construction of prostitution as the condition of all women,[7] Jorge and Marcos Bergner—albeit in an unclear sort of way—seem to connect the security of male identity with the domination or objectification of women. However, in Donoso, while there is a similar pattern of desire and imposition, the boundaries of gender and sexual identity are much more obscured. Most notably, the male hero has a woman's name and is referred to via feminine pronouns, and at the moment that he acts out the assertive male role to defend his daughter from an unruly client in the brothel, he "rescues" her by putting on a dress and attempting to seduce the client in question. In Onetti, to some degree, masculine identity is defined in relation to or opposition to the woman, the whore. In Donoso, the male effectively becomes or wishes to become the woman, the whore. Once again, the relationship of the individual to his environment gives way to an apparent dissolution of the very notion of individual identity.

Let us go on, then, to examine in turn the Onettian and Donosian hero and, briefly, some of the narrative strategies that support their conception. Larsen and Jorge, in *Juntacadáveres*, are essentially inverted representations of the vocational hero or the hero-as-apprentice of the nineteenth-century novel. Larsen, for example, "pensó que había nacido para realizar dos perfecciones: una mujer perfecta, un prostíbulo perfecto" ["felt that he had been born to achieve two perfections: a perfect woman, a perfect brothel"] and that "había que vivir para el momento en que tropezara con la muchacha o pudiera inaugurar el perfecto prostíbulo" ["he had to live for the moment when he would come across the right girl or could open the perfect brothel"] (920–21). This dream is described as both an "ideal" and a "vocation," a vision he has struggled for and, after a long period in the metaphorical wilderness, finally achieved. This is, of course, doubly ironic: firstly because it is clearly a mock or inverted ideal and also because it is doomed from the very moment of victory (the whores are grotesque and not up to the job so that "fundar el prostíbulo era ahora, esencialmente, como casarse *in articulo mortis*, como creer en fantasmas" ["to found the brothel was now essentially like getting married *in articulo mortis*, like believing in ghosts"] (831). Jorge, meantime, is a teenager undergoing a process of initiation into the adult world and, more specifically, undergoing a process of sexual education through his sister-in-law Julita. Yet his growing-up is also presented ironically: he fails as a figure of assertiveness and rebellion, his sexual experience is followed by the suicide of the woman and even just before he makes love to Julita, he accepts the unavoidable "soledad" ["solitude"] of human existence realizing that "estoy solo" ["I am alone"] (917). In both cases, the inversion of the ideal indicates a break with the assumptions of order and established positive values underlying the realist tradition. Yet, in another sense, both characters do assert a positive identity in their respective acts of rebellion. They are portrayed against a background of an irretrievably petty and hypocritical small-town environment and Jorge rejects the values of his bourgeois family and identifies with Larsen whom he sees as the incarnation of an antibourgeois mentality. In the end, Larsen might be seen as a species of absurd hero achieving a kind of dignity and nobility in his struggle against limitations, while Jorge might be seen as graduating from his existential apprenticeship with a sharper sense of awareness than any of those around him.

The ambiguity concerning identity in Onetti, particularly male identity, is explained by Millington in straightforward psychoanalytical terms as a conflict between the Imaginary and the Symbolic in which "the Imaginary seeks to avoid the Symbolic, whose constraining laws and norms disrupt its narcissistic goals" thus "articulating something of the drive of the male characters in Onetti to seek an escape or relocation which implies the search for a (re)new(ed) identity and a plenitude of being."[8] In the text, then, there is a feeling that people are no more than the roles they enact, yet equally there is a strong sense of yearning for or even faith in a unitary self or identity. Díaz Grey, the pseudoneutral outside observer, often appears to perceive identity as constructed. Of Barthé, for example, he comments: "no es una persona; es, como todos los habitantes de esta franja del río, una determinada intensidad de existencia que ocupa, se envasa en la forma de su particular manía, su particular idiotez" ["he isn't a person; he's like everyone else who lives on this side of the river, just a given intensity of existence that fills up the space of, that takes the form of, his particular obsession, his particular idiocy"] (792). He refers to "la expresión austera que [Barthé] había construido" ["the austere expression that (Barthé) had constructed"] (794). Of Larsen, he says that "hablaba refrenando con facilidad la furia o tal vez fingiéndola" ["he spoke, easily holding back his fury or perhaps feigning it"] and describes him as "construido con sustancia de tedio y absurdo" ["constructed from a substance made of tedium and absurdity"] (808). Jorge talks of observing Marcos and Rita, in the sexual act, in a similar way: "mirarlos empujar mientras tratan de mezclarse, o de simular que se mezclan" ["watching them pushing as they tried to fuse together, or to simulate fusing together"] (815). The motif of observation implies objectification and the reduction to role, but it can also include the observer himself. Díaz Grey, for instance, in one chapter, remarks of himself that "no comprendo, lo reconozco, a este yo trepado junto al mostrador de un hotel de Santa María con el bastón y el sombrero entre las piernas" ["I don't understand, I recognize, this me propped up against the bar in a Santa María hotel with his stick and his hat between his legs"] (843), referring later to one of "todos los Díaz Grey que hubieran sido posibles" ["all the Díaz Greys that had been possible"] and "el más Díaz Grey de los Díaz Grey" ["the most Díaz Grey of all the Díaz Greys"] , even ending up describing himself in the third person: "Díaz Grey fuma" ["Díaz Grey smokes"] (851). Junta Larsen sees himself in a similar sort of way. His life now is no more than "una serie de actos reflejos" ["a series of reflex acts"] and, objectifying himself as "el difunto *Junta*" ["the deceased *Junta*"], he feels that "sólo le era posible hablar de *Junta* con sí mismo. Preveía los ademanes medidos, los ojos inmóviles y rojos de los soliloquios, el esfuerzo desesperado, la voluntad de abstención " ["it was only possible for him to talk about *Junta* with himself. He could foresee the measured gestures, the motionless red eyes of his soliloquies, the desperate effort, the will to abstention"] (895).

On the other hand, however, many references in the novel, including some of those just quoted, suggest particularity and individuality at the same time as they suggest the arbitrarily constructed persona. The aforementioned account of Larsen is also "la historia única, insustituible de aquel hombre llamado de varias maneras, llamado *Junta*" ["the unique, irreplaceable history of that man called various names, called *Junta*"] (894). In the scene involving Díaz Grey he is, despite his detachment, enjoying "el puro placer de entregarse a sueños elegidos por absurdos" ["the sheer pleasure of giving himself over to dreams chosen precisely because they are absurd"] (796) and observes because "debo ver qué cosa única hay dentro" ["I must see what there is within that is unique"] (793). So there is a sense of individual identity in the novel. Indeed, much of the novel is about the need to assert that identity, or, as Jorge says, "imponerse a los demás, abolirlos, ser en ellos y obligarlos a ser en nosotros" ["to impose your identity on others, to wipe them out, to be in them and to oblige them to be in us"] (814). This illuminates the relationship of the male "hero" to the female or whore in the novel. The male construction of the female other is implicit in Belsey's words on desire: "the subject itself, already redoubled and split in its imagined, imaged, speculary wholeness, and divided again in its own utterances between the 'I' who speaks and the 'I' who is put on show there, longs for an 'other' (person, way of life, mode of being) which would make it truly whole and unified. . . . The desire of the Other is (or includes) the longing to be the undifferentiated origin of difference, to occupy the place of the deployment of speech, to *be* or to *control* the condition of the possibility of subjectivity—and in consequence of desire itself" (198–99). The other of the male subject is usually, of course, woman. Irigaray's project, for instance, is, in part, "to go back through the masculine imaginary, to interpret the way it has reduced us to silence, to muteness or mimicry," in other words to deconstruct the tendency "to write woman as man's other, his negative, a mirror for reflecting his masculinity."[9] Women, by and large, in Onetti's novel are presented as blanks. On the opening page, in an image later echoed in the figure of the model Sylvia Corday in Donoso's *Tres novelitas burguesas* [*Sacred Families*], the whores are seen to be literally drawing their features on the their faces with lipstick and make-up. An earlier woman of Larsen's is called Blanca and is nothing more than "una cara, en blanco como el nombre" ["a face—a blank whiteness like her name"] (871). Larsen's whores are merely things or objects, bodies or corpses, "cadáveres," "cuerpos doblados y deformes," "restos de mujer" ["cadavers," "bent, shapeless bodies," "leftovers of woman"] (827), "el cadáver gordísimo, apenas verdoso, maloliente, . . . esta presencia" ["the hugely fat, barely greenish, smelly corpse, . . . this presence"] (829). Furthermore, all women seem to be equated with whores from a certain male point of view. Marcos refers to Ana María and *la Nena* as a "maldito par de putas" ["damned pair of whores"] (898) and "yeguas" ["bitches" (lit., "mares")] (901) and later comments that "después de todo, las mujeres son la misma cosa, cualquier mujer" ["after all, all women are the same thing, any woman"] (937). Women, then, become whores, mere objects or blanks upon which to inscribe male desire and identity. Identity through assertion becomes central to the male's sense of self.

During his relationship with Blanca, Larsen spends his wages on male pursuits only, like drinking, because it is essential that his money "no fuera útil para ella" ["should not be of any use to her"] (870) and she becomes one of a chain of women-as-objects he uses for his own ends (later, "se separó de Blanca o de la mujer que sustituía a Blanca" ["he separated from her or from the woman who had replaced Blanca" (871)]). He subsequently goes on to define his identity, *Junta-cadáveres*, through the collecting of whores. But even the seemingly more sensitive Jorge Malabia repeats a similar pattern. His growing-up (or acquisition of identity) is inextricably linked to self-assertion with regard to women. "Necesito una mujer," he says, "lo único que me importa es una mujer" ["I need a woman, the only thing that matters to me is a woman"] (860). His problematic relationship with Julita is disturbing because she controls him through her half-crazy games, to which he acquiesces and in which she encourages him to deny his own identity and adopt the role of another man, his dead brother Federico. The climax to the relationship comes when he and she assume his own name, he makes love to her and slaps her. More-over, he fingers his knife in a number of the sexually charged scenes with Julita. The knife is a phallic symbol of male power and violence, but is also concealed, suggesting insecurity of identity, and frequently displaced by the image of the pipe that he also toys with, an image of a weaker and perhaps falsely assumed masculine identity. Moreover, between the slap and the moment Jorge places the knife beneath Julita's pillow is a scene where Marcos (Julita's truculent brother and a sort of perverted older male role model and sidekick for Jorge) talks of his vague urge to kill someone in the context of his violent emotions toward women (chapters 23, 24, 26). Julita's death indeed comes shortly after Jorge's sexual initiation with her. None of this is terribly clear in its implications, but there is some sense in which Jorge's attempted construction of his identity as a man has something to do with the othering of women and the erection of power over them, even if Julita's suicide may ultimately suggest the elusiveness of that quest as much as its success.

Behind, then, the novel's playing with the notion of the uncertainty and arbitrariness of identity, is an assertion or attempted assertion of some kind of solidity of male identity based on power or control. This is a slippery concept and Millington, for example, argues that "just as . . . Larsen discovers that to evade the power of the bourgeois symbolic order through fantasies of perfect women and the perfect brothel is an imaginary and unsustainable objective, so Jorge discovers that his independence and capacity for self-determination are strictly limited. . . . There is no plenitude of fulfilled self here—the self is caught between its roles and its desire, and hence it is split, it differs from itself."[10] Such a psychoanalytical reading of the characters of *Juntacadáveres* is highly convincing, but it is perhaps less clear which side of the equation is given emphasis by the text's narrative perspective. Millington's exhaustive account of the novel's proneness to decentring, its nonlinearity and its switches of focalization and narrator suggest difference and fragmentation. Yet this surface difference may cover some degree of underlying consistency of perspective. The role of Díaz Grey, a role sometimes paralleled by other characters such as Jorge, privileges the idea of detached outside observation, hinting at a unified consciousness beyond the events portrayed. Indeed the parallels between the characters are such that one sometimes has the impression that they are basically the same, part of a single consciousness. Above all, there is an extraordinary passage in the twentieth chapter—ostentatiously flagged by asterisks breaking the narrative—that appears to clarify the narrative perspective of the novel as a whole. A narrator, assuming, it might seem, the identity of the figure of the, or an, author, intervenes to describe how he has invented or created the town of Santa María and its inhabitants, determining their exact nature and characteristics (910–11). While the enigmatic comment that "es imposible que intervenga y altere" ["it is impossible for me to intervene and make alterations"] (910) may imply a degree of powerlessness, the passage as a whole may seem to reinstate the sovereignty of individual consciousness. *Juntacadáveres* certainly raises questions about the nature of identity, but it does not seem fully to have abandoned the idea of the primacy of the individual.

In *El lugar sin límites* the male hero is a complete inversion or fragmentation of his nineteenth-century counterpart. The central character Manuela also runs a brothel but cannot be seen as attempting to assert a cohesive male identity in relation to women or whores. Instead he is a weak and ugly homosexual transvestite who longs to be a woman and dances at the brothel in a colorful Spanish dress. Indeed his identity is obscured to the extent that he is referred to by feminine pronouns and adjectives so that the reader perceives him initially as a woman and is, for much of the novel, confused as to his sexual identity. In fact, much of the power of his presentation depends on the interplay between his biological sex and his wider sense of identity. Though he sees himself as a woman, the fact that he has sired a child, Japonesita, constantly threatens his sense of self:

> Porque cuando la Japonesita le decía papá, su vestido de española tendido encima del lavatorio se ponía más viejo, la percala gastada, el rojo desteñido, los zurcidos a la vista, horrible, ineficaz, y la noche oscura y fría extendiéndose por las viñas, apretando y venciendo esta chispita que había sido posible fabricar en el despoblado, no me digái papá, chiquilla huevona. Dime Manuela, como todos. ¡Que te defienda! Lo único que faltaba. ¿Y a una, quién la defiende?[11]

> [Because when Japonesita called her dad, her Spanish dress hanging over the washstand grew older, the fabric worn, the red faded, the darns plainly visible, horrible, useless, and the black, cold night spreading through the vineyards, squeezing and crushing the one little spark that it had been possible to create in this deserted place, don't call me dad, you goddamn brat. Call me Manuela, like everyone does. You want me to defend you! And what about me? Who's going to defend me?]

The relationship between maleness and identity, then, is much more problematic than in *Juntacadáveres*. There is a certain similarity with Larsen, though, in that Manuela has been seen, most notably by McMurray,[12] as an absurd hero, clinging nobly to his image of himself and a positive spirit despite the appalling limitations of his circumstances. "Vieja estaría pero se iba a morir cantando y con las plumas puestas" ["She might be old but she was going to die singing and wearing her feather dress"] (14) is the phrase that perhaps sums up this aspect of his personality. However, this optimistic utterance undergoes a cruel and ironic twist: when he dresses up and dances to seduce Pancho Vega near the end, he is brutally beaten to death, realizing that he is, as a matter of fact, Manuel, and that this will be the name on his gravestone. The cohesive feminine identity he seeks is a myth and it is his very maleness that provokes the beating that leads to his death. The name on the headstone is a reminder that he has been little more than a biological body with no unitary psychic identity beyond it. The potentially positive reading of Manuela is comprehensively undone at the end when, after his death, the novel closes instead with the lonely, failed, and miserable Japonesita. She is the reminder of Manuela's biological identity and her plea for a father's protection provoked his death. She now extinguishes the light, metaphorically the futile brightness associated with Manuela, and retreats into darkness as the brothel slips into terminal decline and the entire town begins finally to disappear into oblivion.

The other two principal male protagonists in the novel, though seemingly more obviously masculine, also dissolve conventional expectations of the male hero. The object of Manuela's unease and sexual fascination is the burly trucker Pancho Vega. Inspiring fear and erotic desire in the female or feminine characters, penetrating the darkness with his big red truck, with his hand on his throbbing gear-stick and his piercing honking of his horn making the women and Manuela pulsate with emotional energy, he may seem the macho romantic hero. However, he is wracked by guilt, in a crisis of dependency with regard to Don Alejo, terrified of the landowner's dogs and cowardly in facing up to him, and, most dramatically, he is a latent homosexual secretly drawn to Manuela. Don Alejo, meantime, the tough and manly all-powerful *terrateniente* ["landlord"], Mr. Fix It and protector of Manuela, turns out to be powerless and able to fix very little: the town's economy is collapsing, he is unable to fulfill his promise to bring in electricity, he fails to rescue Manuela from Pancho as had been expected, and turns out to be old, weak, and dying. Indeed, these characters form part of a pattern of inversion in the novel that suggests the absence of any sense of unitary psychological identity. The apparent woman Manuela is a man who nonetheless acts like a woman when making love. The macho man Pancho is a closet homosexual. The powerful landowner and politician is feeble and powerless. The young woman Japonesita acts and looks like an old crone, wants to leave the village but always stays, yearns for Pancho but hates him, runs a brothel but is a virgin, is an adult but has no breasts or pubic hair, and wants to be a mother but has not yet even begun to menstruate. The binary male-female distinction, essential to the attempted construction of identity in *Juntacadáveres*, is thoroughly blurred here. Whereas the title of Onetti's novel is a name that in some senses defines a unitary male identity, the space of this novel is a *lugar sin límites* (lit., "place without limits"), a world without boundaries, binary logic, or cohesive identities. Limits are constantly shifting: the center of the town has moved, the railway station is in decline as the new road bypasses the town, the economic focus switches to the road, the economic boom is over and the lack of electricity will mean perpetual and all-encompassing darkness, the brothel is no longer a social center and is literally sinking into the ground, the vineyards will swamp and devour the town. As the epigraph from Marlowe and the characterization of Alejo as evil God and as creator and provider in an infernal world suggest, even Heaven and Hell are here one and the same. The ultimate boundary is meaningless because all is fluid, unstable, and arbitrary.

The narrative focus of the novel tends to underpin this pattern of uncertainty. The narrative voice repeatedly changes and, as Morell has shown, even the narrative person does not clearly indicate narrative voice.[13] There is no implied focal narratorial or pseudo-authorial consciousness as in the twentieth chapter of *Juntacadáveres*. Moreover, the novel draws attention to the process of framing or delimiting, but only to underline its status as a process of perception and as therefore illusory. This is rather different to the case of *Juntacadáveres*, which is, in large part, predicated on the idea of external observation (even if the process of observation does often yield ambiguous results). Magnarelli has studied the use of flashbacks and the motif of looking through windows or doors in the novel, convincingly demonstrating that "what appears to be a limit (the frame that simultaneously marks a center, that which is framed), like artistic authority in mimetic art, is precarious and ever shifting, a product of the viewer's perspective and position (both spatial and temporal)."[14] Furthermore, Magnarelli notes that what frequently predominates in the framing process is the sense of "theater, the spectacle, directed and orchestrated (to a large degree 'framed') by the gaze of the male" (73). Thus the problematization of the framing process in Donoso suggests another degree of difference with Onetti where observation and narrative focus are often linked to the construction of male identity in relation to an objectified other. The most obvious example of the framing male gaze in *El lugar sin límites* is the performance of copulation between Manuela and Japonesa Grande (itself seen in flashback) staged and watched by Don Alejo as part of a bet. Yet the controlling gaze of the powerful male is thoroughly subverted by a scene that generates multiple, contradictory, and unexpected connotations. The strong male Alejo is, ironically, reduced to the passive role of spectator and indeed is actually undone by the performance in that he loses control of his brothel when Japonesa Grande wins the bet, proving, against indications, her own powers of feminine seduction and Manuela's potential masculinity. Manuela meanwhile is substituting for Alejo in the sexual act by penetrating Japonesa Grande, yet Japonesa Grande is substituting for Alejo too insofar as Manuela would like to have been in bed with him. Moreover, as Magnarelli has pointed out, "Japonesa and Manuela became so engrossed in their roles that their performance (the theater, the mask) became their 'reality'; instead of pretending to copulate, as was the plan, they did" (71). Identity is reduced to a series of gestures, performances, roles, and substitutions that merely deflect attention away from the underlying inconsistency, disunity, and fragility of personality or identity.

Juntacadáveres and *El lugar sin límites*, then, are both novels that break with tradition by questioning secure categories of identity through the foregrounding of the unruly element of desire and sexuality. If there is a difference of emphasis it is that the former novel betrays a yearning for fixity of identity in a hostile and contradictory outside world, while the latter radically problematizes the inside-outside dialectic, subverting the very notion of identity itself. This may be illustrated briefly by the way in which Onetti's text continues to pay lip service, albeit rather sardonically, to the utopian ideal while Donoso's presents a vision of a hell on earth. Larsen's utopian ideal of the perfect brothel has its echo in Marcos Bergner's more conventionally utopian phalanstery, "una comunidad cristiana y primitiva basada en el altruismo, la tolerancia, el mutuo entendimiento" [a primitive and Christian community based on altruism, tolerance, mutual understanding] (884). Both fail, of course, and are in any case presented against a background of day-to-day drudgery and sordidness. But the ambiguous portrayal of Marcos and the heroic dimension to Larsen's character differentiate them to some degree from the imploded *mundo al revés* ["world upside down"] of El Olivo in Donoso's novel. The abolition of money and property is usually implicit in the utopian project, but both are clearly central moving principles in the novels discussed here, driving the brothel-owners in particular. This raises the whole idea of exchange value and the idea of women circulating as commodities in an exchange economy. Property and ownership may relate to the elusive ideals of identity and control, especially in Onetti, but "exchange" also suggests fluidity and uncertainty, particularly in *El lugar sin límites*, which is set against a background of unnerving socioeconomic change radically destabilizing the identity of a small town. Yet the comprehensive problematization of the utopian ideal in Onetti versus its absence in Donoso does suggest that the distance between the two texts is small. And, in the same way, Onetti's text clearly problematizes the question of identity even if identity as a category is subjected to a more rigorous scrutiny in Donoso. Though the distinction made at the beginning between a modernist and postmodernist consciousness may remain by and large valid, the porosity of the terms used and of the nuanced nature of the textual differences alluded to here refers us to a "moment" of response to traditional models and underlines the complexity and liquidity of the processes of cultural-intellectual evolution. Belsey concludes her study on desire by arguing that "desire remains finally uninscribed, in excess of its own performance," but that it "is the metonym of a discontent which envisages utopia, a continuing restlessness that motivates change, whether for better or worse" (209). The utopia of plenitude of being and identity is undermined to different degrees in both texts. What remains is the sense of discontent and change, be it in the restlessness of the individual in modernism or in the permanent restlessness of identity in postmodernism.

NOTES

1. See José Donoso, *Historia personal del "boom,"* 54.
2. José Donoso, "Prólogo," in Juan Carlos Onetti, *El astillero* (1970), 11–15.
3. Edmund Smyth, "Introduction," in *Postmodernism and Contemporary Fiction*, ed. Edmund Smyth, 10.
4. Catherine Belsey, *Desire: Love Stories in Western Culture*, 5.
5. See Philip Swanson, *José Donoso: The "Boom" and Beyond*.
6. Shannon Bell, *Reading, Writing and Rewriting the Prostitute*, 2.
7. See Bell, 88.
8. Mark I. Millington, *An Analysis of the Short Stories of Juan Carlos Onetti*, 4.
9. See Bell, 87. She quotes Luce Irigaray from *This Sex which is not One*, trans. Catherine Porter (Ithaca: Cornell UP, 1985), 164.
10. Mark Millington, *Reading Onetti*, 283–84.
11. José Donoso, *El lugar sin límites*, 51–52.
12. See George R. McMurray, *José Donoso*.
13. See Hortensia R. Morell, *Composición expresionista en "El lugar sin límites" de José Donoso*.
14. Sharon Magnarelli, *Understanding José Donoso*, 75.

WORKS CITED

Bell, Shannon. *Reading, Writing and Rewriting the Prostitute Body*. Bloomington and Indianapolis: Indiana UP, 1994.

Belsey, Catherine. *Desire: Love Stories in Western Culture*. Oxford: Blackwell, 1994.

Donoso, José. *El lugar sin límites*. Barcelona: Seix Barral, 2nd ed., 1981. (*Hell Has No Limits*, in *Triple Cross*. Trans. Suzanne Jill Levine. New York: Dutton, 1973.)

Donoso, José. *Historia personal del "boom."* Barcelona: Seix Barral, 1983. (*The Boom in Spanish American Literature: A Personal History*. Trans. Gregory Kolovakos. New York: Columbia UP and Center for Inter-American Relations, 1977.)

McMurray, George R. *José Donoso*. New York: Twayne, 1979.

Magnarelli, Sharon. *Understanding José Donoso*. Columbia: University of South Carolina Press, 1993.

Millington, Mark I. *An Analysis of the Short Stories of Juan Carlos Onetti*. Lewiston, N.Y.: Edwin Mellen, 1993.

Millington, Mark. *Reading Onetti*. Liverpool, U.K.: Francis Cairns, 1985.

Morell, Hortensia R. *Composición expresionista en "El lugar sin límites" de José Donoso*. Río Piedras: Universidad de Puerto Rico, 1986.

Onetti, Juan Carlos. *El astillero*. Madrid: Salvat, 1970.

Smyth, Edmund, ed. *Postmodernism and Contemporary Fiction*. London: Batsford, 1991.

Swanson, Philip. *José Donoso: The "Boom" and Beyond*. Liverpool, U.K.: Francis Cairns, 1988.

4

Otherwise, or Reading
Onetti with Borges

Mark I. Millington

In the context of a collection of essays called *Onetti and Others* my concern is precisely with the concept of "the other," and specifically the structure and dynamics of the subject in its relation with the other. Via two stories I intend to explore that relation and to point up a particular gender inflection. My purpose is to stage a textual juxtaposition between Onetti and Borges: what is revealed in the juxtaposition is that a subject may act decisively to dismiss an other but is in fact crucially reliant on that other for its constitution. A subject "others" the other but thereby also incorporates the other as part of its identity. My concern is to use Onetti and Borges as vehicles for an exploration of the workings of the effect of the other: I do not seek to "tell truths" about Onetti or Borges, as if Borges might be used somehow to cast definitive light on Onetti (or vice versa). Their juxtaposition is factitious—a similar exploration of the other (differently staged and focused) could be carried out by pairing Onetti with Cortázar, or Hammett, or Faulkner, or Céline, or Hemingway. In other words, I make no claim for a "special relationship" between Onetti and Borges: although they did both live in the Plate region between the 1900s and the 1970s, they do not as writers apparently share very much. But juxtaposing them (*not* factitiously) via two stories does create certain shapes and constructs certain perceptions. In particular, the pursuit of the effect of the other will enable the posing of questions about the definition and delimitation of the subject: What are its boundaries and how stable are they?

In fact, my exploration involves a third party and a third text. I shall be analyzing two stories (Onetti's "Jacob y el otro" ["Jacob and the Other Man"] and Borges' "La casa de Asterión" [*The House of Aster-*

ion]) in conjunction with another text (apparently not fictional) by Emir Rodríguez Monegal. In his introduction to the 1970 Aguilar edition of Onetti's *Obras completas* (which were not complete even then), Rodríguez Monegal devotes a section (OC 14–16) to a rather curious encounter between Onetti and Borges.[1] The singling out of this one incident, in an introduction devoted almost entirely to literary history and criticism, signals its striking quality. The encounter (emphatically not a meeting) is intriguing insofar as it shares many of the underlying structural and dynamic features of the relation of subject and other in "Jacob y el otro" and "La casa de Asterión" that I wish to explore. I start with Rodríguez Monegal's account.

STAGING AN ENCOUNTER

Some time in the summer months of 1948–49 and at the request of Onetti, Rodríguez Monegal (who knew both writers) arranged a meeting with Borges. At this time Borges was already an important literary figure in the Plate region; by contrast, Onetti's major work and reputation were still to be created. Rodríguez Monegal staged the meeting in a Buenos Aires café, "La Helvética," a name (misleadingly) suggestive of Swiss impartiality or neutrality. He and Borges arrived late for the meeting and Rodríguez Monegal soon suspected that Onetti had drunk a few beers while he was waiting, which contributed to his being in a difficult mood. Whether the mood was due to the long wait, Onetti's shyness, or the beer, Rodríguez Monegal describes that mood as funereal: "Estaba hosco, como retraído en sí mismo, y *a la defensiva*. Sólo salía de su isla para *atacar* con una virulencia que nunca le había visto" ["He was sullen, as if withdrawn in himself, and *on the defensive*. He only came out of his shell to *attack*, with a virulence that I'd never seen in him before"] (15, italics mine). The fighting imagery here is striking and will be crucial to some of my later reflections. However, as a result of Onetti's attitude, the conversation did not settle, but leapt around without making constructive headway, until Onetti abruptly asked a rather aggressive and dismissive question about Henry James: "—Y ahora que están juntos, díganme, explíquenme, ¿qué le ven a Henry James, qué le ven al coso ese?" ["And now that we're together, tell me, explain to me, what you see in Henry James, what do you see in that jerk?"] (15). Ingenuously (as Rodríguez Monegal subsequently saw it), he and Borges tried to give helpful explanations to "enlighten" Onetti, but they were hardly appropriate and missed the point of Onetti's question. Like Rodríguez Monegal's whole staging of the meeting, the explanations were doomed attempts to build a bridge, to reconcile two writers, two subjects, whose relations were fraught with temperamental and aesthetic incompatibilities. And those incompatibilities even extended to Borges' not accepting Onetti's implicit invitation to enter an outright sparring match over Henry James. The apparent gap between Onetti and Borges, the unbridgeable gulf, the conflict of value and identity, can be traced into the content of the two stories that I have chosen to examine, which, however, rely on an intriguingly similar underlying logic. In both stories, the boundary between subject and other is not as sharp as, at first sight, appears, and the complexity of underlying reciprocity will eventually lead us back to the encounter in "La Helvética."

SPACES OF SUBJECTIVITY AND OTHERNESS

My point of entry into the discussion of "Jacob y el otro" and "La casa de Asterión" is space(s). More especially, what interests me is the way in which space(s) can be read (allegorically) as articulating the structure of subjectivity. In "La casa de Asterión," the key spaces are Asterión's "casa" ["house"] and its implied location in an urban context. Hence if the "casa" is an inside, an urban space is clearly its outside. The "casa" is never named as a labyrinth, but when, at the very end of the story, Theseus definitively names Asterión as the Minotaur, the "casa" is automatically identifiable as the Cretan labyrinth of Greek mythology.[2] As a result also, the urban space outside is identifiable as Cnossus. As deployed in the story, Asterión's labyrinth is a place that sets him apart, in which he draws a line between himself and the world, taking refuge from what is outside.

The characteristics of the "casa" as described by Asterión are significant. It is a place of some austerity, having no furniture and none of the "bizarro aparato de los palacios" ["splendid display of palaces"],[3] though there is an infinite number of "pesebres, abrevaderos, patios, aljibes" [mangers, drinking-troughs, courtyards, cisterns"] (71). In his disdainful reference to the display of palaces, Asterión alludes to his divine lineage, his mother Pasiphae being the daughter of Helios, the sun. Asterión's currently humble state hardly reflects that lineage but he endeavors to control the perception of his "casa" by suggesting that it is sober or restrained, and this characterization is gendered as masculine since the visitor "no hallará pompas mujeriles aquí" ["will find no womanly ostentation here"] (69). Asterión insists (with suspiciously excessive force) that the "casa" has no (literal) closed doors and no (literal) locks, but this implied openness is strangely combined with his assertion that when he went outside he quickly returned having seen the fear that his appearance inspired in others. There is manifest ambivalence here: on the one hand, defensive assertions that the "casa" is open, that others' perception of his being a prisoner is utterly erroneous, but, on the other, a clinging to a self-imposed seclusion from others, the result perhaps of his fear of others' fear. That ambivalence between openness and closure, freedom and imprisonment, is reinforced by the disorientation, the lack of precise coordinates within the "casa" because of its infinitely repeated features (71), which preclude any certain identification of location. And yet, despite these confusing characteristics, Asterión is clear about one thing: he insists that his "casa" is unique, denying strenuously that there is another like it in Egypt. That insistence ties in with his view that there are only two unique things in the world: the sun and Asterión. He is unique and appropriately the "casa" is unique also. The space that he inhabits is entirely in accord with his identity. But that uniqueness can also be read as isolation, and, in this context, the space and the character can be seen as displaying the illusion of a sovereign masculine subjectivity: supposedly autonomous and self-determining. The unique character encloses itself in its unique labyrinthine space, rejecting others and creating a tensely defensive and brittle, manichean structure of identity.

Although "Jacob y el otro" is at first sight very different from "La casa de Asterión," appearing less cerebral and less self-consciously intertextual,[4] there are very striking common features in the deep structures relating to space and the other. "Jacob y el otro" is highly literary in its own way: its play on perspectives and narrative voices is very sophisticated. Space is articulated in terms of an inside/outside polarity, just as it is in "La casa de Asterión." In this case, the "inside" is a wrestling ring and the "outside" the provincial town of Santa María. This polarization is articulated through the ex-champion wrestler Jacob van Oppen, who, as part of a Latin American tour in which he takes on any challenger, arrives in the less than spectacular setting of Santa María. By contrast with "La casa de Asterión," the urban context is given a modicum of attention, at least insofar as its conservative values are concerned. It is a small, banal town and Jacob's rather incongruous arrival says much about his decline. The tone of the doctor who narrates chapter 1 sets the mood of routine boredom in Santa María, in which an aging wrestler immediately becomes the main focus of attention. The principal element from Santa María that comes into contact with Jacob is the relationship between Adriana and Mario, who are about to marry. Adriana calculates that Mario can easily beat Jacob and sees the challenge as a way to make money for their wedding. And there is a symbolic dimension here: for Mario to beat Jacob will ease the path of marriage in Santa María. In that sense, Jacob threatens a particular social convention.

Just as Jacob "opens" Santa María to the outside world—however briefly—so the apparently closed nature of the wrestling ring is an illusion. For the ring is just one link in a potentially infinite chain: it is a synecdoche for the endless series of challenges in countless wrestling rings stretching backwards and forwards in time. This is an unending chain of repeating and identical spaces in which Jacob is open to any challenge. This complex combination of an unending chain of rings (with the connotation of Jacob's being trapped or enchained) and also of openness (with the connotation of Jacob's having no fixed identity) is reminiscent of the infinite, indecipherable repetition of Asterión's labyrinth and its paradoxically entrapping openness. Moreover, just as Asterión's labyrinth is empty except for "pesebres," "abrevaderos," and "aljibes" ["mangers," "drinking-troughs," and "cisterns"] (which hardly furnish a home), so the wrestling ring is empty except for the (perhaps Jamesian) figures on the mat described by struggling male bodies. As Asterión waits for his visitors, none of whom survives the encounter with him until Theseus arrives, so Jacob has defeated all those with the temerity to penetrate his space by entering the ring, although the play of perspectives in the story at first misleads the reader into believing that he has been defeated. In both cases, the space—labyrinth, wrestling ring—belongs to the sovereign male, the only escape from which appears to be death or ignominy, so tightly drawn is the desired boundary. Despite the multiplicity of rings, however, there is a strict uniformity in their significance: each is the space for the same desperate scenario in which Jacob enacts his desire to stand alone and undefeated, the embodiment of a unique, all-conquering authority; he would be the champion whether the wrestling ring were in Santa María or in Colombia, Peru, Ecuador, or Bolivia (1366). The scenario of the fight is always the same and the resulting uniqueness/isolation of Jacob is unchanging, just as Asterión's labyrinth is unique and his loneliness clear. Further, Asterión's bravado in rejecting all criticism is equivalent to the ritual performance of physical strength and suppleness that Jacob provides daily in Santa María: in both cases, we witness masculinity projecting itself as beyond vulnerability. In that sense, the imaginary spatial division into inside and outside is crucial: both Asterión and Jacob are trapped in structures of identity that leave them no way to adapt or change, and they are identities that are heavily freighted with gender conformity.

THE OTHER IN IDENTITY

In the constitution of Asterión's and Jacob's identities the other is an indispensable element, and its position and effectiveness are not perhaps what either of them might think. Asterión is at pains to underline his status as a special, rather superior being. His arrogance comes through, for instance, as he points out that trivia do not lodge in his mind since his disposition is for what is grand, a point that may again allude to his descent from the gods. That allusion and his arrogance are consolidated when he likens himself to the sun, who is his grandfather, Helios. He openly talks of others' accusations about his arrogance, misanthropy, and perhaps imprisonment and madness (69–70). He meets these accusations with aggression: outright rejection and contempt characterize his attempts to create a polarity between himself and others. These initial polarizing gestures and antagonism are soon complemented by hints at reciprocity: when he ventures out of the labyrinth he experiences fear, a feeling that is evidently also shared by those who see him:

> Por lo demás, algún atardecer he pisado la calle; si antes de la noche volví, lo hice por el temor que me infundieron las caras de la plebe, caras descoloridas y aplanadas, como la mano abierta. Ya se había puesto el sol, pero el desvalido llanto de un niño y las toscas plegarias de la grey dijeron que me habían reconocido. La gente oraba, huía, se prosternaba; unos se encaramaban al estilóbato del templo de las Hachas, otros juntaban piedras. (70)

> [Besides, one afternoon I stepped out into the street; if I returned before night, I did so because of the fear which the faces of the masses inspired in me, colorless, flat faces, like an open hand. The sun had gone down, but the desperate crying of a child and the crude prayers of the faithful told me that they had recognized me. People prayed, fled, prostrated themselves: some climbed on to the stylobate of the temple of the Axes, others gathered stones.]

Although the elements of panic and prayer here do create an Old Testament quality that is soon to seem entirely appropriate, the boundary marking off the other may not be as clear and stable as was thought. Furthermore, Asterión says that he plays games in which he is visited by unknown others and by another Asterión to whom he shows the house (70), both of which are games suggestive of a desire for contact with the other. This desire for visits by others is (at least partially) realized in the regular arrival every nine years of nine visitors. Asterión talks of freeing them from all evil, as if he were himself a redeemer, but this phrase turns out to mean that he kills these interlopers, a combination that suggestively repeats the previous ambivalence between aggression toward and desire for the other. His aggression, the effort to eliminate the other, indicates the attempted renewal of a boundary, of an absolute separation. On the other hand, his response to the prediction that his redeemer will come is to long for that other, to regret his isolation, and to toy with the permutations of the other's identity. These permutations produce a complex mirroring that projects the redeemer, Asterión, awaiting his own redeemer—a self desiring an other that is already itself:

> Ignoro quiénes son, pero sé que uno de ellos profetizó, en la hora de su muerte, que alguna vez llegaría mi redentor. Desde entonces no me duele la soledad, porque sé que vive mi redentor y al fin se levantará sobre el polvo. Si mi oído alcanzara todos los rumores del mundo, yo percibiría sus pasos. Ojalá me lleve a un lugar con menos galerías y menos puertas. ¿Cómo será mi redentor?, me pregunto. ¿Será un toro o un hombre? ¿Será tal vez un toro con cara de hombre? ¿O será como yo? (72)

> [I do not know who they are, but I know that one of them prophesied, at the hour of his death, that one day my redeemer would come. Since then my solitude does not hurt me, because I know that my redeemer lives and finally he will rise above the dust. If my ear could capture all the sounds of the world, I would perceive his steps. I hope that he takes me to a place with fewer galleries and fewer doors. What will my redeemer be like?, I wonder. Will he be a bull or a man? Perhaps he will be a bull with a man's face? Or will he be like me?]

The identity of the desired other is full of possible permutations, which express uncertainty over who the other will be and therefore necessarily how Asterión can relate to it. The permutations of the bull, man, bull/man, man/bull are versions of *being otherwise* and that also manifests itself in Asterión's desire to be acted upon rather than taking action. In encountering the other, the question is whether Asterión will meet the self or another, whether he will be reflected back to himself or refracted in a new way. He toys elliptically with a number of ways in which self and other might relate: these encompass mirroring half of a divided, bimorphic self (either bull or man to man/bull), inverting the self's division (bull/man to man/bull) or reflecting the self exactly (man/bull to man/bull). The anxiety over the relation undermines Asterión's certainty about who he is, but the (illusory) promise of an other who will engage in a reconfiguring of Asterión's identity is that of potential release from the labyrinth of identity in which he is caught.

Asterión contributes to the change in his identity by hardly putting up a defense: he submits passively to Theseus and having done so is renamed as the Minotaur. Where Asterión had been othered by the troublesome identity conferred by his given name, this renaming, the attachment of a proper name, others him again, undermining all pretense to a sovereign self-possession. Theseus creates a frame in which to locate him, not personalized—not Asterión—but as a role or type. And to submit to the other in this way is a kind of release, though, in this case, tragically fatal. So paradoxically, the killing of Asterión and Theseus' taking of the voice of the story for the final paragraphs (72) are an othering of Asterión, a rendering strange—an abrupt switch of perspective. They also open the way for another reading of the story as a killing of the beast, a symbolic elimination of the half-man half-bull: Theseus represses the animal in himself. This is no mirroring, inverting or reflecting of self and other (as Asterión had speculated), but a solipsistic splitting of the mirror, a reduction to an imaginary wholeness in part of identity. In killing Asterión Theseus emerges—he literally becomes a character by this act—and acquires a given name. But this is yet another (albeit miniature) version of the attempted elision of the interplay between self and other. Theseus gains an identity by killing the beast, by eliminating the other, but the other/beast was essential to the birth of that identity. He was a role, he was the awaited redeemer and he becomes Theseus; by contrast, his victim was Asterión and becomes a role, a proper name, becomes the Minotaur. Personal identity is constituted out of the illusion of suppressing an other, which is nonetheless crucial to that identity.

The same kind of ambivalence underlies Jacob's identity and relation with the other. On the surface, Jacob is defined by his role as ex-champion, although in the provincial context in which he is working it is hoped that the "ex" has no effect. No doubt, the role of (ex-)champion implies incomparability, uniqueness, and arrogance. Jacob's commitment to these attributes is not so evident as Asterión's because he is seen in the alien perspectives of Orsini and the doctor, for both of whom he is a strange and dangerously unpredictable lump of flesh. The nearest that Jacob comes to Asterión's explicit claim to uniqueness is his parading sedately around Santa María wearing a vest displaying a large letter "C" and his daily performance of his training exercises in public: in both respects he performs a spectacle that sets him apart. That spectacle is reinforced much more overtly by the grotesque posturing of Orsini as he condescends elaborately (and futilely) to Santa María. But Jacob's position as (ex-)champion relies on his being continuously open to the challenge of others, which means the constant possibility of defeat (as both he and Orsini are aware), and moreover defeat by a nonprofessional. This is manifestly an ambivalent relation: the other is desired, for without the possibility of a challenge from the other there can be no identity as (ex-)champion; but the other also has to be rejected and defeated, for this subject depends on setting itself above the other. A fragile logic is articulated in a win/lose polarity: there is no middle way. And in Jacob's case, there is no dream of a redeemer or salvation from his entrapment: he commits himself strongly to his established identity. The dependency on the other is the truth behind the facade of masculine strength and confidence. But an awareness of dependency is suggested by Jacob's dangerously excessive drinking, as well as by his more or less explicit self-doubt:

> —Estoy esperando. Siempre estoy en un lugar que es una pieza de hotel de un país de negros hediondos y siempre estoy esperando. Dame el vaso. No tengo miedo; eso es lo malo, nunca va a venir nadie. (1367)

> ["I'm waiting. I'm always in a place that is a hotel room in a country of stinking blacks and I'm always waiting. Give me the glass. I'm not afraid; that's the bad thing, nobody is ever going to come."]

> Nadie—dijo—. El *footing*, las flexiones, las tomas, Lewis. Por Lewis; por lo menos vivió y fue un hombre. La gimnasia no es un hombre, la lucha no es un hombre, todo eso no es un hombre. Una pieza de hotel, el gimnasio, indios mugrientos. Fuera del mundo, Orsini. (1368)

> ["Nobody," he said. "Jogging, press-ups, holds, Lewis. For Lewis; at least he lived and was a man. The gym isn't a man, fighting isn't a man, all that isn't a man. A hotel room, the gym, filthy Indians. In another world, Orsini."]

It is such (at times almost incoherent) statements of negativity that provoke Orsini's acute anxiety about the state of Jacob and his decaying flesh; and it is Orsini's increasingly desperate efforts to forestall a genuine encounter with the other that are the truth behind his facade of self-assurance. As Jacob ages, he and Orsini not only depend on the potential other who might fight Jacob but also grow to fear what that other might do. And that fear is apparent in the final encounter: where Asterión gladly submits to Theseus, Jacob defends himself and apparently alleviates his and Orsini's doubts (at least they are not fulfilled). But this "victory" over Mario comes at a high price: in fact, all Jacob manages is to avoid defeat since, in ejecting Mario from the ring, he does not truly win the bout because he breaks the rules:

> Abrió los brazos y esperó al turco [Mario] que parecía haberse ensanchado. Lo esperó sonriendo hasta que lo tuvo cerca, hizo un paso hacia atrás y de pronto avanzó para dejarse abrazar. *Contra todas las reglas,* Jacob mantuvo los brazos altos durante diez segundos. Después afirmó las piernas y giró; puso una mano en la espalda del desafiante y la otra, también el antebrazo, contra un muslo. Yo no entendía aquello y seguí sin entender durante el exacto medio minuto que duró la lucha. Entonces vi que el turco salía volando del *ring* atravesando sin esfuerzo los aullidos de los sanmarianos y desaparecía en el fondo oscuro de la platea. (1395, italics mine)

> [He opened his arms and waited for the Turk [Mario] who seemed to have grown wider. He waited for him with a smile until he was close,

he took a step backwards and suddenly went forward to let himself be clasped. *Against all the rules*, Jacob held his arms up for ten seconds. Then he steadied his legs and spun round; he placed one hand on the challenger's back and the other, and also his forearm, against his thigh. I couldn't understand what was happening and I couldn't understand for the whole of the thirty seconds that the fight lasted. Then I saw the Turk fly out of the ring, pass effortlessly over the shrieks of the people of Santa María and disappear in the darkness at the rear of the pit/stalls.]

In the past, Orsini has bought off the other, deflected the dangerous challenges; now Jacob cheats and so manages to throw the challenger out of the ring.[5] The effect is similar. Jacob can only survive as (ex-)champion by simultaneously wanting the other to challenge him, while being unable to sustain his openness to a real challenge. His dependency on and growing vulnerability to the other can only be concealed by increasingly desperate efforts at denial, denials that reinforce the rigid structure of his commitment to this form of masculinity.

There is an intriguing variant of the story of Theseus and Asterión/the Minotaur that strengthens the structural links between Borges' and Onetti's stories. The variant recasts the detail of Theseus' attempt to curtail the regular sacrifice of Athenian "youths and maidens" in Crete.

The Cretans, however, refuse to admit that the Minotaur ever existed, or that Theseus won Ariadne by clandestine means. They describe the Labyrinth as merely a well-guarded prison, where the Athenian youths and maidens were kept in readiness for Androgeus's funeral games. Some were sacrificed at his tomb; others presented to the prizewinners as slaves. It happened that Minos's cruel and arrogant general Taurus had carried all before him, year after year: winning every event in which he competed, much to the disgust of his rivals. He had also forfeited Minos's confidence because he was rumoured to be carrying on an adulterous affair with Pasiphae, connived at by Daedalus, and one of her twin sons bore a close resemblance to him. Minos, therefore, gladly granted Theseus's request for the privilege of wrestling against Taurus. In ancient Crete, women as well as men attended the games, and Ariadne fell in love with Theseus when, three times in succession, she saw him toss the former champion over his head and pin his shoulders to the ground. The sight afforded Minos almost equal satisfaction: he awarded Theseus the prize, accepted him as his son-in-law, and remitted the cruel tribute. (Graves, 340)

The basic elements here are similar to the better-known version of the story, the name Taurus clearly echoing the identity of the Minotaur and suggesting a man with bullish attributes. But what is uncanny, in the context of my juxtaposition of Onetti and Borges, is the inclusion of a wrestling match. Physical combat against an imposing athletic champion is the key device, the so-far undefeated Taurus being a man with a reputation as large as Jacob's: they have both been peerless champions. In each case, the decisive action in the wrestling ring involves the raising of the opponent above the head, but in the Greek version it is the challenger who is victorious. Theseus' victory means not only freeing Athens from the burden of tribute to Cnossus but also winning the hand of Ariadne in marriage. Specifically, she witnesses his display of physical prowess and falls in love. In defeating Taurus, Theseus eliminates a man who is antisocial (he is cruel and arrogan.) and who is also a threat to Minos (suspicions of an adulterous affair with Pasiphae): Taurus was attempting to be a law unto himself. So the challenger, Theseus, positively asserts social bonds by defeating the champion and embracing a conformist norm as he himself integrates into a dominant social practice: he marries Ariadne where Taurus had been undermining marriage. Nothing could help point up the basic issues in "Jacob y el otro" more clearly (the two stories help to define each other's identity): where Theseus in effect fights for conformity, Jacob fights for disjuncture and alienation. Theseus defeats the other who is a social danger and thereby asserts his position within the "Same," and he is rewarded for so doing.[6] Jacob "fends off" the other who represents Santa María, and in so doing undermines the institution of marriage, since Mario fights for the money on offer in order to further his marriage plans. In this context, Adriana plays the role of Ariadne—intriguingly, Adriana is virtually both an anagram and a homonym of Ariadne—to Mario's Theseus: both women urge on their men in the fight with the antisocial male opponent. In this light, it is no wonder that the conservative Santa María crowd pour derision on Jacob for what he does. He is not defeated but he is utterly rejected by this society.

REREADING ONETTI WITH BORGES

We can now return to Onetti, Borges, and Rodríguez Monegal in "La Helvética." The two stories and their surrounding intertextual spaces enable the drawing out of another example of the intricate relation between subject and other. It was Onetti who asked Rodríguez Monegal to arrange a meeting with Borges but who then rebuffed him. The rebuff, the challenge to fight, takes the form of a complex literary game with Henry James only superficially the object of discussion. In Rodríguez Monegal's speculation, what is at stake underneath the encounter is a set of literary values and traditions of writing. Moreover, reputation is involved, for Onetti at least. As Rodríguez Monegal puts it: "Sólo salía de su isla para atacar con una virulencia que nunca le había visto" ["He only came out of his shell to attack, with a virulence that I'd never seen in him before"] (15). There is a fundamental asymmetry here which makes Onetti's behavior—desire for a meeting, rebuff, excessive virulence of challenge—appear as that of a literary tyro trying to spar with a heavyweight.[7] In this "match," Onetti is the challenger fighting above his weight and Borges the urbane champion, but, in this case, it is the challenger who does not play by the rules: Onetti subverts the normal conversational rules of cooperation—he provokes without explicitly taking on Borges, deflecting the challenge on to Henry James. Here—by contrast with the two stories—it is the challenger who is the isolated, antisocial figure, not the established name: Asterión, Jacob; to quote Rodríguez Monegal again: "[Onetti] estaba hosco, como retraído en sí mismo, y a la defensiva" ["He was sullen, as if withdrawn in himself, and on the defensive"] (15). It is the "challenger" who now isolates himself, insisting on the other's otherness and attempting to provoke Borges. Borges avoids the provocation, he sidesteps the challenge, but nonetheless he also provides Rodríguez Monegal with the first pointer to an interpretative key. After the abortive encounter, Borges asks: "—¿Por qué habla como un compadrito italiano?" ["Why does he talk like an Italian hoodlum?"] (16). This question leads Rodríguez Monegal to see that what Onetti has been doing is to enact the challenge of one literary mode on another. Onetti has performed on behalf of his predecessor, Roberto Arlt, and challenged the literary tradition of Borges: "Comprendí sólo entonces que Onetti había sido esa noche una personificación de Roberto Arlt, aquel genial y loco narrador porteño, contemporáneo estricto de Borges (nacieron a sólo un año de diferencia) y al que Borges también había ignorado" ["It was only then that I understood that Onetti had been that night a personification of Roberto Arlt, that mad narrator of genius from Buenos Aires, a strict contemporary of Borges (they were born just a year apart) and of whom Borges had also taken no notice"] (16). Borges' apparently ingenuous, direct response to Onetti's question about the sophisticated and highly literary Henry James now comes to seem like a deft ducking of explicit conflict: given his position, he could not be seen to engage in a discussion of the unidentified, unnamable Arlt—that would be to acknowledge the (literary) other, one that, anyway, is unread, ignored. In his own way, Borges contributes to the avoidance of reconciliation, the overcoming of othering, since he, like Onetti, may implicitly rely on othering, even belittling, to maintain his sophisticated location apparently "above" the literary "fight."

So, who wins the "match" between Onetti and Borges? As in "Jacob y el otro," no one can be said to win. Both parties survive by avoiding defeat. Onetti may reveal his insecurity but he is no more "floored" by Borges or Rodríguez Monegal than Borges is brought low by Onetti's virulence. However, as with Asterión and Theseus in "La casa de Asterión," each needs the other in order to define some kind of identity, even though the identity constituted through that need will turn out to be incomplete and ambivalent. All that can clearly be said to remain are my staging (an echo of the staging for which Rodríguez Monegal was the impresario) with its figures created by the juxtaposition of three texts, and also, perhaps, the possibility that this fourth text will enable both Onetti and Borges to be read (however marginally) otherwise.

NOTES

1. Rodríguez Monegal's account is largely repeated in María Esther Gilio's and Carlos María Domínguez's *La construcción de la noche. La vida de Juan Carlos Onetti*, 104–6, where they add one or two new details and some speculation.

2. The degree to which this identification appears to be delayed depends, according to Laurent Thirouin, on the reader's knowledge of Greek mythology. Thirouin analyzes the manipulation of information in the story, which he sees as designed to postpone any reader's perception of the link to the well-known Greek myth. However, one might argue against Thirouin that that may not preclude the reader's seeing the "casa" (and indeed the story itself) as constructed like a labyrinth. There is an additional dimension to the "casa"/labyrinth link in that, in one version of the myth, the labyrinth appears to have been the palace at Cnossus: "One element in the formation of the Labyrinth myth may have been that the palace at Cnossus—the house of the *labrys*, or double-axe—was a complex of rooms and corridors, and that the Athenian raiders had difficulty in finding and killing the king when they captured it" (Graves, 345). On this reading, the palace or house is the labyrinth.

3. Jorge Luis Borges, *El Aleph*, 69–72 (69). Further references are in the text.

4. However, it does have its own kind of Biblical intertextuality. See Genesis 32:24–25, which refer to Jacob's wrestling match with a stranger.

5. There is a kind of parallel to Jacob's cheating in the Theseus story insofar as, in the best known version of it, he receives secret advice from Ariadne on how to beat the Minotaur.

6. Strangely, the relation between Theseus and Ariadne is a brief one. In all the variants of the story, they are separated soon after leaving Crete. See Graves, 339–40 and 341–42.

7. "La Helvética" is an oddly inauspicious location for the encounter, because it was the regular meeting place for what Rodríguez Monegal calls "una de las más siniestras organizaciones peronistas" ["one of the most sinister Peronist organizations"] and was demolished by tank fire in 1955 during the over-

throw of Perón. In the first part of *Construcción de la noche*, Gilio and Domínguez add the sinister detail that the organization was "un grupo de choque nazi que apoyaba a Perón" ["a Nazi shock force supporting Perón"] (104). Curiously, there is a further twist to the labyrinth of encounters around the names and stories invoked here. For Onetti had another encounter in Buenos Aires four years before the one with Borges. On that occasion he met Colonel Juan Domingo Perón. In 1944, when he was working for Reuter's as a journalist, he and a Chilean journalist interviewed the rising minister. Striking features of the account of this meeting (which echo elements in the other encounters analyzed here) are how Perón himself ushered the two journalists into his space/ministerial office and proceeded to exercise a powerful, manipulative effect on them despite the Chilean's prior intention to give Perón a difficult interview. There is no doubting who comes out on top in this sparring match. See *Construcción de la noche*, 101.

WORKS CITED

Borges, Jorge Luis. *El Aleph*. Madrid: Alianza, 1974. (*The Aleph and Other Stories*. Trans. Norman Thomas Di Giovanni in collab. with the author. New York: Dutton, 1970; London: Cape, 1971; London: Picador, 1973.)

Gilio, María Esther, and Carlos María Domínguez. *La construcción de la noche. La vida de Juan Carlos Onetti*. Buenos Aires: Planeta, 1993.

Graves, Robert. *The Greek Myths*. Harmondsworth, U.K.: Penguin, 1992.

Thirouin, Laurent. "Astérion, ou l'impatience de lire." *Poétique* 55 (1983): 282–92.

5

"But my writing has nothing to do with Arlt's": Trace and Silence of Arlt in Onetti

Paul Jordan

The indebtedness of classic Onettian narrative, which begins with *El pozo* [*The Pit*], written in 1939, to the work of his precursor in the River Plate urban narrative, Roberto Arlt, is universally recognized, not least by Onetti himself, specifically in the article "Semblanza de un genio porteño" ["Portrait of a Buenos Aires Genius"], which, rather surprisingly at first sight, is also the source of the statement I have used as my title.[1] Of the elements that have clear antecedents in Arlt's novels, perhaps the most fundamental is the use of alienated, urban *fracasado* [failed] protagonists. Yet the two authors' typical expressions of urban experience are very different. In his best-known work, *Los siete locos* [*The Seven Madmen*], for example, Arlt deploys an eclecticism of style, and uses the melodramatic events of the life of an anguished, hallucinating protagonist, Erdosain, to explore possibilities of meaning as well as the problems of living in the rapidly changing and politically unstable metropolis that was Buenos Aires in the late 1920s. Onetti, by contrast, writing a decade later, is characterized by a more controlled, polished prose; and his prototype protagonist, Linacero, occupies a limited, non-descript urban space, compensating for failure with a single obsessive dream. Where archetypal Arltian alienation is in large measure anguish, in Onetti it is *abulia* [apathy].

According to an anecdote related by Onetti in "Semblanza," his surprising denial of a link to Arlt's work was uttered within a specific context in the past. Onetti reports that he made the observation "en aquel tiempo, allá por el 34" ["back in about 1934"] (*Réquiem*, 128) in

Buenos Aires, to a character called Kostia, before they called on Arlt at the offices of *El Mundo*, to seek his opinion of Onetti's recently completed first novel, *Tiempo de abrazar* ["Time to Embrace"].[2] Onetti describes Arlt's favorable impression, but says that the manuscript, "nunca llegó a publicarse, tal vez por mala, acaso, simplemente, porque la perdí en alguna mudanza" ["was never published—perhaps because it was no good, or simply because it got lost during one of my moves"] (*Réquiem*, 128). The implication that "no tiene nada que ver" ["it has nothing to do"] signals modesty, is strengthened by the reply: "—Claro que no tiene nada que ver—sonreía Kostia con dulzura—. Arlt es un gran novelista" ["'Of course not', said Kostia, smiling sweetly, 'Arlt's a great novelist'"] (130). If there were other possibilities, in 1971, three years before the eventual publication of *Tiempo de abrazar*, they could not be explored.

A second text that is invisible, or missing, although in a different sense, is Arlt's fourth novel, *El amor brujo* ["Love the Magician"], which was published in 1932, one year before *Tiempo de abrazar* was written. Among the many references in "Semblanza" to Arlt's works, Onetti states that: "Entre 30 y 34 yo había leído, en Buenos Aires, las novelas de Arlt—'El juguete rabioso,' 'Los siete locos,' 'Los lanzallamas,' algunos de sus cuentos" (128) ["I had read Arlt's novels, "The Rabid Toy," *The Seven Madmen*, "The Flame-throwers," as well as some of his short stories, when I was in Buenos Aires, between 1930 and 1934"].[3] In one sense the absence of *El amor brujo* from the list of "las novelas de Arlt" is not surprising, since it is the least known.[4] Nevertheless, around the period 1932 to 1934 it was well known, even controversial;[5] it is unlikely that Onetti would not have read Arlt's latest novel. Further, it is strange that in his homage to an author whom he admires and promotes precisely for the authenticity of his portrayal of *porteño* [Buenos Aires] life, Onetti should omit all mention of this striking, if not celebrated work. The main purpose of this essay is to demonstrate previously unobserved links between Onetti and Arlt, through a comparison of *El amor brujo* and *Tiempo de abrazar*.

As their titles indicate, both novels are about love affairs. Arlt's narrative is strongly political and nihilistic: intimate relationships are portrayed as being largely fantasy or lie, with behavior in reality essentially in the service and under the control of an impersonal social machine. However, the stagnation, repetition, alienation, hypocrisy, and compensatory fantasy that characterize social relations in this version of the Arltian universe are also portrayed as artificial and absurd, and hence, fragile. Secondly, while faulty communication and cynicism characterize relationships, especially between the sexes, the other person is not blamed or belittled, but is understood as a comrade, a fellow ant in the machine, and an equal if inaccessible emotional fantasist and sufferer. While alienation is as important in *El amor brujo* as in the earlier novels, here there are no extravagant events or characters, and the work acquires a coherence of vision lacking in Arlt's earlier novels, through the quasi-authorial protagonist, Balder, who as bored office worker, would-be visionary architect, husband and fiancé, diarist and eventual narrator observes, records, and acts simultaneously on multiple levels.

Balder, an engineer in his late twenties with a dead-end job and failed marriage, meets and goes out with Irene, a teenaged music student. They soon lose touch, but two years later, Irene contacts Balder and the relationship is resumed. When they are discovered, possibly through Irene's betrayal, they are forced by her family into an official courtship. Balder, who is suspicious, gambles: he agrees to divorce his wife Elena and marry Irene, but on the secret condition that she is a virgin. When he eventually discovers that she is not, he breaks his commitment and returns to his wife. The plot is circular: there is no personal growth, triumph, or tragedy. Balder and Irene simply enact a formal game, in which one seeks the excitement of an affair, and the other tries to catch a breadwinner.[6] The condition (virginity) and the goal (the *entrega* [sexual surrender] and establishment of the couple) are pretexts permitting the focus on the physical, social, and ideological aspects of a typical courtship that takes place in the real Buenos Aires of neon signs, cafés, trams, railway stations, and suburbs. The city's life is a system that forces individuals into miserable, poverty-stricken couples, and where the cultural and social attitudes, products, and behaviors that serve the economic machine, also provide the individual an illusion of escape. The novel is prefaced by a quotation from the translation of Oscar Wilde's *De Profundis*, which, written in the second person, appears to communicate directly with the 1930s *porteño* readers, challenging them to examine their society, if not their own behavior.[7]

Tiempo de abrazar, by contrast, concerns an individual's abandonment of social institutions, in a personal search for authenticity and fulfillment. The protagonist, Jason, a student, sees salvation from his meaningless existence through the pursuit of the teenaged Virginia.[8] Success, for Jason, equals conquest: "Quería la vida. . . . Llegar a tener la energía necesaria para tomar la vida como a una mujer" ["Life was what he wanted. . . . He wanted to be strong, to reach out for life, as if it could be taken, like a woman"] (*Tiempo*, 148), and the route to the goal can be summarized as follows. The protagonist recreates himself by escaping from modern urban society, and by purging his previous, supposedly inauthentic, experience. The modification of self is paralleled by an operation practiced on the world, principally represented by the required other, Virginia; she enters the narrative in response to the protagonist's perceived requirements, and then is assimilated as she is conveniently discovered not to have certain characteristics that he finds undesirable. Onetti's use of a conventional, authoritative third-person narrator, focused entirely on the protagonist, raises problems about subjectivity that Arlt's mixed narrative technique and broader perspective avoid, in spite of the fact that in his novel, too, there is direct access only to the protagonist's thoughts.

In the light of this summary, and before analyzing in detail Jason's progress against the background of Arlt's novel, it is useful to mention some views of the role of female characters in Onettian narrative. Many critics identify the lack of autonomy of characters other than the main protagonists, especially when these are female. Fellow Uruguayan novelist Mario Benedetti, whose own work emphasizes the political and affective dimensions, unsurprisingly diagnoses in Onetti a general alienation from the world and its inhabitants,[9] while a product of Mark Millington's careful analysis of Onetti's major novels is a typology of female Onettian characters, which the critic concludes are "marginal to the male center."[10] As a series of interviews shows, Onetti does not deny the accuracy of these types of observations; but he does not accept their premises.[11] Two critics who have specifically considered *Tiempo de abrazar* take different lines. María Milián-Silveira, for example, tracing the origins of Onetti's art, is a somewhat generous apologist who proposes that his first novel should be viewed as "el símbolo del destete psicológico de un adolescente [the protagonist, Jason]" ["symbolizing an adolescent's psychological weaning"] (66). Jorge Ruffinelli, in his introduction to the novel, seems to acknowledge the major criticisms, and offers the following explanation of the place of the adolescent girl in Onetti's work: "La *muchacha* aparece en la literatura de Onetti como negación, en un gesto romántico de resistencia a las leyes del mundo y de la vida. De la realidad, en suma. De ahí que sea siempre un personaje irreal, creado por esa necesidad, y no una figura encarnada verosímilmente en personajes literarios centrales" ["The adolescent girl in Onetti's work is an emblem of negation, invoked in a kind of romantic gesture of defiance of the laws of the world, of life—of reality, in short. Hence she is always unreal: a creation specifically answering this need—rather than a rounded, plausible, major protagonistic figure"] (*Tiempo*, xxx).

Although their situation is in many ways similar, the initial outlook of the two authors' protagonists differs significantly. Jason seeks to escape from his routine, or "puerca vida" ["rotten life"] (studying Rousseau with an elderly teacher, presumably signifying a sclerotic culture, is its first representation) by creating an idealized erotic figure. A more urgent text than Rousseau's, a girl's confession of love scrawled on the washroom wall, spawns his voyeuristic fantasy: "Imaginaba a la muchacha en cuclillas . . . con los ojos brillantes de miedo y vergüenza; . . . semidescubiertas las piernas blancas y las diminutas ropas, más blancas aún" ["He imagined the girl squatting there . . . her eyes shining with her fear, and her shame; . . . he imagined her half-exposed white legs, and that scanty clothing, whiter still"] (147). Jason's fantasy child-woman contrasts with his memory of a real lover, Cristina: "Era muy linda, muy linda. Sí; estúpida, charlatana, vulgar. . . . Con ella, nada de dudas ni problemas filosóficos" ["She certainly was beautiful. True, she was stupid, vulgar, a chatterbox. . . . At least, with her, there was no hesitation, no philosophical hang-ups"] (149). Evidently, Cristina represents the past, although it is not yet clear why Jason rejects this aspect of his *puerca vida*; while Cristina's conversation does not amuse him, physically and morally she seems to please. Arlt's protagonist, Balder, on the other hand, has left behind his university days, actually does lead a *puerca vida*, and is, in spite of his youth, "un hombre de aspecto derrotado" ["a man defeated by life"] (*El amor*, 23). Moreover, unlike Jason, or Arlt's earlier protagonists, who also create fantasy women, it is Irene who confronts or discovers Balder. Loitering, self-absorbed, surrounded by the bustle of the busy Retiro station, "al levantar los ojos del suelo, encontró la mirada de una chiquilla fija en él. Era una colegiala" ["chancing to look up from his contemplation of the station floor, he saw a young girl staring at him: a schoolgirl"] (24).

Jason emerges as a confident individual, whose dissatisfaction is simplistic, and lacking sociological or psychological perspectives. Arlt's protagonist is very different, and his more comprehensive and comprehending malaise emerges rather less abruptly than Jason's. In the chapter "La voluntad tarada" ["Crippled Willpower"] he describes his circumstances, and makes observations about his social group: "Sobrellevaba la monotonía de su vida con resignación de cadáver" ["He endured his monotonous life with the resignation of a corpse"] (*El amor*, 54); his male colleagues are "odiosos" ["hateful"]; his marriage is empty: "¿Qué relaciones existían entre un piso encerado o una albóndiga a punto, y la felicidad?" ["Quite what happiness had to do with the immaculately polished floor of the apartment, the meatballs served up for his dinner, he couldn't fathom"] (55); his *programas* ["casual affairs"] disappoint: "Las mujeres le desilusionaban por la esterilidad mental de su existencia" ["Women were such a disappointment as their minds were empty and sterile"] (48).

Jason's ideal woman, Virginia, appears not in the city but in a private space: at a reunion of friends, where the debate over politically committed literature versus more personal aims is rehearsed. Condescendingly, Jason guesses that: "Versitos, debía de hacer" ["No doubt, she penned her little verses"] (*Tiempo*, 160) and judges her as "una lite-ratilla, claro; pero no debía estar muy contaminada todavía" ["having literary pretensions, of course, but perhaps not yet totally corrupted"] (168). Frequently in Arlt's fiction, too, a young woman's literary or other artistic inclination lacks the earnestness associated with male characters, being, rather, a badge of social class, and a useful accomplishment for attracting a spouse.[12] Irene is unusual in that she studies piano as a profession. For Jason, however, such attributes are sinister: literary dabbling, and an innocent exterior—a profile which is "puro, infantil, dulce de inocencia" ["pure, childlike, sweet, innocent"] (164)—are a mask, concealing a different nature. In reality Virginia is a woman: "¿Cómo podía ella tener a la vez aquel suave gesto can-doroso y un cuerpo de mujer? . . . [T]enía sexo y fingía no saberlo, sosteniendo un hipócrita gesto de pureza" ["How could she have that gentle, artless expression—and yet have a woman's body? . . . [S]he had a vagina and pretended to be unaware of it, hypocritically keeping up that innocent expression on her face"] (164). This revelation both echoes and contrasts with a scene in *El amor brujo*. As Balder and Irene ride in the electric train, the train itself and the stations and suburbs provide the background for and interruptions to Balder's stream of thought. This mental interior is partly a reverie in which an ecstatic Balder forgets Elena and deifies Irene, abasing himself (like a courtly lover he imagines himself as a hound at her feet), and partly cynical observation of his own feelings. As with the first meeting with Irene, and again in contrast to Jason's case, an external event prompts the important revelation: "Pinos y eucaliptos empenachaban transver-salmente la distancia. De pronto, la curva de los rieles se acentuó y una mancha de sol amarillo cayó sobre el regazo de seda blanca de Irene, mientras Balder pensaba: —Ella tiene sexo . . . sexo como otras mujeres" ["Pines and eucalyptus processed across the distant view, almost like plumes. Then suddenly, as the track curved round further, a patch of yellow sunlight fell on the white silk of Irene's lap. Balder thought: 'She's got a vagina—just like other women"] (*El amor*, 32). Here, the realization of femaleness is not exclusive, as in Onetti's text, but merely suggests that it is a reality which is in some way connected with the different aspects of Balder's ruminations, of Irene's own hidden thoughts, and of the reader's expectations.

Returning to *Tiempo de abrazar*, Virginia's establishment as the object of Jason's desire is preceded by a contrastive parting scene with Cristina. Here, the impersonal term "hembra" ["female"] occurs frequently, and in the eventual sexual encounter, the woman is presented as negative, and purely physical: "Cuando quiso girar tuvo un seno en la mano. El cuerpo desnudo se apretaba contra sus ropas. Caliente, macizo, con un agresivo olor de hembra joven" ["Turning round, his hand cupped a breast. The naked body pressed up against his clothing. The hot, full flesh, gave off the powerful scent of young female"] (*Tiempo*, 186). The impersonality of the encounter is amplified by association in Jason's imagination with the pullulating urban mass, represented by the inhabitants of a hotel opposite his flat: "Toda la torpeza humana, todas las pasiones, libres en el interior de las discretas alcobas. Hombres y mujeres. . . . Vestidos, semidesnudos, desnudos, amontonados en el edificio" ["All human weaknesses and passions were there, in the privacy of discreet bedrooms. Men and women. . . . Dressed, undressed, half-dressed—hundreds of them in the building"] (186).

In contrast to this scene, whose sense of revulsion is reminiscent of earlier Arltian protagonists, in *El amor brujo* estrangement of the existing couple (Balder and Elena) contains no such quality. A restrained narration intensifies a personal alienation: "Silencio. Balder es un cuerpo horizontal con los ojos desencajados en las tinieblas. Elena llora calladamente bajo el embozo de las sábanas" ["Silence. Balder a horizontal body, wild-eyed, in the darkness. The sound of Elena's weeping stifled by the bedsheets"] (*El amor*, 117).

In the remainder of *Tiempo de abrazar* the protagonists are prepared for the *entrega*, which will initiate Jason's new life. Virginia's difference from Cristina is emphasized, as she is made less female; Jason observes: "Sería interesante saber cómo hacía para no tener senos" ["How had that girl managed to avoid growing breasts?"] (*Tiempo*, 188). Jason, on the other hand, seeks heightened manliness. First, he escapes to the countryside, where he emits a tirade against modernity that begins: "Monstruosa mentira la civilización, la falsa y sórdida civilización de los mercaderes" ["What an enormous lie civilization was, the false, sordid civilization of the market economy"] (195). The city is replaced by a vision of fruits, cows, and honeycombs, and the wish to "Reintegrarse a la tierra negra, al pasto verde, el cielo azul" ["Get back in harmony with the dark soil, the green grass, the blue sky"] (196). This is indeed very different from the experience of Arltian characters, who hallucinate or dream toward the future, and for whom the city is an inescapable and complicated reality, a landscape of nightmare, desire, and routine. For Jason, however, modernity is a tiresome but straightforward problem: "La ciudad iba castrando a los hombres, neutralizando su virilidad, domesticando sus almas" ["The city castrated men, destroying their virility, domesticating their souls"] (196).

Jason's virile fantasy develops into an overtly sexual dream, as his body, now a ship, is launched by Virginia with a bottle of champagne. Clearly, from this point, his objective is to get Virginia into bed—

although, rather as the full sexual act is continually deferred in the typical courtship that Arlt describes, so Jason's rhetoric defers the unambiguous statement of his goal:

> Estaba resuelto a no estropear la sensación que le daba la muchacha convirtiéndola en una novia. . . . [S]e amarían en una forma absolutamente personal . . . sin consejos, vigilancia y toda la interminable serie de elementos que van ensuciando el amor hasta hacerlo costumbre. . . . Transó con tomar a Virginia. (207–8).

> ["He was determined not to spoil the feelings she aroused in him by getting engaged to her. . . . [T]hey would love each other in their own way . . . free of the advice, supervision—that whole set of customs that are used to dirty and cheapen love, until it just becomes a habit. . . . He wanted to take Virginia's body."]

Certainly, Jason explicitly rejects the hypocrisy of the supervised courtship as it is presented in *El amor brujo*. However, the management of Jason's supposed idealism, and his undoubted pragmatism or cynicism, is problematical. There are three elements that could easily coexist in a cynical actor/observer character like Balder, but that sit uncomfortably in one like Jason, whose overt moral development is a conscious rejection of the cynical, in favor of the straightforward and wholesome. On the one hand he believes in Virginia's perfection: a unique quality in her "le daba una irrazonable seguridad que solamente así, en la forma limpia y pura en que él lo deseaba concebía ella el futuro de su amor" ["made him certain, although the certainty was quite irrational, that she saw the future of their love as he did: as pure, uncontaminated desire"]; on the other he suspects that her qualities are really a figment of his imagination: "Acaso una gran parte de la manera de ser que le mostraba la adolescente fuera producto cerebral" ["It could just be that most of her behavior toward him was simply the product of his own imagination"]. Third, his speculation that, once Virginia is no longer a virgin, "a la muchacha fresca e incontaminada sucediera la señorita honesta, arrepentida" ["the pure, uncomplicated girl would turn into a reproachful, respectable young lady"] (208) is simply cynical—quite Arltian, in fact. Presumably the introduction into the narrative at this point of Jason's flatmate, Lima, the roué who contrasts with Jason, is a tactic employed by Onetti to smooth over the difficulty. However, the two characters are clearly more likely to be associated than dissociated by the reader, with the result that Jason's unclear moral position is not resolved.

In Arlt's novel, by contrast, hypocrisy is usually comic and in some senses open: for example, when Balder assures Irene's mother of the purity of his intentions, it is quite clear that the mother is acting out a bargaining role in a predictable manner, probably in complicity with Irene, while Irene's sexual glance to Balder invites the reader into the complicity between the two protagonists.

Thus far, Jason, through his escape to the countryside and through his dream, supposedly has been purified and fortified, while Virginia, through the observation that she has no breasts, has been to some extent neutralized. However, this virtually breastless, inexperienced sixteen-year-old is still too female even for a reinvigorated Jason. Virginia voices her suspicion: "—Bueno, ¿te gusta sentirme un muchacho? . . . —Sí. . . . Me parece que estamos más juntos; como si fuera más fácil entender-nos" ["'Tell me, do you prefer to think of me as a boy?' . . . 'Yes. . . . We seem so much closer, it's as if it's easier to understand each other'"] (*Tiempo*, 215–16). Now, Jason neither declares homosexuality, nor does he propose a Platonic relationship with a woman; in fact, he demands that the woman he desires should be a species of female neuter, a creature devoid of characteristics that he attributes to females. He seems to dislike anything he can associate with women, in fact: "No me gustaría que fueras como todas, cien por ciento mujer, hasta la satu-ración. . . . A veces . . . todo lo femenino llega a darme náuseas" ["I'd hate you to be like the others, a woman through and through, one hun-dred percent. Sometimes, absolutely everything associated with women makes me feel sick"] (216).

This complete reduction of Virginia is complemented by an equally extreme operation on Jason. In what seems to be a final attempt to wash away time, and the experience it brings, Jason returns to his family home, and mentally regresses almost back to birth, presumably seeking a guarantee of his good faith from the one figure who is beyond reproach: "Inmóvil bajo las cobijas, estafaba años al tiempo y Mamá volvía a tener un niño melancólico y tierno" ["Motionless, beneath the bedclothes, he mentally regressed, back to being Mummy's sweet, melancholy baby boy again"] (233).

Although there is a gap in the chapter sequence of *Tiempo de abrazar* between this, the twelfth, and the final, nineteenth chapter, it is difficult to imagine what further preparation the protagonists could undergo. Perhaps the gap itself is fictitious (to this point I shall return), and if so, an interesting parallel with *El amor brujo* emerges. The first incident of chapter 19 is a confrontation with Virginia's father, the final representative of the corrupt status quo. Now, *El amor brujo* begins with Balder's confrontation with Irene's mother, an incident that is, evi-dently, out of sequence. Jason's resolution to rescue from society "una Virginia a la que limaron, cepillaron, deformándola, haciéndola igual a los miles de muchachas de la ciudad" ["a polished, brushed, deformed Virginia, a standard city girl, one of the thousands"] (*Tiempo*, 237) is very similar to Balder's judgment of the lot of women in his society: "La conciencia de ellas estaba estructurada por la sociedad que las había deformado en la escuela" ["Their minds were molded by this society that had taken them as schoolgirls, and deformed them"] (*El amor*, 55). Of course, in his dealings with the Loayza family, Balder pretends to no moral action, but plays the game in order to expose it to the reader.

The main focus of the final chapter of *Tiempo de abrazar* is the postcoital idyll. Initially, events seem to have followed Jason's plan: exultant, he beats his chest, while Virginia, who confesses that she has been ashamed of her virginity, has no regrets: "—Yo presentía lo lindo de esto, vida. . . . Tenía que ser contigo . . . contigo, vida querida" ["Oh darling, I knew how wonderful it would be. . . . It had to be with you though, with nobody but you, love of my life"] (*Tiempo*, 240). Such conventional, submissive language is new to Virginia, but is typical of Balder and Irene's conversation: "—Tené paciencia, querido. Yo quiero entregarme a vos. Lo deseo. Creeme. Ése será para mí el día más lindo de mi vida" ["Be patient, darling. I do want you to make love to me. I really do want it. Believe me. It will be the most wonderful day of my life, when we do"] (*El amor*, 134).

At this point *El amor brujo* and *Tiempo de abrazar* seem to converge. While Virginia actually makes the announcement that might be expected from Irene in the context of the *entrega* (in fact in Arlt's novel the event is only alluded to retrospectively and in passing), she does so in language that is new to her, but that is typical of Irene. Thus, Onetti completes a void in Arlt's text, and the six-chapter hiatus in his own might be seen as implying a series of events bearing some similarity to Irene's and Balder's courtship. Both novels, although from different perspectives, focus on courtship, whose culmination, the surrender of virginity, is supposed to be the consecration of the couple, the initiation of a predefined new phase of life. While Arlt clearly exposes the myths from the beginning, it is difficult to interpret Onetti's text, until the very end, as other than an affirmation of the notion of the ideal couple, however mutilated the characters may seem. However, the success of Jason's project eventually becomes doubtful, and the text thus abandons the myth at the culminating point, the *entrega*. Jorge Ruffinelli considers the *entrega* a communion, a moment of "plenitud y franqueza" ["fulfillment and openness"] (*Tiempo*, li), nostalgia for which informs Onetti's future narrative. However, it can also be seen as a moment of loss and an escape: while Jason does not go so far as to apply to Virginia the ominous term *hembra*, she clearly is no longer contained by the copious diminutives he still employs, such as *nena*, *niñita* [little girl], *animalito* [little creature], or *muchachita* [little adolescent girl]: "Miraba ahora entristecido los hombros débiles e inclinados de la muchacha. Alejada de él, era más fuerte. Hundida por completo en el espejo, podía olvidarlo . . . abandonada a su destino de gracia y belleza. Él necesitaba de ella; pero no le era necesario a Virginia" ["Sad now, he looked at the girl's delicately sloping shoulders. There, apart from him, she was stronger. Wholly absorbed by herself in the mirror, she could forget him . . . engrossed in her own beautiful, graceful destiny. He needed Virginia, but she didn't need him"] (244). Where Cristina had been displayed in the mirror for his gaze, Virginia contemplates herself.

The text ends equivocally. Jason's future is uncertain, as his doubt finally turns inwards: "Se había engañado a sí mismo, urdiendo pretextos, complicando las cosas, incapaz de un momento de sinceridad" ["He had deceived himself, inventing pretexts, making things more complicated; he'd been incapable of sincerity, even for a moment"] (246). The woman's return, too, is uncertain, at least in the current guise: "—¿Hasta . . . ? Ella comprendió y le alargó la mano, con un recio apretón de camaradas. —No sé. Pero quiero verte mañana" ["'When shall we . . . ?' She understood, reached over, gave him an affectionate squeeze. 'I don't know. I'd like to see you tomorrow, though'"] (245).

Before moving on to my conclusions, the question of the nature of *Tiempo de abrazar* must be addressed. Its publication was not the simple retrieval of substantial fragments of a previously forgotten early text (as posthumous publication might have been), but an authorial act that was the culmination of a series of related acts. *Tiempo de abrazar* was reinvented in "Semblanza de un genio porteño" (this seems to have led to its eventual publication) as well as being mentioned in various interviews; and on occasion it has been confused with *El pozo*.[13] The complete, but not definitive novel consists of thirteen chapters, reproduced with the author's permission, together with Onetti's various suggestions for its expansion, which are justified by the notion of a potentially remembered complete text (of 1933 or 1941).[14] One such apocryphal narrative is Onetti's suggestion for how the space between the two parts of chapter nineteen might be filled:

> RUFFINELLI—*La versión de que disponemos se detiene en una discusión entre Jason y el padre de Virginia. Éste se opone a la relación de los muchachos. Y una vez me dijiste que la novela finalizaba cuando Jason se marchaba al interior, al campo. ¿Se va solo?*
> ONETTI—Solo.
> RUFFINELLI—*Entonces, ¿qué sucede con Virginia?*
> ONETTI—Él se va, se va de linyera.
> RUFFINELLI—*¿Fracasa su idilio?*
> ONETTI—Sí, fracasa. Y yo no me puedo acordar por qué fracasa. (*Réquiem*, 232).

[RUFFINELLI: The version that we have finishes with an argument between Jason, and Virginia's father, who is opposed to the relationship. Once you told me that the novel ended when Jason leaves the city for the countryside. Does he go alone?
ONETTI: Yes.
RUFFINELLI: So what happens to Virginia?
ONETTI: He abandons her and just goes off wandering.
RUFFINELLI: So the idyll failed?
ONETTI: Yes, it doesn't work out. I don't remember why.]

Onetti also suggests how the novel continued after chapter 19: "Y después [de la entrega] venía la parte burguesa, que ensuciaba lo que para ellos, los muchachos, era de absoluta pureza. Y entonces el chico, ensuciado, mancillado, podrido, se va al campo, se va, se va." ["Then, afterwards (after they have made love) came the conventional part, that soiled what for the young people had been uttely pure. So Jason, feeling dirty, corrupted, besmirched, goes off to the country, just goes away"] (233). However, perhaps a different kind of continuation and return should be considered.

The final words of *Tiempo de abrazar* are "Tres pasos, vuelta, tres pasos" ["Three steps forward, turn round, three steps back"], while *El pozo* begins, as if emerging from the same scene: "Hace un rato me estaba paseando por el cuarto" ["A while ago I was pacing the room"]. The separation of Jason and Virginia and Jason's abandoning of his dream then perhaps represent the understanding and abandonment of a wishful, escapist mode of thinking (which seems to have been a reaction against the cynical, nihilistic turn that Arlt's writing had taken). Jason and Virginia's substitution by the violence and failure of the estranged figures, Ana María and Linacero, marks the beginning of the recognized Onettian vision, one that undeniably and strongly (although, as this paper has shown, rather less directly than is commonly supposed) connects with Arlt's classic novels of urban alienation. The belated reappearance of *Tiempo de abrazar*, a curiosity that can neither enhance nor damage Onetti's standing, appears to have been prompted by his affirmation in "Semblanza" of a debt to Arlt. It is fitting, and quite possibly intended, that the recovery of *Tiempo de abrazar* should in turn lead to a new evaluation of the influences exerted on Onetti by Arlt's writing in the period leading to *El pozo*.

Returning to "Semblanza de un genio porteño," the key text in the reconstruction of *Tiempo de abrazar*, it can be observed that Onetti, unsurprisingly, was thoroughly conversant with the myths about Arlt's life and works, the most important in this context being that of missing texts, and their possible recovery. As well as *El amor brujo*, the text that Onetti himself mislaid, there are two obvious choices in Arlt's oeuvre that could correspond to *Tiempo de abrazar*: an early novel, *Diario de un morfinómano* ["A Morphine Addict's Journal"], rumored to exist in about 1920; and the rest of *Vida puerca* ["A Rotten Life"].[15] Although Onetti's missing early novel has in reality been recovered and created in the senses I have discussed, there are further dimensions to the novel's reappearance. During Onetti's first period of residence in Buenos Aires from 1930 to 1934, according to Jorge Ruffinelli he wrote some film reviews that were published in *Crítica*, under the direction of Conrado Nalé Roxlo. Since Nalé Roxlo was a friend of Arlt's of long standing, and Arlt, too, had written for *Crítica*, Onetti and Arlt should have known each other. The possibility thus arises that the anecdote in "Semblanza" of the first meeting between the two is, in fact as well as content, a fiction, albeit one with a purpose.

An interesting view of the conceit of myths (or even myths about myths) generating realities, including real texts, is found in Ricardo Piglia's *Prisión perpetua* ["Life Imprisonment"]. That text contains a narrative, "Nombre falso" ["False Name"], whose two components are a mixed-genre narrative, "Homenaje a Roberto Arlt" ["Homage to Roberto Arlt"], and a short story, "Luba" ["Luba"], supposedly by Arlt, the narration of whose discovery or recovery is one of the elements of "Homenaje a Roberto Arlt." Like Onetti's companion on the visit to Arlt's office, the fictional intermediary through whom "Luba" is recovered is a friend of Arlt's called Kostia. Although the identity of Piglia's Kostia is different from Onetti's (Saúl Kostia according to Piglia, Ítalo Costantini according to Onetti), it is nevertheless the same character, since Piglia provides a footnote to the effect that this is the Kostia from [Onetti's] "retrato de Roberto Arlt que sirvió de prólogo a la traducción de *Los siete locos*" ["portrait of Roberto Arlt that was used as a prologue for the translation of *The Seven Madmen*"] (Piglia, 161). Furthermore, Nalé Roxlo, who incidentally is a main source of the tales of the existence of *Diario de un morfinómano*, mentions in his memoirs both a poet called Constantino, and a mysterious character known to Arlt, called Constantini (Nalé Roxlo, 87). Strangely, and unlike the prototypes of some of Arlt's more colorful characters, whom he claims to have known, apparently he never met Constantini. One wonders which version or versions of this multiple fictional character might correspond to the Juan Costantini to whom Arlt dedicated his fiction-essay "Las ciencias ocultas en la ciudad de Buenos Aires" ["The Occult in Buenos Aires"], which was published in 1920.

Through his suggestion that the two Kostias (in fact, they are five) are the same character, even though their identities are different, Piglia joins in a game that has been evolving for many years, and signals Onetti's participation. This leads back to the starting point of this essay:

that "Semblanza" is not a traditional critical prologue to Arlt's work, a point that Onetti himself makes. "Semblanza" is of course an important testimonial document that directly conveys much information about Onetti's appreciation of Arlt. But it also is a fiction containing fictions; none more blatant, mischievous, and rich in possibilities than the casual line—ostensibly remembered from almost half a century previously, but probably invented, uttered to a character whose existence is to say the least dubious—than the statement: "—Pero lo que yo escribo no tiene nada que ver con lo que hace Arlt" ["But my writing has nothing to do with Arlt's"].

NOTES

1. Written as a prologue to the Italian translation of *Los siete locos* (*I setti pazzi*, Milan: Bompiani, 1971), "Semblanza de un genio porteño" also appeared that year in *Marcha* (Montevideo) and in an issue of *Macedonio* (Buenos Aires) devoted to Arlt. It has been used as a prologue to an edition of *El juguete rabioso* ["The Rabid Toy"] (Barcelona: Bruguera 1979), and appears in a collection of Onetti's articles, *Réquiem por Faulkner y otros artículos* ["Requiem for Faulkner and Other Articles"], 127–37. Page references in this article are from *Réquiem*.

2. J. C. Onetti, *Tiempo de abrazar* (incomplete text: chapters 1–12, 19) with introductory study: "Onetti antes de Onetti," by Jorge Ruffinelli; referred to in this article as *Tiempo*. Three fragments were previously published, in 1943, in *Marcha*.

3. Onetti's first period of residence in Buenos Aires was from 1930 to 1934. During this time Arlt's third novel, *Los lanzallamas* (1931), and his first collection of stories, *El jorobadito* ["The Little Hunchback"] (1933), were published. Onetti also mentions *Aguafuertes* ["Etchings"], short pieces published mainly in *El Mundo*, and his first play, *Trescientos millones* ["Three Hundred Million"] (1932).

4. Most Arltian criticism focuses on the first three novels; however, there is some interesting, more recent work on *El amor brujo*. Jaime Giordano's article, "El espacio en la narrativa de Roberto Arlt," explores Arlt's imaging of movement; Beatriz Sarlo, in *La imaginación técnica*, is interested in the architectural aspect; Aníbal Jarkowski, in "*El amor brujo*: la novela 'mala' de Arlt," explores the relationship with the 1920s and 1930s *novela rosa* ["romantic novel"].

5. Lázaro Liacho's *Palabra de hombre* contains a seventy-page diatribe against Arlt and *El amor brujo*: "Roberto Arlt, dentro y fuera de *El amor brujo*."

6. The most powerful statement of the circularity is perhaps in the protagonist's name: Balder. Irene's previous lover's name was almost identical: Walter. Observations in which (courtship and family) behaviors customarily viewed from an individual perspective are described as if practiced on an indus-

trial scale are fundamental to the novel. The name Balder may also be the inspiration for that of the protagonist of one of Onetti's early stories, "El posible Baldi" ["The Possible Baldi"], published in 1936.

7. "Si tu pálido rostro que acostumbra a enrojecer ligeramente bajo los efectos del vino o la alegría, arde de cuando en cuando de vergüenza al leer lo que aquí está escrito, cual bajo el resplandor de un alto horno, entonces, tanto mejor para ti. El mayor de los vicios es la ligereza; todo lo que llega hasta la conciencia es justo." *La tragedia de mi vida*, trans. Margarita Nelken, Madrid. Biblioteca Nueva, 1925, p. 87. There is also an earlier (1920) translation by the Uruguayan Álvaro Armando Vasseur: *El alma del hombre*. The original reads as follows: "Your pale face used to flush easily with wine or pleasure. If, as you read what is here written, it from time to time becomes scorched, as though by a furnace-blast, with shame, it will be all the better for you. The supreme vice is shallowness. Whatever is realized is right." (Oscar Wilde, *De Profundis*, in *Complete Works*, 896.) *The Autobiography of Lord Alfred Douglas* (replying to the full version of *De Profundis*) appeared in 1929, was re-edited in 1931, and was widely translated.

8. In spite of the obvious association of the name, and his own summary of the direction of the plot, Onetti maintained that virginity was not a primary characteristic of Virginia: "—Lo de 'Virginia' es deliberado, porque 'Cras' en latín quiere decir 'mañana.' Entonces, en mi locura, pensé en la 'virgen del mañana.' Es decir, desprovista del fetichismo de la virginidad, es la virgen del mañana que se da a quien quiere, de quien esté enamorada. Ahora, uno de los capítulos más importantes de la novela es aquel en que Virginia Cras es desvirginizada; . . . la novela iba hacia eso." ["The business about Virginia's name was quite deliberate: you see, 'Cras' means 'tomorrow' in Latin, So, rather crazily, I had the idea of 'tomorrow's virgin.' In other words, having abandoned the fetish of virginity, she becomes the virgin of tomorrow, who gives herself to whomever she wishes—to whomever she is in love with. Now, one of the most important chapters of the novel is the one in which Virginia Cras loses her virginity; . . . that's what the novel's plot was moving toward"]. "Creación y muerte de Santa María" ["Creation and Death of Santa María"], in *Réquiem*, 233.

9. "Cada novela de Onetti es un intento de complicarse, de introducirse de lleno y para siempre en la vida, y el dramatismo de sus ficciones deriva precisamente de una reiterada comprobación de la ajenidad, de la forzosa incomunicación que padece el protagonista y, por ende, el autor. El mensaje que éste nos inculca, . . . es el fracaso esencial de todo vínculo, el malentendido global de la existencia, el desencuentro del ser con su destino." ["Each of Onetti's novels is an attempt at involvement, at getting right inside life, once and for all; the drama of his fiction is found precisely in the repeated realization of alienation, the inescapable inability to communicate that is suffered by his protagonists— and hence by Onetti himself. His message . . . is the fundamental failure of all attempts to relate, the universal failure of comprehension which is human existence, the failure of the self to realize its destiny"]. Mario Benedetti, "La aventura del hombre," 21–22.

10. Mark Millington, "No Woman's Land; The Representation of Woman in Onetti," 358.

11. See the series of interviews with M. E. Gilio, "Entrevista en cuatro tiempos."

12. Elena, Balder's wife, is more typical: "bordaba excelentemente, cocinaba muy bien, hacía un poco de ruido en el piano" ["She was an expert needlewoman, an excellent cook, she played the piano a bit"] (*El amor*, 56).

13. Jorge Ruffinelli (*Tiempo*, xxiv) mentions an early version of *El pozo*, supposedly lost in Buenos Aires in 1932. Elsewhere Onetti (*Réquiem*, 234) dismisses this suggestion:

RUFFINELLI—¿*La escritura de esta novela* [Tiempo de abrazar] *es anterior a la de* El pozo?
ONETTI—Sí, sí, muy anterior. La escribí en el 33.
[RUFFINELLI: Was *Tiempo de abrazar* written before *El pozo*?
ONETTI: Oh yes, long before. I wrote it in 1933].

14. While, as we have already seen, Onetti gives the casual explanation for the failure to publish his novel as "tal vez por mala, acaso, simplemente, porque la perdí en alguna mudanza" ["perhaps because it was no good—or simply because it got lost during one of my moves"] (*Réquiem*, 128), he did not simply forget it. On the contrary, and surprisingly, in view of the major works that Onetti had completed by 1941, a version of *Tiempo de abrazar* was that year entered in a literary competition (*Tiempo*, xliii).

15. *Vida puerca* is the title of an early version of *El juguete rabioso*. Two chapters, "El Rengo" ["The Lame"] and "El poeta parroquial" ["The Parochial Poet"] were published in *Proa*, in March and May 1925, respectively. A version of "El Rengo" is incorporated in *El juguete rabioso*.

WORKS CITED

Arlt, Roberto. *El amor brujo*, in *Obra completa*, vol. 2. Buenos Aires: Lohlé, 1991, 9–178.

Benedetti, Mario. "La aventura del hombre." *Onetti*. Ed. Jorge Ruffinelli. Montevideo: Biblioteca de Marcha, 1973. 21–47.

Gilio, María Esther. "Entrevista en cuatro tiempos." *Crisis* (Buenos Aires), October 1986: 23–29.

Giordano, Jaime. "El espacio en la narrativa de Roberto Arlt." *Nueva Narrativa Hispanoamericana* 2 (1972): 119–48.

Jarkowski, Aníbal. "*El amor brujo*: la novela 'mala' de Arlt." *Historia social de la literatura argentina*. Gen. Eds. Viñas and Tabakián. Vol. 7: *Yrigoyen entre Borges y Arlt*. Buenos Aires: Contrapunto, 1989. 109–28.

Liacho, Lázaro. *Palabra de hombre*. Buenos Aires: Porter, 1934.

Milián-Silveira, María C. *El primer Onetti y sus contextos*. Madrid: Pliegos, 1986.

Millington, Mark. "No Woman's Land: The Representation of Woman in Onetti." *Modern Language Notes* 102 (1987): 358–77.

Nalé Roxlo, Conrado. *Borrador de memorias*. Buenos Aires: Plus Ultra, 1978.

Onetti, Juan Carlos. *Réquiem por Faulkner y otros artículos*. Ed. Jorge Ruffinelli. Buenos Aires: Calicanto, 1976.

Onetti, Juan Carlos. *Tiempo de abrazar*. Ed. Jorge Ruffinelli. Montevideo: Arca, 1974.

Piglia, Ricardo. *Prisión perpetua*. Buenos Aires: Sudamericana, 1988.

Sarlo, Beatriz. *La imaginación técnica*. Buenos Aires: Nueva Visión, 1992.

Wilde, Oscar. *Complete Works of Oscar Wilde*. 2nd ed. Intro. Vyvyan Holland. London: Collins, 1966.

6

The Thin and the Fat: Onetti and Felisberto Hernández

Gustavo San Román

Onetti (1909–94) and Felisberto Hernández (1902–64) are generally regarded in current critical thinking as the two most important Uruguayan prose writers since the 1930s. Their work, which overlapped for about twenty years, has some features in common. Both authors were inclined to write stories based on their protagonists' fantasies, a fact explained by one critic with reference to the relatively stable and uneventful times they grew up in;[1] also, both produced some highly ambiguous texts, as several studies have shown.[2] But the task of the present piece is to contrast rather than compare the two writers and it is based on the premise that the motives and the authority behind their narratives are quite different.

Although both authors produced highly dense writing, Onetti's work offers an impression of ultimate control and objectivity behind its textual complexity that Hernández's lacks; Hernández's stories, on the other hand, seem to be dictated by more urgent and subjective preoccupations. This claim could be tested through the analysis of a pair of texts such as Onetti's *La muerte y la niña* ["Death and the Girl"] (1973) and Hernández's *Diario de un sinvergüenza* ["Diary of the Scoundrel"] (left unfinished on his death), both highly ambiguous but in fundamentally different ways: briefly, in terms of narrative technique in one case and by dint of the exploration of an eccentric mind in the other. But this essay has taken, as it were, a negative path, and will examine two stories where the signs of narrative cohesiveness are in fact strong: Onetti's *Para una tumba sin nombre* [*A Grave with No Name*] (1959) and Hernández's *La casa inundada* [*The Flooded House*] (1960). I shall therefore consider ambiguity where it is at its most controlled rather than at its most overt.

The present essay builds on two observations. The first is that there is a difference in attitude in the two authors toward the physical shape of their characters: while Onetti favors figures who are thin, Hernández is partial to fat ones. The second stems from an article Onetti wrote on his countryman in Madrid in 1975 where he paid particular attention to his subject's transformation from slim as a young man to obese in his maturity; although central to the piece, the reference remains intriguing on a first reading. It is proposed that the reference will be better understood in the light of the discussion of the two texts selected for the present article. The argument that follows is based on the premise that the apparently superficial difference in predilection as regards body shape in Onetti and Hernández is a sign of a more profound contrast in their work. In the first section I explore the contrast in actual writing practice, with reference first to the associations affecting fat and thin figures in each writer in general, and then to the position of the narrator and the role of food in the two selected texts. I next relate the findings to the wider cultural context in which the two authors wrote, bearing in mind both the contemporary critical reception of their work and the image that each writer projected in terms of local notions of masculinity. Finally, I turn to Onetti's article on Hernández.

FAT AND THIN CHARACTERS AND DISCOURSES

Onetti prefers his characters thin. In his texts people who are fat tend to be treated contemptuously or pitifully. One clear example is Tito Perotti, who in "El álbum" [*The Photograph Album*] (1953) is described by Jorge Malabia as "Gordito, sonrosado, presuntuoso, servil, . . . idiota" ["Chubby, pink-cheeked, presumptuous, . . . an idiot"] (OC 1276). A similar assessment applies to more important characters who seem to carry the implied author's sympathy, at least partially or temporarily. Such is the case of Larsen, whom Onetti considered an "artista fracasado" ["failed artist"];[3] his plumpness is a sign that his goals are doomed to fail. Larsen is "el hombre gordo" ["the fat man"] (81) when we first meet him at the beginning of *Tierra de nadie* [*No Man's Land*] (1941), and he appears even heavier when he returns to Santa María at the opening of *El astillero* [*The Shipyard*] (1961), in what seems to be an indication of his increased conformism: "tal vez más gordo, más bajo, confundible y domado en apariencia" ["perhaps fatter, shorter, more run-of-the-mill and tamed in appearance"] (1049). A similar treatment affects the older and more conservative Jorge Malabia in *La muerte y la niña*, where Díaz Grey says that Jorge "estaba aprendiendo a ser imbécil. . . . Su cara y su vientre estaban engordando" ["was learning how to be stupid. . . . His face and his belly were getting fat"] (CC 377–78). Later in the same text there is some indication of the significance of fat when the doctor is disappointed at Jorge's surrendering to bourgeois values: "Le dolía que el otro engordara, que se mezclara . . . con la estupidez y la mugre del porvenir que le ofrecía la ciudad" ["He was disappointed to see him getting fat, getting mixed up . . . with the stupidity and dirt of the future that the city offered him"] (382).

Onetti's posture on obesity also applies to female characters, as his first and last novels show. At the beginning of *El pozo* [*The Pit*] (1939), when Linacero expresses disgust at the people he can see in the yard outside his window, his eyes focus on a fat woman: "Las gentes del patio me resultaron más repugnantes que nunca. Estaban, como siempre, la mujer gorda lavando en la pileta, rezongando sobre la vida. . . ." ["The people in the yard seemed to me more repugnant than ever. There were, as usual, the fat woman washing in the sink, grumbling about life]" (49–50). Similarly, the decline of the little girl Elvirita in *Cuando ya no importe* [*Past Caring?*] (1993) is predicted by the narrator in terms of her gaining weight: "Imaginé a la muchacha gorda, obesa, perdiendo por los mofletes el encanto de la inocencia" ["I imagined the girl was fat, obese, losing through her chubby cheeks the charm of innocence"] (*Cuando ya no importe*, 77). Fat in Onetti, then, seems to be associated with materialism and bourgeois values in the case of men, and with the loss of sexual innocence for women, who tend to either become whores, or mothers, as Linacero expounds in a notorious passage of *El pozo* (63).

Onetti's attitude toward overweight women is quite contrary to Felisberto Hernández's, whose texts are often peopled by matronlike female characters who are surreptitiously or overtly desired by the male protagonists. There are two stories where this sexual preference is most strongly felt: *La casa inundada*, the last work to be published in Hernández's lifetime and perhaps his most popular, and the posthumous "Úrsula" ["Ursula"] (1969). In the latter the narrator likes to remember Úrsula's "cuerpo grande" ["large body"] walking along a narrow street when "a cada paso sus pantorrillas se rozaban y las carnes le quedaban temblando" ["at every step her calves rubbed each other and left her flesh trembling"].[4] Using a similar image, the narrator of *La casa inundada* fantasizes about being married to the voluminous señora Margarita and being mocked by his previous girlfriends who "se reirían de mí al descubrirme caminando por veredas estrechas detrás de una mujer gruesísima" ["would laugh at me when they spotted me walking along narrow pavements behind a very stout woman"] (82).

This picture of a large woman interfering with the narrator's steps along a narrow path is one that points to the potential of seeing "fat" and "thin" as wider categories of writing. In fact, at least one study so far has found it useful to pursue the wider implications of "literary fat ladies": Patricia Parker's interesting essay on that figure in English Renaissance texts, where she pursues in particular the notion of rhetorical *dilatio* and its associations with deferral and excess in the discourse of romances.[5] I would like to explore here the idea that "fat" and "thin" texts not only privilege or ill-treat obese or lean characters, but that they also differ in terms of their relative density of discourse and single-mindedness of plot. To bring in an older compatriot of Onetti and Hernández and author of several pieces on the ars poetica of the short story, Horacio Quiroga (1878–1937), we may say that a text is the "thinner" the more it displays directness of plot and economy of means.

Quiroga's explicit advice to budding writers insists on the desirability of a slim and controlled plot: "No empieces a escribir sin saber desde la primera palabra adónde vas"; "No adjetives sin necesidad"; "Toma a tus personajes de la mano y llévalos firmemente hasta el final. . . . No abuses del lector." ["Do not start writing without knowing from the first word where you are heading"; "Do not use unnecessary adjectives"; "Take your characters by the hand and lead them firmly to the end. . . . Do not abuse your reader"]. For him, the short story should be "una sola línea, trazada por una mano sin temblor desde el principio al fin" ["a single line, traced by a steady hand from beginning to end"] or "una flecha que, cuidadosamente apuntada, parte del arco para ir a dar directamente en el blanco. Cuantas mariposas trataran de posarse sobre ella para adornar su vuelo, no conseguirían sino entorpecerlo" ["an arrow that, carefully aimed, leaves the bow directly toward the target. Any butterflies that might try to settle upon it in order to adorn its flight, would only manage to interfere with it.].[6] Although Onetti and Hernández are quite different writers from their predecessor, Quiroga's views on the ideal short story are helpful to distinguish between them. This essay aims to show that Onetti is more likely than Hernández to produce "thin" texts such as the one widely regarded as his masterpiece, *El astillero*, where the plot gives an impression of high precision in the making. Such precision is rarely apparent in Hernández, where the dominant aesthetic tends instead toward the "fat." Two aspects that seem particularly appropriate to test this idea will be considered below: the role of the narrator and the function of food.

The two texts to be confronted here, Onetti's *Para una tumba sin nombre* and Hernández's *La casa inundada*, were published in Montevideo within a few months of each other (1959–60), and have certain traits in common. Though fairly carefully drawn and so relatively "thin," both works self-consciously build upon a plot not entirely in the hands of the first-person narrator. In *Para una tumba*, the narrator is doctor Díaz Grey (though he remains nameless), a common voice in Onetti's works from the Santa María cycle and the one most easily identifiable with the implied author. Díaz Grey presents the versions he hears about the tale behind the death and burial of Rita, who had been the maid of the Malabia family. His main source of information is Jorge Malabia, who arranged Rita's funeral and looked after her ailing goat until the animal died a week after its owner. The other main source of information about the plot is Jorge's friend and fellow student at university in Buenos Aires, Tito Perotti. The two secondary narrators provide versions that are in part contradictory, and the doctor himself adds missing information in one chapter, as well as warning at the end that he is making no firm claims about the truth of the story.

In *La casa inundada*, the anonymous narrator reports the story of Señora Margarita, a rich and corpulent patroness who hires him as her boatman for trips in a canal around an island in her garden, during which she provides some background about her peculiar relationship with water. From other sources the narrator cites, it appears that the water also helps Margarita to reminisce over her disappeared husband, José. The narrator, like Díaz Grey, makes no claim to have reported the story in all true details. He is a writer and shares certain features with other narrators in Hernández that make him, like Díaz Grey for Onetti, a likely representative of the author.

THE NARRATIVE VOICE

Since both stories are concerned with filling a gap in the knowledge of the narrator, his position invites special attention. Two aspects of that position are particularly relevant: degree of control over the plot and relationship with other characters.

The two narrators differ in the strength of their grip on the plot. A hint of this can be gleaned from the first of two curious parallels between the stories. At the center of each text there is a remarkably similar intrigue: the status of both Rita and José, who motivate the plot in each story, is far from clear. They may or may not be dead; their graves in each case, the plot in Santa María's cemetery and the fountain in the flooded house, may after all be only cenotaphs, empty tombs. In *La casa inundada*, the ambiguity is announced early on when the narrator vacillates about the possibility that José might be buried in the fountain-turned-island (68) and it is maintained until the very end in the closing words of Margarita's dedication of the story to José: "Esté vivo o esté muerto" ["Whether he be alive or dead"] (89). As with much of the reported story, this is an area that the narrator acknowledges as falling beyond his understanding and control.

In Onetti's story, unlike Hernández's, the last word is firmly by the narrator, who dismisses both Jorge's latest version of events, now reduced to "Hubo una mujer que murió y enterramos, hubo un cabrón que murió y enterré. Y nada más" ["There was a woman who died and whom we buried, there was a goat who died and whom I buried. Nothing else"] (1044), and Tito's letter (whose contents contradict Jorge). It is Díaz Grey who declares that there may not after all have been a body in the coffin that was buried in the graveyard: "no me extrañaría demasiado que resultara inútil . . . toda pesquisa en los libros del cementerio" ["I wouldn't be too surprised if any search in the cemetery records turned out to be fruitless"] (1046), a declaration that amounts to beating Jorge, the putative originator of the tale, at his own game of adding variations. Indeed, as we look back in the story, there is a prefiguration of this statement and of the narrator's control over the plot in Díaz Grey's impression at the burial that the coffin was surprisingly light: "Éramos sólo cuatro personas y bastábamos. . . . Era, casi, como llevar una caja vacía . . . como transportar en un sueño dichoso . . . el fantasma liviano de un muerto antiguo . . . el ataúd de peso absurdo." ["We were only four people and that was more than enough. . . . It was, almost, like carrying an empty box . . . like transporting in a happy dream . . . the light ghost of a dead friend . . . the coffin of absurd weight"] (995–96). Such a commanding presence of the narrator is absent in *La casa inundada*, where his voice is often replaced by that of Margarita.

There are two more instances of the narrator's firm control on events in *Para una tumba*. The first is Díaz Grey's recurring judgment over the way Jorge Malabia tells his story, which includes criticism of the young man's showiness (998), irony, pride and harshness (1008), cocksureness, cynicism and self-righteousness (1026–31).[7] His overall assessment is that Jorge is "un mal narrador" ["a bad storyteller"]: he is too slow and fails to perceive that his audience needs to be told events and not his own rather vague reflections (1012). He then proceeds to prod Jorge into spelling out missing information (1012–13). But since Jorge does not take up the offer, Díaz Grey puts on the second demonstration of his control over the plot by providing his own imagined version of how Rita came to be in charge of the goat. Not only is Díaz Grey's account, including his christening of the inventor of the goat ploy as Ambrosio, accepted by Jorge and Tito as valid; his telling is altogether "thinner" than Malabia's: "Es muy corto. . . . Unas pocas páginas" ["It's very short. . . . Just a few pages"] (1026). The higher degree of succinctness is denoted by the difference in length between the two chapters: chapter 3, by the doctor, is almost half the size of chapter 2 where

Jorge tells the original tale. The other main difference is in plot development, which is direct in Díaz Grey's version and vacillating in Jorge's, a fact confirmed by the young man himself when at the end of chapter 2 he declares that all he has said is merely preliminary material: "no era el final de un capítulo sino el final del prólogo" ["it wasn't the end of a chapter but rather the end of the prologue"] (1014).

No such tight grip on the plot is apparent in *La casa inundada*. The boatman adds no factual information to the story Margarita supplies, and confesses his inability to report reliably what he has heard. Unlike Díaz Grey, the boatman's role is confined to taking note of what Margarita says rather than making contributions. This is evident when he declares his puzzlement soon after the "velorio" ["wake"] episode: "Esta vez ni siquiera comprendía por qué la señora Margarita me había llamado y contaba su historia sin dejarme hablar ni una palabra" ["This time I did not even understand why Señora Margarita had summoned me and was telling me her story without allowing me to say a word"] (88). A further difference is illustrated by the boatman's frequent vacillations, a feature of "fat" discourse that distances him from Díaz Grey and rather approximates him to the less single-minded teller of that story, Jorge Malabia. *La casa inundada* begins with a preamble that seems, paradoxically, to have been unplanned, judging by the statement that closes it: "Pero ahora yo debo esforzarme en empezar esta historia por su verdadero principio, y no detenerme demasiado en las preferencias de los recuerdos" ["But now I must make an effort to start this story at its proper beginning, and not detain myself too long on the preferences of my memories"] (69). This amounts to a confession of the narrator's inability to keep control over the plot (and also echoes another famous beginning by Hernández, that of *Por los tiempos de Clemente Colling* ["For the Times of Clemente Colling"], of 1942).

His hesitation is evident in the connections between sentences, as in the case of the second paragraph of the story (68), which opens with the hypothesis that José might be buried in the island in the middle of the canal. This is followed by one supporting statement ("Por eso ella me hacía dar vueltas por allí" ["that's why she made me go around it"]), but in the next sentence the hypothesis is denied ("sin embargo, el marido no podía estar en aquella isla" ["however, the husband couldn't be in that island"]) and several reasons are given for the new position (Alcides had said José had fallen off a cliff in Switzerland; the previous boatman had said that he had helped make the island by filling an old fountain with earth; Margarita's head movements as the boat went past the island were not consistent with her husband being buried there). In a new reversal, however, the paragraph ends with a statement that appears to support the original claim: Margarita's thick glasses could conceal her true feelings and the place, covered with a glass dome, would be suitable to hold a corpse after all.

A second area of difference between the stories involves the relationship between the narrator and the other characters. Díaz Grey's authority cuts through a highly polyphonic text made up of a collection of voices whose status can be discerned according to a range of attributes that include smoking, drinking alcohol (positive features), materialist values and, of course, body weight (negative traits). On a scale of narratorial partiality, near the bottom go Godoy and Caseros (obese and nonsmoker respectively), followed closely by the fat and pragmatic Tito. Next comes Jorge Malabia, who is thin but there are hints that this may change in future: at the beginning of the story he is "flaco, joven, noble" ["thin, young, honest"] (996); at a second meeting he is "más grande pero no más gordo" ["larger but not fatter"] himself, but his horse is gaining weight (1023–24). Since Díaz Grey gradually changes his appreciation of Jorge as the young man becomes increasingly associated with materialism, it is not far-fetched to expect him to be gaining weight in the time of the story, a prediction corroborated in later texts such as *La muerte y la niña*, already cited. Near the top in the narrator's estimation is his own invention, Ambrosio, who unsurprisingly is also thin. We are told this, appropriately enough, when he brings home the goat after nine months of mental gestation: "parecía más delgado, un poco ojeroso, con un aire de liberación y amansado orgullo" ["he looked thinner, a little haggard, with an air of relief and a tamed pride"] (1019). This description clearly improves on Rita's impression of his insecurity when she first met him: "tenía el aire de haber perdido a la mamá entre un gentío" ["had the air of having lost his mummy in a crowd"] (1016), thus marking Ambrosio's progression toward self-confidence.

Other secondary characters are also distinguished through features that can be related to gluttony or frugality. Thus of two funeral directors, Grimm, preferred by the narrator, is blunt and straightforward: "la brutalidad o indiferencia de Grimm . . . su falta de hipocresía . . . enfrentando a la muerte como un negocio, considerando al cadáver como un simple bulto transportable" ["the bluntness or indifference of Grimm . . . his lack of hypocrisy . . . confronting death as a business, considering a corpse was a simple bundle to be transported"] (987). Miramonte, by contrast, is hyperbolic and showy: "confía todo, en apariencia, a los empleados y se dedica, vestido de negro, peinado de negro, con su triste bigote negro y el brillo discretamente equívoco de los ojos de mulato, a mezclarse entre los dolientes, a estrechar manos y difundir consuelos" ["he leaves everything, apparently, to his workers, and devotes himself, dressed in black, with his black hair combed back, his sad black mustache and his discreetly equivocal shining mulatto eyes, to mingling with the mourners, to shaking hands and proffering condolences"] (987–88). The connotations of thinness and fatness sometimes overrule actual physical characteristics, as when the old Nordic priest Bergner is preferred to the Italian successor who, though slight of frame, has negative traits of excess: "Favieri, chico, negro, escuálido, con su indomable expresión provocativa, casi obscena" ["Favieri, small, black, scraggy, with his untamable, provocative, almost obscene expression"] (988). Similarly, Miramonte's employee, Caseros, physically fit on account of his sportsmanship, is the butt of irony worthy of overweight characters: "Exageraba, mentía un poco, andaba buscando alarmas. . . . Tiene largos los bigotes y los puños de la camisa, mueve las manos frente a la boca como apartando moscas con languidez" ["He was exaggerating, he was lying a bit, he was looking for something to alarm me. . . . He has a long mustache and the sleeves of his shirt are long, he moves his hands in front of his mouth as if wearily shooing flies away"] (989).

Finally in the hierarchy of *Para una tumba*, Díaz Grey's own superiority over the other characters corresponds to his status within the social context of the story. He is a well-respected figure in his community, as indicated most explicitly by the attitude of the lesser characters who report events to him, Caseros and Fragoso. Apart from the overt high regard they show toward him, both characters pay for his drinks and are willing to pass on to him the information they have, implicitly asking for the doctor's approval. He, in turn, does not issue any comments but, in a gesture of superiority, keeps his judgment to himself.

The position of Hernández's narrator is quite different: he is an employee of Señora Margarita, who has hired him to write her story. During his stay at the flooded house, the narrator constantly obeys Margarita's orders even when unhappy to do so, as happens during the third outing: "Parece mentira, la noche es tan inmensa, en el campo, y nosotros aquí, dos personas mayores, tan cerca y pensando quién sabe qué estupideces diferentes" ["I'm puzzled, the night is immense upon the countryside, and here we are, two grown-up people, so near each other and yet each thinking who knows what stupid and different thoughts"] (76). It is also significant that not only is he unable to articulate to Margarita his displeasure at being there, but that his nearest move in that direction is to quote the words of others: "Yo me ahogaba y me venían cerca de la boca palabras que parecían de un antiguo compañero de orquesta que tocaba el bandoneón: '¿quién te hace ninguna pregunta? . . . Mejor me dejaras ir a dormir . . .'" ["I was drowning and words reached my mouth that seemed to belong to an old fellow musician who played the accordion with me in an orchestra: 'who is asking you anything? . . . I wish you let me go to sleep . . .'"] (76). That this statement should remain unuttered is confirmation that the narrator's real feelings are repressed in the presence of Margarita. And the fact that her name is always prefaced by the title "señora" underpins his lower status and further contrasts him to his counterpart in *Para una tumba*, who is typically addressed as "doctor" by the other characters.

A further illustration of her power in *La casa inundada* is that Margarita need only request his writing of her story indirectly: "si por casualidad a usted se le ocurriera escribir todo lo que le he contado, cuente con mi permiso" ["if by any chance you are thinking of writing down all that I have told you, you have my permission"] (89). And her tacit superiority over the narrator is overtly inscribed in the last sentence of the story, which is a quotation of her dedication of the tale to José and represents her final appropriation of the text. This contrasts with the ending of *Para una tumba*, when the narrator imposes his own assessment: "Y cuando pasaron bastantes días de reflexión . . . escribí, en pocas noches, esta historia. . . . Lo único que cuenta es que al terminar de escribirla me sentí en paz" ["And when enough days of reflection had passed . . . I wrote this story in a few nights. . . . All that counts now is that once I had finished writing it I felt at peace"] (1045–46).

FOOD

Bearing in mind the associations highlighted so far, the difference in goal between the two narrators should be corroborated in the stories' references to food. The subject is indeed treated quite differently in the two texts. In *Para una tumba* there is little mention of eating, and much mention of drinking alcohol, although the impression given is that consumption has not been extravagant. By contrast, food is an important preoccupation in *La casa inundada* (and in Hernández's texts more generally).

The difference in attitude toward food in the two texts can be gleaned from the second of the two curious parallels between them: also at the center of each story there are a wake and a goat, real in *Para una tumba* and metaphorical or pictorial in *La casa inundada*. Whatever other meanings these elements may have in each text, two aspects are relevant to the argument being pursued here.[8] One is the fact that the "velorio" ["wake"] in *La casa inundada* is closely associated with food. The first piece of furniture the boatman sees on arrival is a food trolley ("trinchante" [86]), the candles are placed into pudding basins and the ceremony is triggered off by the sound of a gong. The second aspect is complementary to the first: in *Para una tumba*, the goat appears to represent both Ambrosio's achievement and the opposite to Jorge's uncertainty and shortcomings ("símbolo de algo que moriré sin comprender" ["a symbol of something I shall die without understanding"] [1011]); it is also, in the opinion of Díaz Grey, the motor that triggered the plot ("El cabrón, que es lo que cuenta" ["the goat, which is what counts/recounts"] [1023]). According to the logic that has emerged from things "fat" and "thin" in the two stories, it should follow that the goat, as a positive figure in Onetti's text, must be slim. Although this is not stated openly, it is the case that the animal lives up to its idealized image by dying of self-imposed inanition. As he arrives at the cemetery, Díaz Grey observes that the animal "refregaba el hocico en los pastos cortos de la zanja, sin llegar a comer" ["rubbed its snout against the short grass in the ditch, without eating it"] (993) and Jorge confirms that it had given up eating a few days previously: "Creo que tiene una pata rota, hace unos días que apenas come" ["I think it has a broken leg, it's hardly eaten for a few days"] (995). When it eventually dies, at lunchtime, it was still fasting: "Murió. Recién hoy a mediodía. No pude conseguir que comiera" ["It died. Only today at lunchtime. I didn't manage to make it eat"] (998). (Relatedly, although no reference is made to the size of the goat in *La casa inundada*, the picture which contains it is "un cuadro enorme" ["an enormous picture"] placed over a bed that is "muy grande" ["very large"] [86].)

There is no comparable intentional dieting in Hernández's text. On the contrary, the main reason why the narrator wanted the post of boatman at the flooded house was to avoid starvation. Alcides, Margarita's nephew, mentioned the possibility of a job to the narrator one day when he was feeling weak with hunger, "Alcides me encontró en Buenos Aires un día en que yo estaba muy débil . . . y me hizo comer de todo" ["Alcides found me in Buenos Aires one day when I was very weak . . . and he made me eat a lot"], and the narrator is grateful to Margarita because of the "cambio brusco que me había hecho pasar de la miseria a esta opulencia" ["sudden change that brought me from poverty to this opulence"] (69). It is significant, furthermore, that the part of the story in which Margarita, after several failed attempts that frustrate the narrator, finally speaks about her past happens on an evening when he had eaten and drunk excessively: "Otra noche en que yo había comido y bebido demasiado" ["On another night, when I had eaten and drunk too much"] (76). It is as if inebriation and gluttony made him more perceptive in the eyes of his landlady. And on reaching his bed after the outing, he has memories of a previous mildly drunken night: "al tantear los muebles tuve el recuerdo de otra noche en que me había emborrachado ligeramente con una bebida que tomaba por primera vez" ["as I was groping the furniture I remembered another night when I was slightly drunk on a beverage I had taken for the first time"] (81). This declaration further undermines the authority of a highly distracted teller who, in a clear contrast with Díaz Grey's position, readily confesses his inability to understand people: "Yo sabía que tenía gran dificultad en comprender a los demás y trataba de pensar en la señora Margarita un poco como Alcides y otro poco como María" ["I knew that I had great difficulty understanding other people and tried to think about Señora Margarita a bit as Alcides would and another bit as María would"] (75).

MAN VERSUS CHILD

This last quotation points to an important feature of the boatman's personality that also markedly opposes him to Díaz Grey, namely his highly diffused sense of self. While in both stories the narrator displays certain parallels with the main character, the two relationships involved are quite different. As we have seen, the doctor eventually stands back from Jorge Malabia and judges him from a position of superiority. This is not the case in Hernández's text, where the narrator often seems unable to disentangle himself from Margarita emotionally and psychologically. This situation obtains throughout, and is perhaps particularly strong during the third outing, when he has been eating and drinking heavily. There we read that his mind takes a path of its own ("La cabeza se me entretenía en pensar cosas por su cuenta" ["My head entertained itself thinking on its own"] [76]), and that he cannot separate his own from Margarita's thoughts: "Después que ella empezó a hablar, me pareció que su voz también sonaba dentro de mí como si yo pronunciara sus palabras. Tal vez por eso ahora confundo lo que ella me dijo con lo que yo pensaba" ["After she started to speak, I thought that her voice also sounded inside me as if I was pronouncing her words. Perhaps that's why now I'm confusing what she told me with what I was thinking"] (77).

This general dispersion of discourse is related specifically to Margarita's large body, again showing that fat discourse and fat bodies tend to coexist, in this case further supported by overindulgence in food and drink. Margarita's body is the site upon which the narrator constructs his fantasies: "su cuerpo inmenso . . . me tentaba a imaginar sobre él, un pasado tenebroso. . . . [E]lla se prestaba—como prestaría el lomo una elefanta blanca a un viajero—para imaginar disparates entretenidos" ["her immense body . . . tempted me to imagine on it a shady past. . . . [S]he lent herself—as a white elephant would lend her body to a traveler—as a site for me to imagine entertaining and absurd thoughts]" (69); "Cuando dijo 'mundo,' yo, sin mirarla, me imaginé las curvas de su cuerpo" ["When she said 'world' I, without looking at her, imagined the curves of her body"] (74).

The boatman's desire for Margarita is linked to several references to him as a child: she looks as if she was asking him "¿Qué pasa, hijo mío?" ["What's wrong, my boy?"] (69); she represents "el sueño fantástico de un niño" ["the fantastic dream of a child"] (73); after seeing her, he climbs the stairs "como un chiquilín" ["like a child"] (74); he sees himself as a satellite attracted by her and wishes to replace José in her eyes (82). The narrator also shares with Margarita an affinity with water (e.g., "los recuerdos de agua que yo recibía en mi propia vida, en las intermitencias del relato, también me parecían fieles de esa religión" ["the water memories that I received in my own life, in the gaps in the story, also seemed to me that were faithful to that religion"] [81]). As Patricia Parker notes at the end of her study of "literary fat ladies," the deferral and excess of the romances she has analyzed echo the claims of *écriture féminine* criticism, among them "the description of women's speech, in Luce Irigaray, as 'dilatable'" (31). A further connection with Irigaray is also relevant to Hernández's text; in particular, Margarita's relationship with water appears to support Irigaray's ideas on liquids as icons of female desire: "Yo debo estar con mis pensamientos y mis recuerdos como en un agua que corre con gran caudal" ["I must be with my own thoughts and memories as if I was being carried by a great flow of water"] (80).[9]

These two tendencies in the boatman, desiring a motherly woman and sharing in her affinity for water, contrast strongly with the tone of control and authority of Díaz Grey, who behaves like a man, not a child. Such a contrast, which is paralleled in a difference in the critical reception of Hernández and Onetti in contemporary culture in Uruguay and beyond, can be related to dominant views of masculinity. Although some critics from the implacable "generation of 1945" in Uruguay took to Hernández (most strongly, the rather benign Ángel Rama and José Pedro Díaz),[10] the majority seemed ambiguous about him (e.g., Ruben Cotelo, Mario Benedetti, and Carlos Martínez Moreno),[11] and some were quite openly hostile, most notoriously Emir Rodríguez Monegal in a review of *Nadie encendía las lámparas* [*No One Had Lit a Lamp*] (1947), to which I return below.

The grounds for critics' disapproval of Hernández appear to be mainly three: bad writing, deviant sexuality, and dependency on others. The first aspect involved not only deficient Spanish, as highlighted in Rodríguez Monegal's review by an addendum listing grammatical and lexical errors, but also poor writing in more general terms. What was criticized in Hernández was, in brief, a tendency toward "excess," which, in the terms of the present analysis, can be related to his predilection for things "fat." Thus in his review Rodríguez Monegal focused on what he saw as Hernández's lack of control over his material: "[El] niño detrás de este relator . . . no puede organizar sus experiencias, ni la comunicación de las mismas; no puede regular la fluencia de la palabra" ["The child behind this narrator . . . cannot organize his experience, nor the communication of it; he cannot regulate the flow of language"] (52). Similarly, Ruben Cotelo criticized *La casa inundada* for its failure to present what was "material . . . potencialmente rico" ["potentially rich material"] in a suitable, and we could say "thin," form; instead, he delivered it "casi en bruto" ["almost in a raw state"] and without having achieved "su debida forma narrativa" ["its proper narrative form"] (107). In each review, the excess in form is coupled with a lack of control, and therefore also "excess," in sexuality: Monegal notices that the author "no se reconoce límites, ni siquiera los impuestos por la sobriedad" ["sets himself no limits, not even those imposed by sobriety"] (51) and that behind him there is a child who "no maduró para el arte ni para lo sexual" ["did not reach maturity in art or in sexuality"] (52). And Cotelo feels that: "A esta altura del siglo estamos curados de perversiones; lo reprochable es que se nos haga partícipes de ellas" ["At this stage in the century we are immune to perversions; what is to be reproached is that we should be made to participate in them"] (107).

By contrast, the value of frugality (and the rejection of "fat") comes through quite clearly in the following assessment by Cotelo of Onetti's "La cara de la desgracia" [*The Image of Misfortune*] (1960), published a week earlier than his review of *La casa inundada*: "Es un placer que pocas veces proporciona la literatura uruguaya: un estilo tenso, la precisión de vocabulario, el pudor expresivo, . . . la ausencia total de adiposidades, vacilaciones y rellenos; . . . una estructura formalmente limpia y cargada de significado, de un ascetismo que no rehúye el humor y la pasión [sino que] más bien los destaca" ["It is a pleasure that is rarely provided by Uruguayan literature: a tense style, precision in vocabulary, modesty of expression, . . . total absence of adiposity, vacillation, and stuffing; . . . a structure formally clean and loaded with meaning, with an ascetic quality that rejects neither humor nor passion [but rather] highlights them"] ("El guardián de su hermano" [41]). Moreover, although neither of these critics particularly celebrated Onetti's preference for idealized pubescent girls, they held back from a strong attack of this aspect. (In one of the subtlest early readings of Onetti, "Muchacha y mujer," Cotelo relates the writer's interest in the figure of the girl with Catholic ideas). As Rodríguez Monegal summed up elsewhere, Onetti inspired unanimous high regard among contemporary local critics: "resulta . . . notorio el caso de Juan Carlos Onetti, cuya fortuna ha ido acentuándose hasta ser hoy el único escritor uruguayo aceptado por tirios y troyanos" ["the case of Juan Carlos Onetti is well known, whose status has been growing to the extent that he is today the only Uruguayan writer accepted in all quarters"].[12] Indeed, it is really only with the advent of feminist criticism that the overwhelming respect for Onetti has been seriously challenged (one recent example being Moreira).

The third criticism of Hernández relates most overtly to contemporary views of masculinity, where Hernández and Onetti occupy extreme poles in a continuum. At one end there is the dependent childlike figure of Hernández, who needed the help of his friends' subscriptions or connections to get his works published or to obtain employment.[13] This trait of Hernández's character was an important factor behind Rodríguez Monegal's negative disposition toward him, as shown in one of his more favorable notes: "siempre pensé que había en Hernández un escritor de grandes dotes, pero malogrado por la adulación de sus amigos" ["I always thought that there was in Hernández a writer of great qualities, but spoilt by the adulation of his friends"] ("Un escritor original"). This contrasts with the position of Onetti at the other end of the continuum, since he saw himself and was perceived by everyone else locally not only as the most important literary figure of his time but also as a strong, detached, and, for his contemporaries, archetypal male.[14]

In an interview for French television a few years before his death, Onetti laughed when told of the claim by one of his countrymen that he was one of the greatest living Uruguayan writers, considering such praise rather insignificant.[15] And in an article incorporating an earlier interview, a young writer who had known Onetti for some time confessed the effect of awe he inspired in others: "No he conocido a nadie (salvo aisladas mujeres) que no se ponga solemne o tartamudo cuando Onetti empieza a burlarse de él" ["I haven't known anyone (save a few women) who didn't become solemn or develop a stutter when Onetti began to mock them"]. This position of superiority was acknowledged by Onetti himself (though not without irony) when the same young interviewer put it to him more directly: "Entonces le repetí mi teoría, ya una vieja convicción: 'A vos no te interesa tener amigos. O no tenerlos. Tanto te da'" ["So I repeated my theory, which is already an old conviction: 'You are not interested in having friends. Or in not having them. It's all the same to you'"] "Puede ser" ["Maybe"] was Onetti's reply.[16]

ONETTI ON HERNÁNDEZ

The images of the two writers that come through in the work of contemporary critics seem quite consistent with those of the two narrators studied above. They seem also to correspond to what we know of the two authors' relationships with their own writing. While Onetti claimed not to have to labor over his texts ("Pues yo le digo que no trabajo ni la sintaxis ni el estilo" ["Well, I tell you that I do not work on syntax or style"], he told Chao[17]), Hernández confessed to his mentor and supporter Jules Supervielle that he had to go over numerous drafts of *La casa inundada*: "le he hecho, realmente, miles de veces" ["I have redone it, literally, thousands of times"],[18] a fact consistent with statements in other letters and with his biographers' comments on his lack of self-confidence.

For a closer assessment of what they thought of each other, we can now turn to the short article by Onetti on Hernández, published in exile in Spain and mentioned at the beginning of the present paper. The article should confirm some of the insights gained through the study of the two stories undertaken above. Two aspects of the piece, entitled "Felisberto, el 'naif'" ["Felisberto, the Naïve One"] are particularly relevant to the present discussion because they highlight a contrast between Onetti and his subject. The first is a comment made in passing: "Felisberto—siempre se le llamó así—" ["Felisberto—that's what everyone called him—"] (31). It is true that, like a child or a woman writer, Hernández was and still is generally referred to by his Christian name. This may have to do partly with the rarity of that appellation, as opposed to the common nature of his surname, but it is also consistent with the image of a man who, like a child, always depended on others for support. By reminding the reader of this fact, the author tacitly confirms the difference in their status, which is endorsed by Onetti's further statement that Felisberto, who was seven years older than him, seemed insecure and lost when they met: "Lo sentí tan descentrado, tan sinceramente inseguro de los pequeños libros que había publicado" ["I felt he was so directionless, so sincerely unsure about the little books he had published"] (31). Hernández's status is thus in clear opposition to that of Onetti himself, who, as it happens, is generally referred to by his surname alone.

The second aspect of interest comes when Onetti ponders on what he calls Hernández's innocence: "su inocencia de aquellos días le hizo preguntarme al despedirse:—¿Usted en qué café habla?" ["his innocence at the time made him ask me as we parted: 'In what café do you speak?'"] (32). After reporting his own reply ("Ninguno" ["There isn't one"]), Onetti makes a curious parenthetical remark that refers to Hernández's physical outlook: "(Y un detalle tal vez desdeñable pero que a mí me importa: cuando se produjo la entrevista recién contada, Felisberto era más flaco que yo)" ["And one detail that is perhaps negligible but that I care about: when the above-related interview took place, Felisberto was thinner than me"]. He then comments on some of Hernández's early texts, saying he was impressed by the spontaneous originality they displayed: "Para resumir, era necesario desgastar otra vez la maltrecha frase: un alma desnuda" ["To sum up: one had to turn again to the old cliché: a naked soul"] (32).

It seems therefore as if Onetti finds a parallel between the innocence of the man and that of the work he produced when he was thin. Onetti's reaction then changes as he mentions some of Hernández's later texts: of *Las Hortensias* [*The Daisy Dolls*], he says that it was "alargado sin necesidad o por empeño en la inocencia" ["stretched unnecessarily or by determination on its innocence"] (32), and of *La casa inundada*, that it was "una sucesión de situaciones absurdas que mostraban, con exceso, la deliberación de conservar la pureza, la sinceridad de sus primeros libros" ["a succession of absurd situations that showed, with excess, his deliberation to maintain the purity and sincerity of his early books"] (33). There then follows a second reference to the size of the now older Felisberto Hernández, which once again ties together writing and the body of the author:

> Y ahora un casi *nota bene* para explicar por qué señalé la flacura del Felisberto inicial. Cuando pasaron años de aquel encuentro, después del viaje a París, el escritor comenzó a engordar, a pedir en los restaurantes cantidades asombrosas de platos. Llegó a deformarse físicamente y eran muchos los amigos del pasado que no lograban reconocerlo a primera vista. (33)

> [And now almost a *nota bene*, to explain why I pointed to the thinness of the early Felisberto. Years after that meeting, after his trip to Paris, the writer started to get fat, to order amazing numbers of dishes in restaurants. He became physically deformed and there were many of his old friends who did not recognize him at first sight.]

Nothing more explicit is said on the link, but the implication is that the older Felisberto had lost the quality of innocence associated with his earlier slimness by Onetti. Instead, Hernández's gaining in weight seems to be contemporary with an increasing artificiality in his writing. The assessments implied by "por empeño" ["by determination"] as regards *Las Hortensias* and "deliberación con exceso" ["with excessive deliberation"] concerning *La casa inundada* are applicable both to the discourse of Jorge Malabia in *Para una tumba* and to that of Margarita's boatman in the story written by the older and plump Felisberto. They also echo the appreciations of contemporary critics, as we have seen. They are clearly a criticism of "fat" discourse.

Onetti's piece thus helps to draw together a number of the features noted above. The conclusion that emerges from the various texts considered is that Onetti's preference for thin characters and Hernández's for fat ones represent the tip of an iceberg that contains models of writing and manliness that contribute to an understanding of the contemporary critical reception of their texts. On the one hand Onetti, like Díaz

Grey, and apart from any other artistic merit of his work, practiced a form of writing that was consistent with a dominant notion of adult masculinity: controlled, detached, self-sufficient, and goal-oriented. Onetti's fantasies, furthermore, were comprehensible to current perceptions, notably the thin girl as an icon of innocence that counteracts the undesirable aspirations of his whores, pimps, or bourgeois young men like Jorge Malabia and Tito Perotti, who are all typically fat figures. Although very different in tone to Quiroga's own work, Onetti's writing is consistent with the exhortations from his "Decálogo" ["Decalogue"] already mentioned, as well as others such as "No escribas bajo el imperio de la emoción" ["Do not write under the rule of your emotions"] and "No pienses en tus amigos al escribir" ["Do not think of your friends when you are writing"], which Hernández's texts and biography would seem to disobey. Quiroga also shared with Onetti, perhaps not unpredictably, an inclination for pubescent girls, as both some of his stories and some biographical details would confirm.[19]

Felisberto Hernández, on the other hand, and regardless of his own aesthetic achievements, failed to live up to hegemonic ideals. He and his characters represented weak figures, needful of supporters and interested in a sexuality associated with children's fantasies: the interminable motherly provider consistent with the appreciation of food and fat figures in his stories. What for Hernández was reassuring plenitude, for others signaled despised and unmanly excess.

NOTES

1. See José Pedro Díaz, *El espectáculo imaginario*, esp. 46–56.

2. See, for example, Arthur Terry, "Onetti and the Meaning of Fiction" and Stephanie Merrim, "Felisberto Hernández's Aesthetic of 'lo otro'."

3. In an interview with Jorge Ruffinelli included in Juan Carlos Onetti, *Réquiem por Faulkner y otros artículos*, 222.

4. Felisberto Hernández, *Obras Completas*, vol. 3, 118. All further references to *La casa inundada* are to this same volume.

5. Patricia Parker, *Literary Fat Ladies*, 8–35.

6. Horacio Quiroga, "Decálogo del perfecto cuentista" ["Decalogue of the Perfect Short-Story Writer"] (1927) and "Ante el tribunal" ["Before the Judges"] (1931), included in *Sobre literatura* ["On Literature"], 87 and 137.

7. On Jorge's transformation, see Mark Millington, *Reading Onetti*, 220–27. Chapter 7 of Millington's book and "Contar el cuento" by Josefina Ludmer, included in her *Onetti o la construcción del relato* (143–85), are essential readings on *Para una tumba*.

8. See Jorge Panesi, "Felisberto Hernández, un artista del hambre," and Gabriela Mora, "*La casa inundada*: hacia una interpretación."

9. See Luce Irigaray, *Ce Sexe qui n'en pas un*, 105–6.

10. See, for example, Ángel Rama, "Felisberto Hernández," *Capítulo Oriental* 29. It is interesting that although Hernández was older than Onetti and started publishing earlier, he should come after Onetti in this collection of installments on Uruguayan literature (the *Capítulo* on Onetti is vol. 28). For José Pedro Díaz on Hernández, see note 1 above.

11. See Ruben Cotelo's reviews of *El caballo perdido* (26 July 1964) and *La casa inundada* (19 December 1960); Mario Benedetti, "Felisberto Hernández o la credibilidad de lo fantástico"; Carlos Martínez Moreno, "Un viajero falsamente distraído."

12. Emir Rodríguez Monegal, *Literatura uruguaya del medio siglo*, 222.

13. For instances of this support see, for example, Norah Giraldi de Dei Cas, *Felisberto Hernández: del creador al hombre*, 52, 66, and 91.

14. See María Esther Gilio and Carlos M. Domínguez, *Construcción de la noche. La vida de Juan Carlos Onetti*, esp. chapters 5 and 6.

15. The interview has been published in French and, expanded, in Spanish; see Ramón Chao, *Onetti*, 78, and *Un posible Onetti*, 117.

16. Álvaro Castillo, "Hacia Onetti," 281.

17. Ramón Chao, *Un posible Onetti*, 30.

18. See Nicasio Perera San Martín, "Alrededor de dos cartas de Felisberto Hernández a Jules Supervielle," 424.

19. An example of a story is "Rea Silvia," from *El crimen del otro*; a famous anecdote about Quiroga's inclination toward young girls is related by Manuel Gálvez in *Amigos y maestros de mi juventud, 1900–1910*, 275. The link between literature and anecdote is noted by Emir Rodríguez Monegal in his biography on Quiroga, *El desterrado*, 125–26.

WORKS CITED

Benedetti, Mario. "Felisberto Hernández o la credibilidad de lo fantástico." *Literatura uruguaya siglo XX*. 2nd ed. Montevideo: Alfa, 1970. 90–95.

Castillo, Álvaro. "Hacia Onetti." *Homenaje a Juan Carlos Onetti*. Ed. Helmy Giacoman. New York: Las Américas, 1974. 277–93.

Chao, Ramón. *Onetti*. Paris: Plon, 1990.

Chao, Ramón. *Un posible Onetti*. Barcelona: Ronsel, 1994.

Cotelo, Ruben. "El guardián de su hermano" (12 December 1960). *En torno a Juan Carlos Onetti*. Ed. Lídice Gómez Mango. 39–44.

Cotelo, Ruben. "Muchacha y mujer" (1964). *En torno a Juan Carlos Onetti*. Ed. Lídice Gómez Mango. 45–53.

Cotelo, Ruben. Review of *El caballo perdido* (26 July 1964). *Felisberto Hernández: notas críticas*. Ed. Lídice Gómez Mango. 81–88.

Cotelo, Ruben. Review of *La casa inundada* (19 December 1960). *Felisberto Hernández: notas críticas*. Ed. Lídice Gómez Mango. 103–7.

Díaz, José Pedro. *El espectáculo imaginario. Juan Carlos Onetti y Felisberto Hernández: ¿Una propuesta generacional?* Montevideo: Arca, 1986.

Gálvez, Manuel. *Amigos y maestros de mi juventud, 1900–1910*. Buenos Aires: Kraft, 1944.

Gilio, María Esther, and Carlos M. Domínguez. *Construcción de la noche. La vida de Juan Carlos Onetti*. Buenos Aires: Planeta, 1993.

Giraldi de Dei Cas, Norah. *Felisberto Hernández: del creador al hombre*. Montevideo: Ediciones de la Banda Oriental, 1975.

Gómez Mango, Lídice, ed. *En torno a Juan Carlos Onetti*. Montevideo: Fundación de Cultura Universitaria, 1970.

Gómez Mango, Lídice, ed. *Felisberto Hernández: notas críticas*. Montevideo: Fundación de Cultura Universitaria, 1970.

Hernández, Felisberto. *Obras Completas*. 3 vols. Ed. José Pedro Díaz. Montevideo: Arca, 1981–83. (*Piano Stories* [includes *The Flooded House*]. Trans. Luis Harrs. New York: Marsilio Publishers, 1993.)

Irigaray, Luce. *Ce Sexe qui n'en pas un*. Paris: Éditions de Minuit, 1977.

Ludmer, Josefina. *Onetti o la construcción del relato*. Buenos Aires: Sudamericana, 1977.

Martínez Moreno, Carlos. "Un viajero falsamente distraído." *Número* (Montevideo) 2a época, 3–4 (May 1964): 159–71.

Merrim, Stephanie. "Felisberto Hernández's Aesthetic of 'lo otro': the Writing of Indeterminacy." *Revista Canadiense de Estudios Hispánicos* 11.3 (Spring 1987): 521–40.

Millington, Mark. *Reading Onetti*. Liverpool, U.K.: Francis Cairns, 1985.

Mora, Gabriela. "*La casa inundada*: hacia una interpretación." *Escritura* (Caracas) 7.13–14 (1982): 161–87.

Moreira, Hilia. "*El pozo* de Juan Carlos Onetti. Yo con yo." *Mujer, deseo comunicación*. Montevideo: Linardi y Risso, 1992. 55–93.

Onetti, Juan Carlos. *Cuando ya no importe*. 2nd ed. Madrid: Alfaguara, 1993.

Onetti, Juan Carlos. "Felisberto, el 'naif'." *Cuadernos Hispanoamericanos* 320 (1975): 257–59. Reprinted in Walter Rela, ed., *Felisberto Hernández. Valoración crítica* (Montevideo: Editorial Ciencias, 1982): 31–33. Latter is the source of my quotations.

Onetti, Juan Carlos. *Réquiem por Faulkner y otros artículos*. Ed. Jorge Ruffinelli. Buenos Aires: Calicanto, 1976.

Panesi, Jorge. "Felisberto Hernández, un artista del hambre." *Escritura* (Caracas) 7.13–14 (1982): 131–59.

Parker, Patricia. *Literary Fat Ladies. Rhetoric, Genre, Property*. London and New York: Methuen, 1987.

Perera San Martín, Nicasio. "Alrededor de dos cartas de Felisberto Hernández a Jules Supervielle." *Felisberto Hernández ante la crítica actual*. Ed. Alain Sicard. Caracas: Monte Ávila: 1977.

Quiroga, Horacio. *El crimen del otro*. Buenos Aires: Emilio Spinelli, 1904.

Quiroga, Horacio. *Sobre literatura*. vol. 7 of his *Obras inéditas y desconocidas*. Ed. Roberto Ibáñez and Jorge Ruffinelli. Montevideo: Arca, 1970.

Rama, Ángel. "Felisberto Hernández." *Capítulo Oriental* 29. Montevideo: Centro Editor de América Latina, 1968.

Rodríguez Monegal, Emir. *El desterrado*. Buenos Aires: Losada, 1968.

Rodríguez Monegal, Emir. *Literatura uruguaya del medio siglo*. Montevideo: Alfa, 1966.

Rodríguez Monegal, Emir. Review of Felisberto Hernández, *Nadie encendía las lámparas*. *Clinamen* (Montevideo) 5 (1948): 51–52.

Rodríguez Monegal, Emir. "Un escritor original." *El País* (Montevideo), 26 January 1964: 8.

Terry, Arthur. "Onetti and the Meaning of Fiction: Notes on *La muerte y la niña*." *Contemporary Latin American Fiction*. Ed. Salvador Bacarisse. Edinburgh: Scottish University Press, 1980. 54–72.

7

Between Man and Woman:
Onetti and Armonía Somers

María Rosa Olivera-Williams

Estaba también la tramposa, tal vez deliberada, deformación de
los recuerdos. ["There was also the deceiving, perhaps intentional,
distortion of memories."]

—J. C. Onetti, "La cara de la desgracia"
[*The Image of Misfortune*] (OC, 1338)

Comprendí que jamás, en adelante, debería comunicar a nadie mi
mensaje. . . . [E]ra necesario liberar también al hombre de mi pro-
pio favor simbólico, tan basto como el de cualquiera. ["From that
moment, I understood that I must never make my message known
to anyone. . . . [I]t was also necessary to release the man from my
own symbolic favor, which was every bit as crude as anyone
else's."]

—A. Somers, "El hombre del túnel"
["The Man in the Tunnel"] (131)

Five years separate the births of two of the greatest Uruguayan authors
of the twentieth century, Juan Carlos Onetti (1909) and Armonía
Somers (1914), and only two months separate the death of Somers (9
March 1994) from that of Onetti (30 May 1994). In her study of the
generation of Uruguayan writers active during the 1970s, Somers noted,
following Malraux, that "cada generación aporta una imagen del
mundo creada por su sufrimiento, por la necesidad de vencer su sufrimiento" ["each generation contributes an image of the world created
through its suffering, through the need to overcome its suffering"].[1]
Onetti and Somers may be considered as fellow members of a generation; hence, the fantastic, impassioned, and painful images that appear
in their literature might represent the fruit of that generation's suffering.

These two writers stand out in particular on account of their unique character, their tendency to rail against the hegemonic literary trends of the moment,[2] and on account of that air of "lobos esteparios" ["steppe wolves"], an expression coined by Somers herself to describe her status as an author.[3] That said, it would not be especially enlightening to approach the work of these writers by merely considering them as members of the same literary group. Of course, as Hugo Verani has already noted, Onetti's fiction belongs to a spiritually derelict universe, a world beset by events that appear to indicate the absence of God. Much the same could be said of Somers; like other great Spanish American writers, her work coincides with the project of many European colleagues, as she too sets about seeking "una justifcación de la vida misma" ["a justification of life itself"].[4]

The works of Onetti and Somers feature hallucinatory worlds that transcend the bounds of reality and touch upon fantasy, but at the same time they convey the distinct personalities of the two authors. For instance, it is not difficult to find an echo of Onetti himself in several characters in his fiction who prefer lying in bed to working in an office. Neither is it hard to envisage the author, perpetually armed with a cigarette and a whisky, his gaze lost in space, inventing the characters who wander through the streets of a provincial town called Santa María and relate unlikely stories as they go. For Onetti, as he points out in *La vida breve* [*A Brief Life*], to write is to save oneself, to write is to live.[5]

It is not so easy to see the petite and demure woman of reality behind the author of *La mujer desnuda* ["The Naked Woman"] (1950), a first novella that scandalized the prudish city of Montevideo, nor to imagine her eagerness to break the taboos that undermine the individual. However, the apparent schizophrenia between the author and the persona she invented is nothing other than a response to the difficulties facing intellectual, middle-class women in Montevideo during that era. Armonía Etchepare de Henestrosa, the teacher dedicated to her profession, the loving wife faithful to the memory of her late husband, almost the perfect model of Uruguayan femininity, had little or nothing in common with Armonía Somers.[6] At first, the personality the author established for herself shocked a readership unaccustomed to witnessing individuals affected by loneliness and repugnance when confronted with an uncaring world or the pretentiousness of human existence.[7] These were not the products of a conventional woman's imagination.

Like the metamorphosis that transforms Rebeca Linke into the naked woman of the eponymous text, Armonía Somers emerges through the process of writing. Reflecting upon her *nom de plume*, Somers stated: "a lo mejor era una protesta que yo hacía contra el hecho de haber nacido sin que me pidieran la autorización y la osadía de seguir sobre-viviendo en un mundo como éste, que no me gusta" ["perhaps I was protesting against the fact of having been born without my consent and against the valor needed to go on living in a world like this one, which I do not like"] (quoted in Risso, 254). If this pseudonym was indeed used to confront a world that displeased the author, it did not serve as a veil to separate her from reality, but as a sort of diving suit to enable her to venture into the waters of reality and of the subconscious in search of the individual as a social and sexual being with dreams and desires. For this reason, as in the case of Onetti, one senses a true love for the human being in the fiction of Somers. In Somers' own words, "a través de la indagación en las profundidades de mis personajes arquetípicos, a través del que llaman por ahí mi despiadado descarnamiento, yo he comprendido a todos los demás que componían el estrato grupal" ["by means of investigating the depths of my archetypal characters, by means of what is called around here my unrelenting starkness, I have come to understand all the others who made up my peer group"] (quoted in Risso, 277).

Now that both writers are no longer with us, we can only attempt an interview with the personalities they projected through their writing. The present investigation is limited to two stories, Onetti's "La cara de la desgracia" [*The Image of Misfortune*] (1960) and Somers' "El hombre del túnel" ["The Man in the Tunnel"] (1963).

Both stories were published in the sixties, and they both engage, from very different perspectives, the topics of love, desire, disillusionment and, especially, that of gaining access to reality through writing. For Onetti, literature "es un arte. Cosa sagrada en consecuencia: jamás un medio sino un fin" ["is an art. A sacred thing, therefore: never a means without an end"].[8] In "La cara de la desgracia," however, it would appear that Onetti is also interested in fiction as a means of arriving at truth, as a way of grasping reality. Nevertheless, even in this story, fictional discourse delights in its fictionality, a fact that does not hinder, but on the contrary facilitates, the attainment of truth. Through the fictionality of the story, an understanding of the anonymous first-person narrator can be reached.

The forty-something narrator of "La cara de la desgracia" records his personal history and recollections after the death of a young girl with whom he fell in love when they met at a seaside resort. The references to the act of writing throughout the story constantly suggest that writing, borrowing a concept from Derrida, appends a significant supplement to simple events, but at the same time replaces them.[9] Through the medium of writing, the narrator of "La cara de la desgracia" tries to address his troubled relationship with his late brother, whose suicide made him go to the resort in the first place, and struggles to come to terms with finding love, with disillusionment and ultimately with death:

Sin embargo, *debo escribir* sin embargo. Pude haber nacido, y continuar viviendo, para estropear su condición de hijo único; pude haberlo
obligado, por medio de mis fantasías, mi displicencia y mi tan escasa
responsabilidad, a convertirse en el hombre que llegó a ser. . . . Libre
de él, jamás hubiera llegado a ser mi amigo, jamás lo habría elegido o
aceptado para eso. *Las palabras son hermosas o intentan serlo cuando
tienden a explicar algo. Todas estas palabras son, por nacimiento, dis-
formes e inútiles*. Era mi hermano. (OC 1334–35, my italics)

[Nonetheless, *I must write*, however. I could have been born, and gone
on living, in order to spoil his status as an only child; I could have
obliged him, though my fantasies, my disdain, and my meagre responsibility, to become the man he ended up being. . . . Free from him, I
would never have chosen or accepted him, he would never have
become my friend. *Words are beautiful or they try to be so when they
aim to explain something. All these words are, by origin, deformed and
useless*. He was my brother.]

Words that attempt to explain something are "por nacimiento, dis-
formes e inútiles" ["by origin, deformed and useless"]. With their added
linguistic value they enrich the object they aspire to explain, but as
Onetti understood, even before Derrida's ideas about the supplement
attained prominence in the academic world, they also inevitably sup-
plant this object, leaving us only with words and more words. Rather
than the actual suicide of the narrator's elder brother Julián, a penalty
described as disproportionate to the crime he committed, namely that of
embezzlement, the greatest impulse behind the narrative is another written account, the newspaper report entitled "*Se suicida cajero prófugo*"
[*"Fugitive Cashier Commits Suicide"*] (1334). The narrator makes a ritual of his continual reading of this report, "la más justa, la más errónea
y respetuosa de todas las publicadas" ["the most fair, the most erroneous and respectful of all those published"] (1334), leading him to seek
an alternative explanation for Julián's fate. However, if the report, "the
most erroneous . . . ," does not do justice to the individual who abused
his position as the humble cashier of a cooperative, neither will his
brother's version. From this point onward, we discover that justice or,
to put it another way, the veracity of written discourse, is nonexistent;
in spite of originating from a desire to grasp the truth, discourse distances itself from this objective through its reliance upon the abstract
nature of words.

The tale spun by the narrator in the quest to explore his existential
culpability for transforming Julián into the corrupt cashier, is believed
by neither the fictitious listener, Arturo, nor by the readers of "La cara
de la desgracia." Arturo states: "Veintiocho días que ese infeliz se pegó
un tiro y vos, nada menos que vos, jugando al remordimiento" ["It's

twenty-eight days since that poor wretch shot himself and you, none other than you, are toying with remorse"] (1335), later adding, "Conozco toda la historia. . . . Explícame qué culpa tenés si el otro hizo un disparate" ["I know the whole story. . . . Explain to me how it is your fault that he did something stupid"] (1337). We cannot believe the narrator's suggestion that he is to blame for his brother's death on account of his own birth, which he claims deprived Julián of his privileged status as an only child. This is especially unbelievable as the narrator was five years younger and posed, therefore, no real threat to his brother's position as the elder. In any case, we do not believe in his culpability because his own story makes it incredible. The use of the subjunctive in the passage quoted above permits the possibility that his explanation could possess another meaning, or that something unsaid can be read into it. "Pude haber nacido, y continuar viviendo, para estropear su condición de hijo único" ["I could have been born, and gone on living, in order to spoil his status as an only child"] (1334) suggests that the narrator is blaming himself for the failure and death of his brother. But equally, this may not be justified, as Arturo perceives. Moreover, if an excess of words is required to explain the apparent truth of the real, this implies a voluntary or involuntary selection not only of words, but of memories too. The narrator writes: "Y estaban, pensaba yo, los recuerdos de infancia que irían naciendo y aumentando en claridad durante los días futuros, semanas o meses. Estaba también *la tramposa, tal vez deliberada, deformación de los recuerdos*" ["And there were, I thought, the memories of infancy which would go on being born and increasing in clarity in the days, weeks and months to come. There was also *the deceiving, perhaps intentional, distortion of memories*"] (1338, my italics). If this double-edged nature of writing, on the one hand enriching the object to be explained, but, on the other, substituting it, replacing it with words of new meanings, allows us access to the plurality of the present, it also prevents the discovery of a single interpretation.

Onetti's story relegates lived experience to a secondary position in order to give primacy to fiction, to the linguistic ecstasy that produces a multiplicity of meanings and readings. The narrator relates a series of events that he tries to explain and understand from an external position. In search of truth, the narrator falsifies and distorts his account, not only altering the chronological order of events, but also his knowledge of certain facts. Let us leave for a moment the Onetti of "La cara de la desgracia," who is the same Onetti we encounter throughout his entire literary production, in order to question the Armonía Somers of "El hombre del túnel" about the function of writing. Let us ask if there is an outbreak of "semantic libido" in her literature; in other words, does she relish the simple pleasure of storytelling?

Firstly, we should note that the act of writing is not mentioned in Somers' story and that the story is related by a first-person narrator who, like the narrator of "La cara de la desgracia," is given no name. "El hombre del túnel" appears to relate a voyage through the tunnel of the subconscious in search of the wholeness of feminine experience, a wholeness that is restricted and denied by the culture of the era and the place. It tells of the emotional relationship between the narrator and a mysterious man, "vestido de oscuro" ["darkly dressed"], with "una ramita verde en la mano" ["with a little green branch in his hand"], wearing an old-fashioned mustache, and who seemed to be immune to the aging process from the time the narrator was seven until her death (128). In the case of Onetti, the narrator found difficulty in describing events not because of their horror, but rather on account of the problems of discourse itself. Hence, when he tries to recreate the image of the young girl outlined against the restaurant window, he writes: "Sólo quedó de la muchacha algo del pelo retinto, metálico en la cresta que recibía la luz. Yo recordaba la magia de los labios y la mirada; *magia es una palabra que no puedo explicar, pero que escribo ahora sin remedio, sin posibilidad de sustituirla*" ["Of the girl there remained only a hint of her dark hair, metallic where the light fell on it. I remembered the magic of her lips and her gaze; *magic is a word I cannot explain, yet I have no choice but to write it now as there is no possibility of replacing it*"] (1342–43, my italics). The narrator of "El hombre del túnel," for her part, delves into her inner experience, restricted by the process of cultural indoctrination that affects every social being, and she tries to rescue herself through language.

The little girl of seven is at an age when the individual gradually begins to venture beyond the security of the family circle, already equipped with a code of values as a talisman against the dangers lurking in the outside world. She enters a concrete pipe and finds the darkly-dressed man with "una sonrisa de miel que se desborda" ["a honeyed smile that bursts forth"] (128), who is, in fact, her own image of masculinity: "Es claro que ni por un momento caí en pensar que era yo quien había estado buceando hacia todo, sino que las cosas se vendrían de por sí a fuerza de tanto desearlas. . . . El hombre de las suelas gruesas y clavetadas en forma burda, estaba sentado, efectivamente. . . . Vestía de oscuro, llevaba un bigote caído de retrato antiguo y tenía una ramita verde en la mano" ["It is clear that I never thought for a moment that it was I who was diving down in search of everything, but that things would arrive by themselves on the strength of my wishing for them so much. . . . The man with the coarse, thick-soled, studded shoes, was sitting still, in effect. . . . He was dressed darkly, he wore a mustache out of an old portrait, and he had a little green branch in his hand"]

(128). Further on, the narrator indicates that her image of the man in the tunnel, her own creation of masculinity, is invisible to others.

At this point, it is tempting to embark upon a psychoanalytic study of Somers' story. The image of masculinity created by the girl and embodied in the man in the tunnel is nothing other than the image of the father: this strong man, with "suelas gruesas" ["thick soles"], "vestido de oscuro" ["darkly dressed"], and possessing a "sonrisa de miel" ["honeyed smile"], is what the child desires, but is forbidden by society, being portrayed to her as a "cosa" "terrorífica" "llamada violación" ["terrifying" "thing" "called rape"] (129). Her desire for the father, the basis of her image of masculinity, the image she will seek throughout her life, is taboo. The strong, good-natured man becomes, thanks to "ellos" ["them"] (impersonal society), dehumanized and dehumanizing; he becomes the "hombre raro," "vago," "violador" ["strange man," "layabout," "rapist"]. Avoiding a digression into psychoanalysis, let us just say that literature is for Somers a means of recovering her individuality, of recuperating her dreams and desires, by describing that which culture and society prohibit ("Violación, hombre dulce. . . . Así fue cómo la imagen inédita de mi hombre permaneció inconexa, tierna y desentendida de todo el enredo humano que había provocado. . . . Hasta que un día decidí no hablar más" ["Rape, sweet man . . . that was how the provisional image of my man remained disconnected, fresh and free from all the human tangle that it had provoked. . . . Until one day I decided to say no more"] [129]). As Cristina Peri Rossi observed when reflecting upon the nature and purpose of literature, describing things is a way of controlling them.[10] Here I would venture to say that the act of describing/writing functions as a way of getting to know oneself, especially in the case of women authors. If words call out to other words in a kind of semantic orgy—something that Dostoevski understood and Lacan complemented with the idea of the receptor, the fact that what one says is determined by the other[11]—engagement in literature, for women in general, and for Somers in particular, is not only an enriching exercise, but also an attempt to describe the indescribable.

The desire of the narrator of "El hombre del túnel" for the masculine other is condemned by society, which transforms this other into a repulsive rapist. Culture denies the narrator the words to describe her desire. Hence, she is forced to immerse herself in her own subjectivity. To achieve this, she must slip into "el túnel" ["the tunnel," down "la escalera" ["the stairway"] and across "el cruce de la calle" ["the road junction"], three lanes that enable her to reach the realm of the desire awakened during infancy. But in order to describe this desire, she must seek recourse in an almost fantastic type of fiction, in which the boundaries of reality are blurred, in which linear time disappears and where the sensuality of the feminine reigns supreme: "—Gracias por la invención de las siete caídas—alcancé a decirle [al 'hombre de la sonrisa de miel'] viendo rodar mi lengua como una flor monopétala sobre el pavimento [resultado del impacto de las ruedas de un vehículo]" ["'Thanks for the invention of the seven sins,' I managed to say to him ('the man with the honeyed smile'), seeing my tongue roll like a monopetalous flower on the pavement (the result of the impact of the wheels of a vehicle)"] (134).

Onetti, himself a cog in the cultural machine, a fact that in no way negates the strong current of social criticism running throughout all his work, became a story-writer through the use of masculine rhetoric, recreated in linguistic labyrinths that never cease illuminating the individual's complex relation with a hostile, alienating world. Somers, on the other hand, marginalized like the character of Rebeca Linke in her first story, perhaps because the weight of masculinity continues to dominate culture even in the twentieth century, explores herself through an essentially feminine discourse, examining the inner self whose escape is prevented by the social self. If the added semantic value of words takes Onetti into an essentially literary world, to the very heart of culture, this same added value permits Somers to divest herself of the archetypal image of the feminine and to slip from word to word, from meaning to meaning, toward a more complete and open image of the female self. Thus, we can say that the masculine rhetoric of Onetti inserts him into the cultural system, whereas the feminine rhetoric of Somers places her on its margins.

Let us now inquire about love, a recurrent theme in the fiction of both Onetti and Somers. For Onetti, love represents the fullness of the moment, but it always ends in misunderstanding and disillusionment, a fact that does not detract from its glory. Love is a feeling that, like dreams and high-brow literature, falsifies reality in an attempt to obtain communication, to recuperate lost innocence.

Recalling his apparent communion with the girl on the bicycle, the narrator of "La cara de la desgracia" states:

Era indudable que la muchacha me había liberado de Julián y de muchas otras ruinas y escorias que la muerte de Julián representaba y había traído a la superficie; era indudable que yo, desde una media hora atrás, la necesitaba y continuaría necesitándola. (1348)

[It was beyond doubt that the girl had freed me from Julián, and from the many other wrecks and messes which the death of Julián represented and had brought to the surface; it was beyond doubt that I, since half an hour earlier, needed her and would continue to need her.]

The death of Julián, that man who had never grown or lived, the man who "desde los treinta años le salía del chaleco olor a viejo" ["since he was thirty the smell of old age had emanated from his jacket"] (1334), represents the death of innocence and leads the narrator to connect the girl with his late brother: "Entonces, sin escuchar, me sorprendí vinculando a mi hermano muerto con la muchacha de la bicicleta" ["Then, without listening, I surprised myself by linking my dead brother with the girl on the bicycle"] (1340). Considering himself in some way to blame for being unable to prevent Julián's suicide, he feels the need to protect the young girl from death: "ambos [el hermano y la muchacha], por tan diversos caminos, coincidían en una deseada aproximación a la muerte, a la definitiva experiencia" ["both (the brother and the girl), by such diverse paths, shared in a desired approximation to death, to the definitive experience"] (1341). Death can be overthrown by love. Love, after all, embodies the mystery of the human condition and is an expression of individual liberty, a process of "caída y vuelo" ["falling and soaring"], to borrow the words of Octavio Paz. In *La llama doble del amor* ["The Double Flame of Love"], Paz writes: "Doble fascinación ante la vida y la muerte, el amor es caída y vuelo, elección y sumisión" ["A double fascination before life and death, love is falling and soaring, choice and submission"] (97).

The sense of fullness experienced by the narrator in the face of love, which enables him to tell the story of his brother to the object of his love in "una seria voz masculina" ["a serious, masculine voice"] (1347)—I think the adjective "masculina" is very important here—and which allows him to speak of his blame and to feel in some way absolved, is, however, condemned to failure. It is doomed not because love is a human phenomenon, and thus subject to the ravages of time—"el amor no vence a la muerte: es una apuesta contra el tiempo y sus accidentes" ["love does not vanquish death; it is a wager against time and its accidents"], says Paz (220)—but because the narrator invents the object of his love and, in doing so, negates her as a person. But is love not always like this? Has Stendhal not already told us that love is a process of crystallization that progressively idealizes and transforms the object of love? All those of us who love or have loved understand this process of magnifying the object of our amour. But love demands freedom, voluntary submission, understanding, and, above all, the unconditional acceptance of the other person. Paz observes: "Se ama a una persona, no a una abstracción" ["One loves a person, not an abstraction"] (107).

The narrator does not realize, or does not wish to acknowledge, that the girl is deaf, despite many indications of her lack of hearing: "La vi fumar con el café, los ojos clavados ahora en la boca lenta del hombre viejo" ["I saw her smoke with her coffee, with her eyes fixed on the slow-moving mouth of the old man"] (1342); "En la playa desierta la voz le chillaba como un pájaro. Era una voz desapacible y ajena" ["On the deserted beach, her voice screeched like a bird. It was an unpleasant and alien voice"] (1345); "sonó trabajosa la voz extraña"; "la voz dura"; "—Qué—roncó. —Hablaste. Otra vez" ["the strange voice sounded wearily"; "her hard voice"; "'What?' she snorted. 'You spoke. Say it again'"] (1346). Neither does he wish to acknowledge the girl's lost innocence, ignoring Arturo's ironic use of the words "nena" ["kid"] and "señorita" ["young lady"]: "—¿Café?—preguntó [el mozo]. —Bueno—sonrió Arturo—; eso que llaman café. También le dicen señorita a la muchacha de amarillo junto a la ventana" ["'Coffee?' asked the waiter. 'O.K. then,' said Arturo with a smile, 'they may call it coffee. They also call the young girl in yellow over by the window "Miss"'"] (1342). He also ignores the comments of the waiter who speaks with a wry smile of the girl's nocturnal bicycle rides, from which she returns with tousled hair and no make-up, and of her reputation among "los muchachos ingleses que están en el *Atlantic*" ["the young Englishmen from the *Atlantic*"] (1343). Through not accepting this reality, the narrator, in a move that resembles the rhetorical function of the simile, makes the connection between the independent life of the girl and that of his brother, who had been stealing from the cooperative for five years despite appearing to have resigned himself to a mediocre existence. Just as some small and insignificant man speaks about the life of the girl, a wretched woman from a squalid café, Julián's lover, prematurely aged by bad living, reveals the story of the fraudulent life of the narrator's brother, hoping, like the waiter in the café, for a financial reward.

For some critics, the girl's innocence is real, and her promiscuous reputation is false.[12] But we cannot ignore the device of the simile, which, as we have just seen, connects and embellishes a series of events through indicating their similarity to others. The narrator, however, after making love to the deaf girl in the wood alongside the beach, states: "tuve de pronto dos cosas que no había merecido nunca: su cara doblegada por el llanto y la felicidad bajo la luna, *la certeza desconcertante de que no habían entrado antes en ella*" ["I suddenly had two things which I had never deserved: her face, overcome with weeping and happiness in the moonlight, and *the unsettling certainty that they had not entered her previously*"] (1347, my italics). We should return now to the use of the adjective "masculina" to describe the narrator's voice as he speaks to the girl. Onetti's presentation of love in this story is essentially masculine. The mature man who falls in love with the innocence of a young girl is the perfect formula for the man to transfer his desires onto her, to realize through the girl, who in Lacanian terms has "denigrated" his soul, his longing to discover the truth.[13] Moreover, he observes the virginity of the girl because, as Georges Bataille indicates, the female partner in eroticism was seen as the victim, the male as the sacrificer, both during the consummation losing themselves in the continuity established by the first destructive act. . . . [The act of violence] is intentional like the act of the man who lays bare, desires and wants to penetrate his victim. . . . The woman in the hands of her assailant is despoiled of her being.[14]

The narrator requires the virginity of the girl in order to save himself and, by destroying her previous being through the act of love, he is able to reinvent her with her face bathed in tears of joy for the love that he has to offer.

There is nothing more startling, yet it goes strangely unnoticed by many astute readers of Onetti, than the expression used by the narrator to describe his desire to undress and possess the girl: "empezamos a enfurecer y besarnos. *Nos ayudamos a desnudarla* en lo imprescindible" ["We became excited and started to kiss. *We helped each other to undress her* only as far as it was essential"] (1347, my italics). The eagerness with which the lovers kiss seems to indicate a sudden outburst of sexuality on the part of the girl, whose deafness had prevented her from hearing the narrator's words. In the case of the narrator, this episode marks the materialization of his desire to dispossess the girl of her being and to transform her into the object of his fantasies. Moreover, it is the narrator who removes the girl's clothes, like Bataille's *sacrificateur*, but the employment of the first person plural ("nos ayudamos" ["we helped each other"]) suggests an encounter of equals. The latter is undermined, however, by the use of the third person feminine singular, "la" ["to her"], as an indirect object. "La" suggests that the girl has become the mere object of the narrator's desire. Through the girl's negation as subject in the act of love, the narrator briefly finds his soul, the same soul with which he wanted to rescue both his brother and the girl from a chaotic world.

The dialogue between the narrator and the girl becomes a monologue, given that the girl cannot hear. The act of love is simply a projection of his desires onto a being that can respond sexually, for this is her only mode of communication with the outside world. We are told that the girl knew how to kiss and that she kissed feverishly. The brutal death of the girl, which is described in a horrifyingly realistic fashion, similar to that of Julián, reveals the impact of a dehumanizing reality that destroys the illusions of the individual. The death of the girl confirms her promiscuous past, but, like the suicide of Julián, it is a grotesque and disproportionate punishment. For this reason, and once again using the language of the simile, "ya nada tenía importancia" ["nothing matters now"] (1348), neither the girl's lie about her punctured tires, which the narrator discovers to be fully inflated, nor the fact that the narrator is accused of killing the girl, a crime he did not commit. "No se preocupen: firmaré lo que quieran, sin leerlo" ["Don't worry: I shall sign whatever you want, without reading it"], the narrator says to the police, "Lo divertido es que están equivocados. Pero no tiene importancia. Nada, ni siquiera esto, tiene de veras importancia" ["The funny thing is that you are mistaken. But it does not matter. Nothing, not even this, really matters"] (1358).

The death of the woman, the impossibility of love, and hence of communication, suggests the absence of God. Faced with the impotence of the individual, Onetti replies with a story in which words create an apparently arbitrary and ambiguous order. Through their "semantic libido," they give meaning to the meaningless aspects of life. Although it may be an illusion, the narrator's dream to momentarily recover purity from the misery of the world is realized through the act of writing.

Can we speak of love in the work of Somers, which, in the words of Ángel Rama, recreates "un universo material sordo y disonante, una experiencia tensa de la crueldad y la soledad" ["a material universe, deaf and dissonant, an intense experience of cruelty and solitude"]?[15] Let us recall that "no hay amor sin erotismo como no hay erotismo sin sexualidad. Pero la cadena se rompe en sentido inverso: amor sin erotismo no es amor y erotismo sin sexo es impensable e imposible" ["there is no love without eroticism, just as there is no eroticism without sexuality. But the chain breaks when turned around; love without eroticism is not love, and eroticism without sex is unthinkable and impossible"] (Paz, 106). The search for desire, for sensuality, for eroticism is present in Somers' characters, especially when they are women. If social circumstances restrain the libido of every individual, that restraint is greater for those who possess the capacity for the reproduction of the species. Woman is dominated by the image of the Virgin Mary, through which she is desexualized and denied erotic pleasure. In other words, she is obliged to reproduce, but like a virgin-mother she is deemed to be passive in the miracle of the creation of life. It is not in vain that Somers asks for the wax effigy of woman's body to be melted down to liberate the inner self.

The narrator of "El hombre del túnel" creates something that very few women have achieved, an ideal of masculinity, an object of erotic desire that she wishes to transform into a living subject. The problems confronting this image of the ideal man come from outside, from culture. To safeguard the image, the narrator opts for silence, as the Somers epigraph of the present paper shows. But silence fails to save the image; rather, it endangers it by burying it in the depths of the subconscious. In order that the narrator's desire for the other can continue, in order that she can go on living, she has to express herself. She must learn how to tell "la verdadera historia" ["the true story"] (129). She must discover a way of describing things in order to control them.

The narrator immerses herself in her inner being; she slips through a tunnel and slides down a banister in search of her sexuality, her eroticism and her femininity. Otherwise she would become the stereotypical woman, the housewife prematurely aged by a routine existence. In other words, she would become a projection of her "yo-social" ["social self"], as Teresa Porzecanski has noted.[16] From within her subjectivity, she can once again discover the image she created in infancy of the man with the "sonrisa de miel" ["honeyed smile"]. But to find the words to describe this image, it must pass into the dimension of the fantastic. Only through a story in which the boundaries of the permissible and the prohibited are blurred, in which time is converted into a eternal present, and in which reality and imagination are confused, can the narrator's desire crystallize in words.

But this desire is not satisfied. The union of the narrator with the man with the green branch on the other side of the street is crushed beneath the wheels of a motor vehicle. Porzecanski states that "la facticidad de lo real-societario" ["the falseness of social reality"] prohibits the satisfaction of the desires of "la sensualidad de lo femenino" ["feminine sensuality"] (103). I would say that this desire goes unfulfilled because, as Freud understood, what matters is not the satisfaction of the self, but rather the drive of desire, which gives meaning to the individual's existence. When the process of desire ends, the life of the individual loses meaning. The narrator ends up going down through a tunnel, the tunnel of death, yet she continues to speak as an indication that desire will return.

We have asked fundamental questions of Juan Carlos Onetti and Armonía Somers, who have answered us through their two stories, revealing their similarities and differences in the art of narrating. But the major point to emerge from this interview, which attempted to focus upon the function of writing for both authors, is the existence of an essentially masculine discourse in Onetti's "La cara de la desgracia," and a discourse that reveals the complexities of women's writing in Somers' "El hombre del túnel."[17]

Translated by Iain A. D. Stewart

NOTES

1. Armonía Somers, "Diez relatos a la luz de sus probables vivenciales" ["Ten Stories in the Light of Their Existential Possibilities"], 114.

2. In his prologue to the anthology of Somers, *La rebelión de la flor* ["The Flower's Rebellion"] Rómulo Cosse states: "Estaba ya cerca la mitad de este siglo

XX, tan rico en cambios y transformaciones, cuando el modelo narrativo imperante en Uruguay [que no era sino la réplica del relato realista europeo occidental y decimonónico], se fisura y estalla. . . . Es precisamente, la escritura artística de Onetti y Armonía Somers, el factor que produce el estallido de aquel modelo" ["It was close to the middle of the twentieth century, a century of changes and transformation, that the prevailing narrative model in Uruguay (which was none other than an imitation of nineteenth-century, Western European realism), fractured and broke down. . . . The artistic mode of writing of Onetti and Armonía Somers was the very factor that produced the collapse of that model"] (3).

3. "Durante veinte años de magisterio no dejé traslucir al lobo estepario" ["During twenty years of teaching, I did not let the steppe wolf shine through"], quoted in Roberto de Espada, "Armonía Somers," *Maldoror* 7 (Montevideo: 1972) (quoted in Risso, 270).

4. Hugo Verani, *Onetti: el ritual de la impostura*, 185.

5. "Pero yo tenía entera, para salvarme, esta noche de sábado; estaría salvado si empezaba a escribir el argumento para Stein, si terminaba dos páginas, o una, siquiera, si lograba que la mujer entrara en el consultorio de Díaz Grey y se escondiera detrás del biombo; si escribía una sola frase, tal vez" ["But I had the whole of Saturday night to save myself; I would be saved if I began to write the screenplay for Stein, if I completed two pages, or even one, if I managed to make the woman enter Díaz Grey's surgery and hide behind the screen; if I wrote a single phrase, perhaps"] (456).

6. In "La insólita literatura de Somers," Ángel Rama notes: "Nada más magisterial, dulce y hasta convencional que la persona que encubre el seudónimo Armonía Somers, casi el prototipo de la maestra de primeras letras de voz aterciopelada, de empaque maternal, de suave tono vital" ["There is nothing more magisterial, sweet, and even conventional than the person behind the pseudonym Armonía Somers, almost the prototype of the primary school mistress with a velvety voice, a motherly presence, and a soft, lively tone"]. Ángel Rama, "La insólita literatura de Somers: la fascinación del horror," *Marcha* 1118 (Montevideo: 1963) (quoted in Risso, "Un retrato para Armonía (cronología y bibliografía)," 262–63).

7. See, for instance, the reviews of *El derrumbamiento* ["The Collapse"] by Mario Benedetti (*Número* 22 [Montevideo: January–March 1953]) and Emir Rodríguez Monegal (*Marcha* 679 [Montevideo: 17 July 1953]). Both critics express their distaste for a style of writing whose rawness they initially judge to be merely a literary pose. Both Benedetti and Rodríguez Monegal would later recognize the authenticity of Somers' voice.

8. J. C. Onetti, "Divagaciones de un secretario" ["Rambling Thoughts of a Secretary"] (1963), in *Réquiem por Faulkner y otros artículos*, 173.

9. "The supplement adds itself, it is a surplus, a plenitude enriching another plenitude, the *fullest measure* of presence. . . . But the supplement supplements. It adds only to replace. . . . Compensatory [*suppléant*] and vicarious, the supplement is an adjunct, a subaltern instance that takes-(*the*)-place [*tient-lieu*]." Jacques Derrida, *Of Grammatology*, 144–45.

10. Cristina Peri Rossi, "Aspectos socioculturales, simbólico-artísticos y místico-religiosos del juego de azar."

11. Dostoievski lamented in a letter written on 27 May 1869 to Maïkov: "The main thing is sadness, but if one talks about it or explains it more, so much more would have to be said." Quoted in Julia Kristeva, *Black Sun*, 186.

12. Verani writes: "También la muchacha presenta una imagen falsa. Se tiene un mal concepto de ella, aparece como poseedora de un ayer tormentoso y promiscuo ante los ojos de los empleados del hotel donde se hospeda el "hombre." Sin embargo, la verdadera imagen de la joven se conoce después del acto de amor en la playa." ["The girl also presents a false image. One receives a bad impression of her; in the eyes of the employees of the hotel in which the 'man' is staying, she appears to have had a turbulent and promiscuous past. However, the true image of the girl becomes known after the love scene on the beach"]. For Verani, the narrator's assertion of the girl's virginity is accurate. See Verani, *Onetti*, 180–81.

13. Jacqueline Rose explains in her prologue to Jacques Lacan, *Feminine Sexuality*: "Lacan sees courtly love as the elevation of the woman into the place where her absence or inaccessibility stands in for male lack, just as he sees her denigration as the precondition for man's belief in his own soul" (48–49). And later, "As negative to the man, woman becomes a total object of fantasy (or an object of total fantasy), elevated into the place of the Other and made to stand for its truth" (50).

14. Georges Bataille, *Eroticism*, 18 and 90.

15. Ángel Rama, "La generación crítica (1939–1969)," in *La crítica de la cultura en América Latina*, 236.

16. Teresa Porzecanski, "Sensualidad y socialidad en 'El hombre del túnel'," in Cosse, ed., *Armonía Somers, papeles críticos*, 101.

17. The author is grateful to the Helen Kellog Institute for International Studies at the University of Notre Dame for a travel grant to attend the *Onetti and Others* conference in St. Andrews, July 1995.

WORKS CITED

Bataille, Georges. *Eroticism*. Trans. Mary Dalwood. San Francisco: City Lights Books, 1986.

Cosse, Rómulo, ed. *Armonía Somers, papeles críticos*. Montevideo: Linardi y Risso, 1990.

Derrida, Jacques. *Of Grammatology*. Trans. Gayatri Chakravorty Spivak. Baltimore and London: The John Hopkins UP, 1976.

Kristeva, Julia. *Black Sun*. Trans. Leon S. Roudiez. New York: Columbia UP, 1989.

Lacan, Jacques. *Feminine Sexuality*. Trans. Jacqueline Rose. New York & London: Macmillan, 1982.

Onetti, Juan Carlos. *Réquiem por Faulkner y otros artículos*. Ed. Jorge Ruffinelli. Buenos Aires: Calicanto, 1976.

Paz, Octavio. *La llama doble del amor: Amor y erotismo*. Barcelona: Seix Barral, 1993.

Peri Rossi, Cristina. "Aspectos socioculturales, simbólico-artísticos y místico-religiosos del juego de azar." Paper presented to the *Congreso nacional de asociaciones y técnicos para el tratamiento y rehabilitación de la ludopatía*. Valladolid, 1994.

Rama, Ángel. *La crítica de la cultura en América Latina*. Caracas: Biblioteca Ayacucho, 1985.

Risso, Álvaro J. "Un retrato para Armonía (cronología y bibliografía)." Cosse, 247–99.

Somers, Armonía. "Diez relatos a la luz de sus probables vivenciales" ["Ten Stories in the Light of Their Existential Possibilities"]. Afterword to *Diez relatos y un epílogo* ["Ten Stories and an Epilogue"], by an anonymous editor. Montevideo: Fundación de Cultura Universitaria, 1979.

Somers, Armonía. "El hombre del túnel," in *La rebelión de la flor: Antología personal* ["The Flower's Rebellion: A Personal Anthology"] (Montevideo: Linardi y Risso, 1988), 127–34.

Verani, Hugo. *Onetti: el ritual de la impostura*. Caracas: Monte Ávila, 1981.

8

"The cadaver raised its head and tried to smile": The Prostitute in Onetti's Juntacadáveres and Luisa Valenzuela's Hay que sonreír

Linda Craig

The image of the prostitute was particularly powerful in the Argentine psyche in the late nineteenth and early twentieth centuries, a historical context that helps throw light on Onetti's work in general, and on *Juntacadáveres* [*Body Snatcher*] in particular; it is also relevant to Valenzuela's first novel, *Hay que sonreír* [*Clara*]. There are also many questions within these novels that lie beyond the parameters of a historical reading, and I shall be referring to Luce Irigaray's *Speculum of the Other Woman* in order to explore some of these issues. A feminist perspective such as Irigaray's is, to my mind, particularly relevant to Valenzuela's novel, and the link between the two works, which is made via the representation of prostitutes, will be read with the support of Irigaray's work.

Juntacadáveres, published in 1964 in Montevideo, is, like many of Onetti's works, set in the fictional town of Santa María, a location that began its life as an imaginary construct, dreamed up by Brausen, one of the protagonists of *La vida breve* [*A Brief Life*](1950). The town is the realization of a recurrent image within the history and mythology of the New World, the possibility of a new beginning in an unmarked empty space. And while this image is disputable as a construct, what is of particular interest, in this case, is the town's name; for the very possibility of a truly new beginning is undermined by the baggage of beliefs and prejudices implicit in the term Santa María. It emphasizes the Christian dimension of its settlers in a way that its literary counterparts, Faulkner's Yoknapatawpha and García Márquez's Macondo, do not. There is also an echo in it of the original title of Buenos Aires: Santa María de los Buenos Aires.

Since Christian mythology so clearly informs the belief systems and behavior of the inhabitants of Santa María, particularly in terms of the images of men and women, it is useful to explore its underlying theoretical sources. As Marina Warner shows in *Alone of All Her Sex*, the Christian concept of woman stems from Greek thought. Warner points out how fundamental Christian thinkers, such as St. Thomas Aquinas, were influenced by Greek philosophers, and most particularly, Aristotle.

> It was . . . Aristotle's view that from the thirteenth century onwards shaped and conditioned Western thinking on human generation and became the authorized teaching of the Church, principally because the Church's greatest theologian, St. Thomas Aquinas, gave it his authority. In *On the Generation of Animals*, Aristotle declared that woman provided the matter for the embryo, while the man gave the matter form and motion. . . . This view of human reproduction gives women an all-important role; but slanted through the glass of the Greek contempt for matter, that role was considered animal and therefore inferior, while the male performed the spiritual function of imparting life. Aristotle himself went so far as to say that women were "a deformity, though one which occurs in the ordinary course of nature." (Warner, 40–41)

When looking at the hierarchy of the protagonists in *Juntacadáveres*, it will become clear that these ideas, which juxtapose men with spirituality and women with matter, are implicit within the text.

Juntacadáveres, in common with all of Onetti's work, has a certain timelessness; no dates are ever given, and its basic themes, a frustrated search for perfection or transcendence and an exploration into the nature of writing, have at least an apparent claim to exist outside the realms of time and space. However, it is clear that these ideas do have a more material basis, and it is this that will provide my main approach to the novel.

In an extremely interesting study, *Sex and Danger in Buenos Aires*, Donna Guy carries out an investigation into the issues surrounding prostitution in Buenos Aires (with some mention of Montevideo too) in the late nineteenth and early twentieth centuries. She describes a demographic situation that reveals that for most of that period there were many more men than women in Argentina. This was a consequence of the intensity and type of European immigration during the period. Prostitution was legalized in 1875, and as Guy puts it: "At the end of the nineteenth century Buenos Aires had a terrible international reputation as the port of missing women, where kidnapped European virgins unwillingly sold their bodies and danced the tango" (5). The city became famous for its white slave trade, and the very name of Buenos Aires struck fear in the hearts of many Europeans. Guy goes on to point out that the number of cases of young girls actually being kidnapped and forced to work in Argentine brothels was greatly exaggerated, but that many women were forced into this situation through economic hardship. But whatever the circumstances, there can be no doubt that prostitution had an importance within Argentine culture at that time that was far beyond the norm for "the oldest profession" in Western society. Francine Masiello, in her study of women and nation in Argentina, also notes that "a commodity consciousness informed the treatises on women."[1]

Controversy around the topic took on religious overtones with groups of British Protestants and European Jews vilifying Argentina for its paradoxical combination of a Catholic heritage and legalized prostitution. In fact, official nineteenth-century Vatican policy also condemned licensed brothels, but Argentine Catholics and anticlerics referred to both St. Thomas Aquinas and St. Augustine in support of their position. Here I quote Guy again:

> Saint Augustine and Saint Thomas Aquinas had recognized that female prostitution, though repugnant, was necessary. Augustine, for example, believed that eliminating brothels would lead to pollution of everything with lust, "a lust at least equal to . . . fornication. . . . In his mind it was better to tolerate prostitution . . . than to risk the perils that would follow the successful elimination of the harlot from society."[2] Thomas Aquinas perpetuated the Augustinian view and compared prostitution to a sewer whose removal would pollute the palace. (13)

The justification for legalization was not made in the interests of the prostitutes themselves, but rather in the interests of the family, that great bastion of national identity, and of society at large.

There are many factors that link *Juntacadáveres* with these historical realities. As I have pointed out above, the particular prevalence of prostitution within the River Plate region at that time might go some way toward explaining Larsen's choice of profession, pimping, and his dream of setting up the perfect brothel. Moreover, before leaving for Santa María, he is described as working at his chosen profession in Rosario, a town cited by Guy as being one of the centers for organized prostitution (Guy, 10). The issue of the legality of the brothel is one that claims considerable importance in the novel. In a further section that deals with Larsen's more distant past in the capital, he mourns the death of a friend, "el pibe Julio" ["the kid Julio"], who was shot for trying to create an organization of Argentine pimps in response to the competition from foreigners, Larsen mentions the very groups of white slave traders, French and Jewish, that Guy refers to:

> Por aquel tiempo . . . todos andábamos separados, cada cual buscando hundir al compañero por roñerías sin importancia. Los marselleses, no; porque es como siempre, a ellos sólo les importaba el negocio y sabían entenderse para defenderlo. Marselleses y judíos y después los polacos que se arrimaron al sol que más calentaba. (OC 873)

> [At that time . . . it was every man for himself, each one trying to screw his buddies for peanuts. Not the Marseilles crowd; because it's always that way, they only worried about business and knew how to work together to protect it. The Marseilles guys and the Jews and later the Polacks, who decided it was better to be friends with whoever was on top. (144–45)][3]

My major reason for emphasizing in this way the historical context for what is, above all, a piece of fiction is to resist an ahistorical and acultural reading of gender roles as presented within the text; and the same reasoning holds true for the exploration of the Christian belief systems referred to above. I shall now look at some of the characters in the novel to see how they correspond to this context.

Returning to Aristotle's view that "man gave matter form and motion," it is clear that the character in *Juntacadáveres* who most closely corresponds to this idea is Larsen, for the central anecdote of the novel is that of Larsen actively realizing his most cherished dream. The importance of this dream is apparent in the following description:

> Estaba viejo, incrédulo, sentimental; fundar el prostíbulo era ahora, esencialmente, como casarse *in articulo mortis*, como creer en fantasmas, como actuar para Dios. (831)

> [He was old, incredulous, sentimental; founding the brothel now was, essentially, like getting married *in articulo mortis*, like believing in ghosts, acting like God. (85)]

That this demiurge's greatest ambition should be the setting up of a brothel is a strange idea, and yet Larsen is not depicted as immoral, rather he is amoral, and his dream has a certain distance, a certain aesthetic quality. Moreover, he is endowed with a level of awareness that allows him the possibility of choice. For Larsen, who could have spent his life working in an office with "la angustia de saberse distinto a los demás" (868) ["the anguish of knowing himself to be different from the others" (137)], rejects that lifestyle for this riskier and for him apparently more meaningful project.

Of the other male characters, perhaps the most striking are Jorge Malabia and Marcos Bergner. Jorge, a mere sixteen years old, is already aware of the possibility of choosing his own life. His father, editor of the local newspaper, is hoping that his son will follow in his footsteps but Jorge is contemptuous of the hypocrisy implicit in the bourgeois lives around him, and by visiting the brothel toward the end of the novel shows his rejection of the life mapped out for him. Marcos, for his part, has already distanced himself from a conventional lifestyle by following his utopian dream of living in a phalanstery that has been organized around the principles of self-sufficiency and free love. This dream has failed and now Marcos is in a state of confusion, torn between a return to a conventional life and further rebellion.

Each of these male characters is constructed around images of ambivalence and uncertainty and each is invested with some level of existential awareness and therefore the capacity to make at least some active choices within their lives. While the concept of spirituality, thinking of the Aristotelian image, is not particularly evident in them, this active existential dimension would seem to make up for it in protagonists who do not appear to hold religious beliefs. When we look at the female figures, however, the picture is quite different.

In the case of Julita, Jorge Malabia's sister-in-law, there would at first appear to be an element of choice in her life, for Jorge says of Julita's madness, "Ella eligió estar loca para seguir viviendo" (797) ["She chose madness in order to go on living" (35)]. But far from being a real choice, an active decision, this is more like a passive reaction. There is no sense of any conscious effort on her part. Jorge's mother is in a similar position; he says of her, "Sabe, desde hace mucho tiempo, que es esposa y madre; yo siempre la he conocido con la cara correspondiente, la mirada dulce e impersonal, la boca bondadosa y amargada" (924) ["For a long, long time she has known that she's a wife and mother; I've always known her with either one face or the other: the sweet, impersonal eyes, the kindly and embittered mouth" (220)], a description that is also indicative of mental inaction. Both of these women have an awareness of the fact that they are playing roles but they are trapped, incapable of escape. Similarly, the schoolgirls who write anonymous letters function within comparable parameters; these girls are not driven by manipulativeness or malice, they are quite simply protecting themselves, for as the narrator says, "eran sinceras y actuaron con limpieza" (877) ["they were sincere and acted cleanly" (150)]. Again the image is one of reaction rather than action.

This general impression assumes an extreme version in the depiction of the prostitutes. Their role in the novel is extensive, and the greatest divide among them is between, on the one hand, the "madams," Tora, who owns her own brothel and is admired by Larsen for her commercial ingenuity, and María Bonita, chosen by Larsen to run the brothel in Santa María for her two salient characteristics (she is "prudente e inmoral" [872] ["prudent and immoral" (143)]), and, on the other hand, the rest of the prostitutes. The latter are almost indistinguishable, and many of the references to them are fairly damning; the section where Larsen visits Tora's brothel is perhaps the most revealing in terms of images of gender in the novel.

Larsen visits this brothel with a view to buying it, and during his survey he makes a note of its imperfections. The first of these concerns an inefficient light; the second, the installation of a bar; and the third, with no change of tone, refers to the three women working there, whose appearance he summarizes as "Demasiado polvo, demasiada pintura, las tres tienen el mismo peinado" (826) ["Too much powder, too much makeup, all three of them have the same hairdo" (78)]. This is an image of complete reification. Further on in the same chapter, Larsen wakes up at midday with one of the prostitutes by his side; referred to as "el cadáver de turno" and "el esqueleto"(829) ["the body on duty," "the skeleton" (82–83)], this woman is ultimately described in the words chosen for the title of this paper, "el cadáver alzó la cabeza y trató de sonreír" (830) ["the cadaver raised its head and tried to smile" (84)].

What more grotesque image, and what greater symbol of pure matter than a corpse? A corpse is human form devoid of spiritual or existential dimension; it is inert matter. This image of woman as matter has been used both by Aristotle and by Christian thinkers and therefore, while in Onetti's hands it is particularly crude and totally shorn of any romantic overtones—indeed, this cruel honesty is one of Onetti's strengths—it is nevertheless a symbol that has its logic within Christian thought. At the lowest possible point of this philosophical hierarchy, these women are depicted as being barely human. The very title of this novel already points to this conclusion: the corpse-gatherer is actually a collector of prostitutes, of women.

My goal so far has been to emphasize the historical and cultural background to *Juntacadáveres*. "But what if the object started to speak?" asks Luce Irigaray in *Speculum of the Other Woman* (135).[4] As a contrast to Onetti's vision of woman, I shall now turn to the text by Luisa Valenzuela. *Hay que sonreír* is Valenzuela's first novel and it lacks the stylistic inventiveness and weight of her subsequent work; nevertheless it is interesting in several ways. Published in 1966 but actually written a few years earlier, at approximately the same time as *Juntacadáveres*, the novel predates much of current feminist thought, and yet it presents a remarkably perceptive and disaffected view of gender roles.

Probably the most notable aspect of *Hay que sonreír* is the fact that its protagonist is not only a woman, but she is also a prostitute. Moreover, she is a prostitute viewed much more sympathetically than her counterparts in Onetti. She does not, however, fall into the classic stereotype within Western fiction and film, "the prostitute with the heart of gold." Rather, she is depicted as the innocent abroad.

Tracing her arrival in the capital from the interior in search of a better life, the novel is divided into three sections under the headings "El cuerpo," "Transición," and "La cabeza" ["The Body," "Transition," and "The Head"]. These titles would appear to denote a progression, but as we shall see, that is not in fact the case. The woman's most apparent characteristic is her passivity. This is seen firstly in her name, Clara, which brings to mind the idea of a blank space; moreover, on arrival in Buenos Aires she is a virgin, untouched; thirdly, the headings in the novel refer at least partly to the differing inscriptions made on her by a series of men.

Apart from the use of flashback, time is conveyed chronologically in the novel. In the first section, "El cuerpo," Clara is working in the streets, having more or less fallen into the world of prostitution, then she is living with a man who gives up his job to live off her takings, and subsequently she moves in with another man who, while their relationship appears to be totally loveless, is at least keeping her; she now lives the life of a housewife. The second section, "La transición," is where Clara finds, to quote Sharon Magnarelli, "that her body can lure the man of her dreams."[5] Tired of her role as housewife, "No vale la pena trabajar para que a una la tomen por esclava" ["It's not worth working if you're only going to be taken for a slave"] (70), and of a world in which men talk while she listens in silence, she begins to search for a relationship in which she is no longer deemed to be no more than a body.

So it is that in the last section of the novel, "La cabeza," Clara finds herself a beautiful man, Alejandro, who is even more capable of silence than she is, and despite the fact that she finds him moody and forbidding, she agrees to marry him. He works as a magician in a fairground, and at last an opportunity arises for Clara to fulfill one of her greatest dreams, namely to work not with her body, but with her head. The ironic twist in this is that Clara's job is to play the part of an Aztec flower in a sideshow, and for this a contraption is constructed with mirrors into which Clara's body is squeezed in order to create the impression of a head with no body. She may have been permitted to use her head, but she can use it only under the condition that it becomes an object. Clara's ambition actually leads to her death, for in what seems like an almost logical progression that separates the recalcitrant head from the more compliant body, Alejandro slits her throat in the last lines of the novel.

What is of interest in the depiction of Clara is the way in which cracks and contradictions arise around her. Although there are moments of awareness in which she subverts traditional expectations, this apparent progression is undermined by the strange depiction of her head as mere matter.

In the first of these ideas, that of subverting traditional expectations, the reader becomes aware, through Clara's perspective, of the contradictory nature of the masculine discourse around her when an older man has sex with her and then says, "No comprendo cómo una chica tan fina como vos pueda andar haciendo esas cosas" ["I don't understand how a refined girl like you can go around doing such things"] (22). The other men that she meets all automatically assume that they are her intellectual and moral superior, and say things like, "Si te dejo hacer lo que se te antoja vos te comprás mil chucherías sin pensar en ahorrar. Y bueno, yo pienso por vos" ["If I leave you to do whatever you like, you'll buy a thousand knickknacks without thinking about saving. Right, so I'll do the thinking for you"] (47). Clara finally appears to accept this, "Víctor tenía argumentos tan aplastantes que más valía darle la razón hasta en el pensamiento" ["Victor's reasoning was so crushing that it was better just to agree with him even in your head"] (32). And yet a chink of light remains, "nadie le impediría continuar un diálogo interno silencioso pero vehemente" ["nobody could stop her from carrying on a dialogue in her head which was silent but vehement"] (31).

Julia Kristeva observes that "the symbolic order—the order of verbal communication, the paternal order of genealogy—is a temporal one. For the speaking animal, it is the clock of objective time."[6] And time is something that Clara finds as controlling and as confusing as men. She spends much of her time waiting for men, but she keeps an imaginary, alternative time in her fantasy so that she observes at one point, "a la una y catorce ya eran las nueve y media" ["At fourteen minutes past one it was already half past nine"] (52), and she attaches great importance to the purchase of a watch, of which she says:

> Pero el reloj era algo tan suyo como sus pies o su boca. Era su condecoración que había ganado en un gesto de valentía que nunca más podría repetir y uno de sus mayores placeres era mirar girar las rueditas mientras se decía que ella había logrado escaparse de una máquina tan endiablada como esa." (33).

> [But the watch was something that was so much her own that it was like her feet or her mouth. It was her medal which she had earned in a gesture of courage which she would never be able to repeat and one of her greatest pleasures was to watch the little wheels go round while she told herself that she had managed to escape from a machine as diabolic as that.]

In the undermining of the apparent progression within Clara's life, time is crucial. For as she becomes more apparently respectable, she realizes that she is losing her freedom. Whereas when she was working as a prostitute, and so long as she earned enough money, her time was her own to use as she wished, later on, as she lives the life of a housewife, she becomes aware that her time is no longer her own, since she is answerable to the man for how she spends her time. This is where she describes her life as one of slavery.

In Valenzuela's novel the possibility of progression within a masculine world is an illusion, traditional values are no more than a trap, and the very idea of a woman's using her head is to cross boundaries that prove to be fatal. The image of Clara as the Aztec flower toward the end prompts the words from Alejandro that give the novel its title, and also echo Onetti's line about a corpse trying to smile. Alejandro begins by reminding her, "Hay que sonreír, hay que sonreír" ["You have to smile, you have to smile" (184), but this soon degenerates to "Sonreí, sonreí, infeliz" ["Smile, smile, you wretch"] (187), and ultimately to, "Hay que sonreír, pedazo de imbécil" ["You have to smile, you little imbecile"] (190).

The similarity of the images used to depict female smiles in the two novels is striking. In both cases the reader is presented with women who have been totally dehumanized, rendered matter, attempting, unsuccessfully, to smile. The very concept of a smile, a spontaneous action, is one that requires an authenticity that is denied them.

Of course this is something of a simplification since men too sometimes force a smile; the image springs to mind of Gálvez in *El astillero*, a man who is constantly showing his teeth in a grotesque attempt at a smile, thus showing that authenticity is also a difficult concept for men. However, there can be no doubt that in both *Juntacadáveres* and in *Hay que sonreír*, the female protagonists are excluded from language and power and even from the myth of authenticity to a much greater extent than are their male counterparts.

So the power of Christian discourse pervades culture far beyond the bounds of any active religious belief, for both of these novels, although they are so very different, do come from the same time and space, from the same cultural interface, and ultimately, almost incongruously, they present almost identical readings of gender stereotypes. Aristotle's images are enduring.

The major difference between Onetti's and Valenzuela's images of women, and particularly of prostitutes, lies in the area of the women's perceptions of themselves. So while Onetti's women have an almost animal-like unawareness of their existence, as we have seen, Valenzuela's is a woman who becomes all too conscious of her entrapment. Although she is far from having any very active or powerful dimension, Valenzuela's Clara is extremely interesting as a protagonist who presents a perception of the world from within these boundaries.

In *Speculum of the Other Woman*, Irigaray argues that "all theories of the subject have always been appropriated to the 'masculine'" (165), and there can be no doubt that Clara is treated by the men in the novel not as subject but as object, indeed a commodity to be exchanged. And yet the very fact of Clara's position in this novel, as its principal protagonist, is a means of endowing her with importance. Even more importantly, the fact that Clara's point of view is given prominence over that of the male protagonists obfuscates the issues of subject and object. However in reply to Irigaray's question, "but what if the object started to speak?," the answer here would have to be that such a step could well prove to be fatal.

The purpose of this essay has been to historicize the issue of gender roles within areas of Christian thought with particular reference to the image of the prostitute within the boundaries of the River Plate region during the earlier part of the twentieth century; it has attempted to show just how culturally bound the gender roles played out in the two novels are. The different perspectives given by the two writers have, I hope, served to highlight how two novels that reach a similar conclusion in terms of their ultimate images of the prostitute, can arrive there by means of such different trajectories, and how the totally negative and denigrating imagery presented in Onetti's novel is no more than one possible rendering. Valenzuela proves that a much more sympathetic representation can be carried out.

Onetti in this sense is harking back to the master narratives of patriarchy and Christianity; by contrast Valenzuela, looking to the future, is taking her first steps toward disrupting these constructs, toward a more postmodern sensibility where the very idea of a seamless reading of reality gives way to levels of awareness that diverge and intersect.

NOTES

1. Francine Masiello, *Between Civilization and Barbarism*, 114.

2. Here Guy is quoting from Vern A. Bullough and James Brundage, eds., *Sexual Practices and the Medieval Church* (Buffalo, N.Y.: Prometheus Books, 1982), 36.

3. The translations from *Juntacadáveres* come from J. C. Onetti, *Body Snatcher*.

4. This question of subject versus object, which is an important strand of Irigaray's thought, is explored in chapters on *Speculum* by both Toril Moi in *Sexual/Textual Politics* and Rosi Braidotti in *Patterns of Dissonance*.

5. Sharon Magnarelli, *Reflections/Refractions*, 6.

6. This line is from Toril Moi, ed., *The Kristeva Reader*, 152.

WORKS CITED

Braidotti, Rosi. *Patterns of Disonance*. Cambridge: Polity Press, 1991.

Guy, Donna. *Sex and Danger in Buenos Aires*. Lincoln and London: University of Nebraska Press, 1991.

Irigaray, Luce. *Speculum of the Other Woman*. Ithaca, N.Y.: Cornell UP, 1985.

Magnarelli, Sharon. *Reflections/Refractions*. New York: Peter Lang, 1988.

Masiello, Francine. *Between Civilization and Barbarism: Women, Nation and Literary Culture in Modern Argentina*. Lincoln and London: U of Nebraska P, 1992.

Moi, Toril. *Sexual/Textual Politics*. London: Routledge 1985.

Moi, Toril, ed. *The Kristeva Reader*. Oxford: Basil Blackwell, 1986.

Onetti, Juan Carlos. *Body Snatcher*. Trans. Alfred MacAdam. London: Quartet, 1991.

Valenzuela, Luisa. *Hay que sonreír*. Buenos Aires: Américalee, 1966. (*Clara; Thirteen Stories and a Novel*. Trans. Hortense Carpentier and Jorge Castello. New York: Hartcourt Brace Jovanovich, 1976.)

Warner, Marina. *Alone of All Her Sex*. London: Picador, 1985.

9

Masculine Impostures
and Feminine Ripostes:
Onetti and Clarice Lispector

Hilary Owen

My concern in this essay is to produce a comparative analysis of the construction of sexuality in Juan Carlos Onetti's "Bienvenido Bob" [*Welcome Bob*] (1944) and Clarice Lispector's "A partida do trem" ["The Departure of the Train"] (1974). At first glance the potential for discovering connections between Lispector and Onetti looks unpromising. An initial reading of their stories seems to confirm that they are irreconcilably opposed. The key to a comparison lies, however, in the very diametricality of that opposition. Onetti consistently deals with men excluding women. Clarice repeatedly, though not so exclusively as Onetti, looks at women marginalizing men. Constructions of sexuality are arguably central to both writers. The exclusion of women systematically points up the centrality of masculinity in Onetti and this partializes and undercuts universalist or humanist readings of his works.

Nearly all of Onetti's narrators and protagonists are men. As Mark Millington puts it in "No Woman's Land," "in Onetti we read a narrative of male subjectivity. It is a narrative founded on male characters' heterogeneity, incompleteness and difficulties. In a crucial sense, women barely exist" (358). Despite the unavoidable recognition that women are the ostensible pretext for man's fall from innocence and the scapegoat for his cosmic frustration, Onetti's predominantly masculine focus has frequently been elided into a human, universal dimension. This elision demands that the reader collude with the suppression of the feminine in order to participate fully in the "human experience" as Onetti reveals it. One effect of this is to naturalize a relationship whereby the male acquires meaning at the expense of woman.[1] In this context, Mark Millington's critical project "to open the texts of Onetti on to the historical moment of his writing, to denaturalize this repeated treatment of women characters" constitutes a significant move in the study of Onetti. As Millington notes, "the investigation of male subjectivity is in itself interesting enough, but it produces this internal contradiction whereby the key problem is simply displaced onto the woman and so perpetuated within male thinking." Consequently "one of the corner-stones" of Onetti's "system" "is placed over the void and . . . will not hold securely in place" ("No Woman's Land," 377, 376–77). Women may be marginal to Onetti's textual concerns but his work focuses on constructions of sexuality. So does Lispector's.

Clarice Lispector's works centralize woman and the feminine. She has been taken as the epitome of French feminist theories of *écriture féminine*, particularly those of Hélène Cixous, who calls for the writing of the body, the practice of difference and an openness to bisexuality in the writing of both sexes. I do not contend that Onetti's fiction is an example of *écriture féminine* with a masculine signature in the manner of Cixous's recuperation of Joyce, Genet, and Proust. Rather I intend, through comparison with Clarice Lispector, to examine how Onetti's texts deploy exaggeration, repetition, and excess to reveal an undercurrent of tension and resistance in relation to the repression, elimination, and closure that Hélène Cixous highlights as emblematic of a "masculine" language constructed on principles of opposition and exclusion. In this sense, Onetti's prose might be taken to epitomize "the masculine" in the very specific sense in which *écriture féminine* renders it visible. Where Lispector textualizes the body, Onetti disembodies the text. Before analyzing the two stories in detail, I will summarize briefly Hélène Cixous's theories of *écriture féminine*, and her refutation of Lacanian psychoanalysis, in order to stress the importance of Onetti's writing, as well as Clarice Lispector's, for the study of sexual/textual politics in Latin American short fiction.

Nelly Furman's "The Politics of Language" points up the key relationship in Lacanian psychoanalysis between entry into language and the split within the subject. According to Furman, "the mirror stage is the initial step in the process of an individual's integration in the social system; it marks the child's entrance into the symbolic order which is the realm of what Lacan calls the Law-of-the-Father or Name-of-the-Father" (70). The acquisition of language is therefore linked to entry into the symbolic order and to the primary repression of the loss of the mother. This is the point at which the father intervenes, the Oedipal crisis occurs and the mother/child unity is broken. For Lacan, the Oedipal crisis has a specific relationship with language. As Jane Gallop writes, "whereas Freud's Oedipal Father might be taken as a real, biological father, Lacan's Name-of-the-Father operates explicitly in the register of language. The Name-of-the-Father: the patronym, patriarchal law, patrilineal identity, language as our inscription into patriarchy" (71).

From a French feminist perspective, signification through binary opposition necessarily negates the feminine. Thus Cixous coins "bisexuality" in a specific sense as "the location within oneself of both sexes, evident and insistent, in different ways according to the individual, the non-exclusion of difference or of a sex." For this reason, it is more probable that women will be open to this nonexclusion of difference as, "for historical reasons at the present time it is woman who benefits from and opens up within this bisexuality beside itself, which does not annihilate differences but cheers them on, pursues them, adds more: in a certain way *woman is bisexual*—man having been trained to aim for glorious phallic monosexuality" ("Sorties," 85). Where Lispector's writing has been comprehensively reworked in terms of its "bisexuality" by Cixous, Onetti's has not been so closely interrogated for signs of a "glorious phallic monosexuality." I will now discuss some of the ways in which Lispector's bisexual practice of difference works in terms of textual specifics before attempting to unbutton the linguistic overcoat that Onetti's Bob wears "cerrado hasta el cuello" ["buttoned up to the neck"] (OC 1222).

The challenge that *écriture féminine* mounts to phallogocentric language and/as knowledge has been variously identified with the following strategies: ellipsis, polyphony, resistance of closure and fragmenting of linear structure (particularly time), symbolic encoding, repetition and cumulative structures, disruption of syntax, ambiguity, multiple-punning, pairing of unconventional opposites, paradox, rhythm and the mixing of genres. I will single out four of these, ellipsis, repetition, paradox, and fragmentation of time, to show how they are developed in the stories by Lispector and Onetti. In both cases, these linguistic strategies are also underscored by explicit, textual reference to the physical body. Lispector's story overtly celebrates the feminine body in terms of power and wholeness, self-possession and life. Onetti's story denies, dissects, and delineates the body in terms of absence and silence, mortality, and loss.

ELLIPSIS

A useful working definition of ellipsis in relation to sexual politics, may be found in Sherry Dranch's revealing analysis of Colette. For Dranch "ellipses" are "the connection . . . between . . . the subliminal style of the flesh—and a forbidden obsession" so that "a subtext consisting of the clearly stated unsaid, or more precisely of an inter-said (interdit: forbidden), is indicated through ellipsis and metaphor" (177). An example of this occurs in "A partida do trem," with the use of the infantile word "dodói" ["a bit poorly"] to refer to "dores menstruais" ["period pains"]. Angela Pralini's boyfriend Eduardo asks her by way of a dismissive euphemism, which obscures and abnormalizes a physical fact, "você está dodói, não é?" ["you are feeling a bit poorly, aren't you?"] (40). It is, paradoxically, the euphemism that makes Angela blush with embarrassment. She recalls his effort to be attentive as "uma coisa horrorosa" ["something horrendous"] (40). With the reference to "dores menstruais" two lines earlier, a clear statement is made of what Eduardo is about to "unsay," so that his words, not Angela's, effectively become a subtextual unsaid or "inter-dit."

REPETITION

As will be noted with reference to "Bienvenido Bob," Onetti disperses repeated images and *leitmotiven* throughout his text in an ever narrowing spectrum. According to Millington, "repetition in Onetti builds and refines on a restricted nexus of concerns which fosters self-referentiality and closure. Repetition becomes a means of limiting or even eliminating new stimuli" (*Fictions of Desire*, 203). For Lispector, in comparison, the repetition process is more localized and intense as words and sounds are repeated serially within the same sentence, or in consecutive phrases. This heightens the rhythmic and assonantal effect and, more importantly, it also fractures the organizing principle of syntax. Consequently the repetitions effect a short circuit, breaking any promise of logical progression that might have been proffered by the syntactical arrangements within which they are framed. For example, "Enquanto isso Angela Pralini efervescendo como as bolinhas da agua mineral Caxambu, era uma de repente. Assim de repente. De repente o que? Só de repente. Zero. Nada" ["Angela Pralini meanwhile, effervescing like the bubbles in Caxambu mineral water, was one all of a sudden. Just like that, all of a sudden. All of a sudden what? Just all of a sudden. Zero. Nothing"] (42). "De repente" ["all of a sudden"] is repeated in such a way as to divorce it from the adverbial function in which it was introduced.

A recurrent pattern of repetition involving the accumulation of verbal structures in sequences of three, specifically traces Angela's revolt against Eduardo's repression of her emotions and corporeality. This begins where Angela recalls Eduardo's incapacity to feel, as she remarks, "Mas ele não segurava nada. Só fazia era: pensar, pensar e pensar" ["But he did not hold onto anything. All he did was: think, think, think"] (32). Angela subsequently responds in triplicate thinking, "Quero fruir de tudo e depois morrer e eu que me dane! me dane! me dane!" ["I want to enjoy everything to the full and then die and then I'll be damned, damned, damned!"] (34) and later, "E me obrigou a saber, a saber, a saber" ["And he forced me to know, to know, to know"] (35). This use of repetition marks out the limits of signification and opens the text onto multiple sensualities through emphasizing sound. As Cixous claims in "Castration or Decapitation," "there's tactility in the feminine text, there's touch, and this touch passes through the ear" (54). The conscious flow of Angela Pralini's reflections is thus periodically submerged in a subconscious enjoyment of rhythm in phrases such as "ela queria a vida, vida plana e plena, bem bacana, bem lendo às abertas as Seleções" ["what she wanted was life, life smooth, full and easy, reading the Seleções (Brazilian version of *Readers Digest*) openly"] (40). The triple repetitions are echoed in a pattern of onomatopoeia where sounds are also arranged in threes. A sense of pleasure in rhythm consoles Angela from fear of death as she creates the imaginary story of a man walking on the shells left by a vast windfall of luscious fruit. The shells make a pleasing "cloc, cloc, cloc" sound and Angela's fear is momentarily beguiled. Similarly, Angela spontaneously recalls her dog barking, "Au, au, au, latira meu cachorro. Meu grande cachorro" ["Wooff, wooff, wooff, barked my dog. My lovely big dog"] (42). This poetic primacy of sound over meaning fits into a broader scheme of sensual correspondences in Lispector's prose.

As Carol Armbruster reminds us, "Lispector plays with all the senses of the body and with their interrelations. She urges her reader to listen to designs and colors, and to photograph the smell of perfume, all in an effort to sensitize every bodily vibration possible" (154–55). This equation of bodily and musical vibration is exemplified when Angela metaphorizes Dona Maria Rita's tremulous aspect by comparing it to accordion music, asking, "Por que os velhos, mesmo os que não tremem, sugeriam algo delicadamente trêmulo? Dona Maria Rita tinha um tremor quebradiço de música de sanfona" ["Why was it that old people, even those who are not actually shakey, seemed faintly tremulous somehow. Dona Maria Rita possessed a kind of brittle tremor, like the sound of accordion music"] (30). The tremor is expanded into an evocation of breaking and the folded multiplicity of the accordion itself. As will be noted later, Onetti also exploits sound and repetition by way of sensual correspondence but his focus rests on singularity not plurality, in a movement of contraction rather than expansion.

PARADOX

Logic and rationality are frequently undermined in Lispector's prose through the juxtaposition of noun and adjective pairings that are not exactly contradictory in the manner of oxymoron, but are unconventional and incongruous. An example of this occurs when Angela imagines bathing naked in the river to mix her own sacred mud with the clay of the earth. "Tomarei banho no rio misturando com o barro a minha abençoada lama" ["I will bath in the river mingling my own sacred filth with the clay"] (33). "Abençoada" ["sacred"] is not conventionally employed with reference to "lama" ["filth"]. The culturally separate realms of the sacred and the untouchable, the pure and the impure are here deliberately juxtaposed in order to force the reader to split open and examine the origins and consequences of the cultural taboo that make this association of "abençoada lama" dissonant, incongruous, or shocking.

Lispector also constructs paradoxes through the combination of logically incompatible images. This occurs in the metaphor that Angela uses to describe her sudden feeling of oneness as "efervescendo como as bolinhas de água mineral Caxambu, era uma de repente" ["Angela Pralini meanwhile, effervescing like the bubbles in Caxambu mineral water, was one all of a sudden"] (42). The multiplicity of bubbling or fizzing contradicts the oneness of feeling whole and yet the two concepts are made to coexist, recalling Cixous's assertion that "if she [woman] is a whole, it is a whole made up of parts that are wholes" ("Sorties," 87). Throughout "A partida do trem" the authority of phallic knowledge is derailed with the undermining of the basic couple, male/female at work behind oppositional signification. Cixous sees death operating in the binary process as she claims: "And the movement whereby each opposition is set up to make sense is the movement through which the couple is destroyed. A universal battlefield. Each time, a war is let loose. Death is always at work" ("Sorties," 64). Thus, conversely, when binary opposition in language is destabilized, death is decanted and the feminine is let loose. This leads to my fourth point about the construction of *écriture féminine* in "A partida do trem," the fragmentation of linear time.

TEMPORAL FRAGMENTATION

"A partida do trem" is not a one-way journey to death, rather it fragments linear time as it does conventional syntax. The departure of the train becomes the point of infinite return in the story. The linear flow returns ineluctably and constantly to the beginning. This is achieved through a series of "false starts" in the story. The movement of setting off is described three times and the impression created that the journey is finally under way, only for the pluperfect to cast the reader back to the moment of departure. Thus the title, "A partida do trem," is an originating moment of convergence, a departure and a breaking point, with all time past and present flowing to the center. Departure marks the beginning of a series of textual circles, not a linear route.

Onetti's "Bienvenido Bob," in contrast, appears to typify the linear in terms of inescapable aging and mortality. The story concludes, however, with a misplaced epithet: "tantos miles de *pies inevitables*" ["so many thousands of *inevitable feet*"] (1228, my emphasis). Death is not an ultimate moment but an ongoing movement, latent in human relationships and interactions. There is a paradoxical open-endedness in the very continuity of the marching feet that pervert traditional expectation by trampling not the graves of the dead but their worn-out dreams or "formas repulsivas" ["repulsive forms"]. The "cadáveres pavorosos" ["fearsome corpses"] referred to are Bob's erstwhile ambitions (1228). The inevitability of death is represented in the final paragraph as the doomed decay of Bob's aspirations and desires. The narrator is not the agent of this mortality, but he is the textual barometer of its progress.

The opposition between Bob and the narrator acts as the structuring device by which death is articulated in the text. This is reminiscent of Cixous's statement that "the movement whereby each opposition is set up to make sense is the movement through which the couple is destroyed" ("Sorties," 64). In the final part of this essay, I would like to interrogate the gaps and pointers in "Bienvenido Bob," in order to illuminate those places where Onetti's fatalist, misogynistic "stated" seems at variance with his slippery, polyvalent "non-said" as he explores the limits of oppositional signification.

In "Bienvenido Bob" most of the communication between Bob and the narrator is maintained through a dialogue of looks and stares. Their encounters take place in public space. Others must be and always are present to see them seeing each other. A sense of voyeurism links with exhibitionism. Cixous claims, "*sexual difference* is not determined simply by the fantasized relation to anatomy, which depends to a great extent on catching *sight* of something, thus on the strange importance that is accorded to exteriority and to that which is specular in sexuality's development. A voyeur's theory, of course" ("Sorties," 82). French feminist theorists such as Cixous and Irigaray counter this "voyeurism" with the primacy of touch. The denial of touching the body is a palpable force within Onetti's text. Emotions are expressed through displacement onto objects, through facial expressions, gestures, body language, and what artists would call the negative space between the symmetrically choreographed profiles and figures.

Ellipsis also acquires a pivotal role as the nonsaid or unsayable speaks loud in this story. The unsaid forms a significant pairing with nontouching. Objects not people are touched and even then only tentatively with one finger, such as the flower by Bob ("tocó una flor con un dedo" ["touched a flower with his finger"] [1222]) and the playing of a single piano key by the narrator at a highly significant moment. The nonsaid and the nontouched meet over the piano. The narrator tries to "llamar" ["call"] or communicate "lo fundamental mío" ["the deepest part of myself"] (1224) to Bob by playing the same note over and over on the piano every three seconds. The rhythmic insistence of the repeated note is involuntary. It comes from an irrational place beyond control of the will. This single note, "al fin encontrada" ["found at last"], is "la única palabra pordiosera con que podía pedir tolerancia y comprensión a su juventud implacable" ["the only miserable word with which I could beg tolerance and understanding of his implacable youth"] (1223). But the word is a nonword and the Spanish for piano key, "tecla" (1222), overlaps teasingly with the verb "tocar" ["to touch"].

Neither Bob nor the narrator is worthy to touch Inés. The narrator toys with the risk of telling Bob about the images stirred in his mind when Bob describes himself as also unworthy to touch Inés or kiss the hem of her robe. The untold of the narrator's imagining is linked to the untouched Inés as he asks himself "cómo hablar a Inés, cómo tocarla" ["how to speak to Inés, how to touch her"] when he meets her empty shell after Bob has destroyed their liaison with yet another untold, as "nunca supe cuál fue la anécdota elegida por Bob para aquello" ["I never found out what story Bob told to achieve this"] (1226). Violent as well as erotic touching is a nonhappening linked with nonsaying. The narrator says, "no podía contestarle nada, no podía deshacerle la cara de un golpe" ["I could not think of a way to answer him at all, I could not smash his face in with a single blow"] (1223). Exchanges of dialogue implicitly fail to make any logical connection as Bob's answers attribute significance to the unstated verbal stimuli to which he responds. For example, when he is challenged as to why he finds the narrator "deshecho" ["worn out"], Bob refutes an unstated imputation of childishness with the words, "no, no . . . no soy tan niño. No entro en ese juego"["no, no . . . I am not childish like that. I'm not playing that game"] (1224–25).

The nonsaid is linked to nondesire. Significantly, the narrator experiences not the desire, but rather, as he repeats several times, the need, "la necesidad," to marry Inés. "Yo no pudiera desear otra solución" ["I could not desire any other solution"] (1223). The desire is in the negative and "la necesidad de casarme" ["the need to marry"] (1224) playfully substitutes Inés as the object of the phrases, "cómo yo había abrazado *aquella necesidad*" ["how I had embraced *that necessity*"] and "Mi amor de *aquella necesidad* había suprimido el pasado y toda atadura con el presente" ["My love of *that necessity* had suppressed the past as well as all links with the present"] (my emphases, 1223). He claims to desire not Inés but rather, in the abstract, the obligatory solution of marriage. Words are dismissed as "nombres marchitos para ir poniendo a las cosas y un poco crearlas" ["worn out names that we go around calling things, to try and bring them to life"] (1225). The process of naming is connected with death when Bob explains that according to his definition of "vejez" ["old age"], "lo que determinaba la descomposición, o acaso lo que era símbolo de descomposición era pensar por conceptos, englobar a las mujeres en la palabra mujer, empujarlas sin cuidado para que pudieran amoldarse al concepto hecho por una pobre experiencia" ["the thing that caused decomposition, or rather perhaps, that symbolized decomposition, was thinking in concepts, carelessly casting all women in the same conceptual mold, formed by insufficient experience"] (1225). Bob refers to old age in terms of "descomposición" ["decomposition"], symbolized by reducing "las mujeres" ["women"] to the single term, "la mujer" (1225). This reductive process of linguistic definition is then associated with de/composition, implying both the physical disintegration of the body and the "unmaking" of music.

In "Bienvenido Bob," music and the body mark out a subtext of unsaid and untouched that are obliquely stated by the accumulation of repeated abstractions such as "necesidad" ["necessity"] (1223) and "descomposición" ["decomposition"] (1225). These abstractions and repetitions intermittently make the reader aware of the outer limits of closure and meaning. Millington describes an analogous relinquishing of mastery in relation to the ending of Onetti's "Jacob y el otro" ["Jacob and the Other"] where "the story's structure (the movement from knowledge established, to knowledge reformulated) does not connote the story's mastery, but the fact that no knowledge is substantively whole, that there is always more, always another reformulation, always an ignorance within knowledge" (*Fictions of Desire*, 111).

From the Cixous/Lispector view of language and knowledge, this continual subsidence of mastery is also the undermining of phallogocentric power. The reader is thus diverted away from the rational as senses and feelings are displaced into sensual correspondences. In "A partida do trem," rhythm, sound, and repetition have the effect of interpellating the physical body, merging narrative perspectives and reducing intersubjective distances. Onetti, conversely, accompanies his explicit alienation of the body with a metalinguistic subtext of cancellation, negation, and neutrality. In "Bienvenido Bob," his repetitions do not exploit their inherently poetic qualities as Lispector's do with rhythm and onomatopoeia. As already noted above, Millington finds that repetition in Onetti "fosters selfreferentiality and closure" (*Fictions of Desire*, 203). Thus Onetti uses the correspondences of music to articulate differences in terms of their reduction to an ultimate "same." Lispector, on the other hand, stimulates sensual awakenings by discarding oppositional difference and seeking multiple differences in apparent sameness. Onetti's single, repeated "profunda nota que tenazmente hacía renacer mi dedo en el borde de cada última vibración" ["deep note which my finger persistently revived as each successive vibration died away"] (1223) is a sombre counterpoint to Lispector's quest for variations. "Bienvenido Bob" may be read as a minimalist parody of masculine (im)posture and as such, I contend, it too seeks a textual space from which to challenge "[man's] grotesque and unenviable fate of being reduced to a single idol with clay balls" ("Sorties," 82).

NOTE

1. An example of this humanist neutrality and its implicit naturalization of female invisibility can be found in John F. Deredita, "The Shorter Works of Juan Carlos Onetti." He writes "Onetti's 'subjective something' consists in a pathetic and ironic recognition of human aging and decay" (113), and later, "perception of this fate is the sign of maturity" (114).

WORKS CITED

Armbruster, Carol. "Hélène—Clarice: Nouvelle Voix." *Contemporary Literature* 24.2 (Summer 1983): 145–57.

Cixous, Hélène. "Castration or Decapitation." Intro. and trans. Annette Kuhn. *Signs* 2.1 (1981): 41–55.

Cixous, Hélène. "Sorties: Out and Out. Attacks/Ways Out/Forays." Hélène Cixous and Catherine Clément, *The Newly Born Woman*. Trans. Betsy Wing; intro. Sandra M. Gilbert. *Theory and History of Literature* 24 (Manchester: Manchester UP, 1986). 61–132.

Deredita, John F. "The Shorter Works of Juan Carlos Onetti." *Studies in Short Fiction* 8 (1971): 112–22.

Dranch, Sherry E. "Reading through the Veiled Text. Colette's *The Pure and the Impure*." *Contemporary Literature* 24.2 (Summer 1983): 176–89.

Furman, Nelly. "The Politics of Language: Beyond the Gender Principle?" *Making a Difference: Feminist Literary Criticism*. Eds. Gayle Greene and Coppélia Kahn. London and New York: Methuen New Accents, 1985. 59–79.

Gallop, Jane. *The Daughter's Seduction: Feminism and Psychoanalysis.* Ithaca, N.Y.: Cornell UP, 1982.

Lispector, Clarice. "A partida do trem." *Onde Estivestes de Noite* ["Where were you at Night?"]. Rio de Janeiro: Nova Fronteira, 1980. 21–43.

Mark Millington. *Fictions of Desire. An Analysis of the Short Stories of Juan Carlos Onetti.* Lewiston, N.Y.: Edwin Mellen, 1993.

Millington, Mark. "No Woman's Land: The Representation of Woman in Onetti." *Modern Language Notes* 102 (1987): 358–77.

10

Conrad and Onetti:
The Two Steins

Peter Turton

A man that is born falls into a dream like a man who falls into the
sea. If he tries to climb out into the air as inexperienced people
endeavor to do, he drowns—*nicht wahr?* . . . No! I tell you! The
way is to the destructive element submit yourself, and with the
exertions of your hands and feet in the water make the deep, deep
sea keep you up. So if you ask me—how to be? . . . I will tell you!
For that too there is only one way. . . . In the destructive element
immerse. . . . That was the way. To follow the dream . . . —and
so—*ewig—usque ad finem.*

—Stein, in *Lord Jim*

Toda la ciencia de vivir . . . está en la sencilla blandura de acomodarse en los huecos de los sucesos que no hemos provocado
con nuestra voluntad, no forzar nada, ser, simplemente, cada minuto. . . . Abandonarse como a una corriente, como a un sueño.

[The whole science of living . . . is in the simple suppleness of fitting yourself into the spaces left by the events that we have provoked by our will, not forcing anything, being, simply, at every
minute. . . . Letting yourself go as if borne by a current or a
dream.]

—Brausen, in *La vida breve* [*A Brief Life*] (OC 646–47)

Joseph Conrad's *Lord Jim* (1900)[1] is a novel about a romantic and
idealistic young man who has spent part of his life running away from
an act of cowardice he committed when once severely tested by circumstances. As chief mate on the ship *Patna*, he has leapt overboard
when it seemed to be sinking, leaving to their fate hundreds of
Moslem pilgrims sailing to Arabia to make the holy journey to

Mecca. Jim, and the rest of the white officers aboard, including the captain, come safely to land in a lifeboat only to witness the later arrival of the *Patna*, which has been towed to safety by a French ship. After a trial, Jim has his mate's license confiscated and is forced to make his living in a variety of shore jobs. But he is driven from place to place in the East because someone always eventually turns up to recognize him. The narrator of the story, Marlow, who is present at Jim's trial, decides to help him and introduces him to Stein, a prosperous German trader in Java, who gives Jim an introduction to some of his native friends in Patusan and the opportunity to set up in business there. Jim becomes very successful in this, partly because he manages to organize the local people to fight a victorious war against the enemies of Stein's native friends. In the process, Jim becomes the best friend of Dain Waris, son of the chieftain Doramin, who had been Stein's main native friend and ally. Jim makes himself practically the ruler of Patusan, being universally admired for his courage, honor, honesty, and intelligence. One day, however, a boat arrives in Patusan carrying a group of criminal white men, headed by Gentleman Brown, who in the process of fleeing justice and taking refuge in Patusan kill some natives. Jim decides to expel these men without punishment, and trusts them to leave quietly, partly because Brown appeals to him as a fellow white man and partly because Brown inadvertently awakens Jim's guilty conscience about his own misdemeanor in abandoning a sinking ship. On leaving Patusan, however, Brown kills some more natives, among them Dain Waris. Jim is appalled at what he has allowed to happen and deliberately permits Doramin to kill him in revenge for the death of his son. In so doing, Jim is acknowledging his debt of guilt to his native allies and washing away the stain on his honor. Jim could have resisted Doramin's act of revenge by fighting, as his native entourage and wife urge him to do, but decides to offer himself up to Doramin in sacrifice. For this act he is cursed by his wife Jewel as a traitor to their love. The narrator Marlow comments in the second to last paragraph of the novel: "But we can see him, an obscure conqueror of fame, tearing himself out of the arms of a jealous love at the sign, at the call of his exalted egoism. He goes away from a living woman to celebrate his pitiless wedding with the shadowy ideal of conduct" (351).

Onetti's *La vida breve* [*A Brief Life*] (1950) tells the story of Brausen, a man in his thirties awaiting the sack from his job in a Buenos Aires publicity agency and estranged from his wife Gertrudis, who has just had a breast surgically removed. Brausen is in a general state of crisis, as the following extract from an interior monologue illustrates. He is thinking:

"A esta edad es cuando la vida empieza a ser una sonrisa torcida,"
admitiendo, sin protestas, la desaparición de Gertrudis, de Raquel, de
Stein, de todas las personas que me correspondía amar; admitiendo mi
soledad como lo había hecho antes con mi tristeza. "Una sonrisa torcida. Y se descubre que la vida está hecha, desde muchos años atrás, de
malentendidos. . . . Fuera de esto, nada; de vez en cuando, algunas
oportunidades de olvido, algunos placeres, que llegan y pasan envene-
nados." (476; Raquel is Brausen's sister-in-law)

["It is at this age that life starts to be a twisted smile," admitting, without protestations, the disappearance of Gertrudis, of Raquel, of Stein,
of all the people that it was my lot to love; admiring my being alone as
I had done before my madness. "A twisted smile. And you discover
that life is made up, from many years back, of misunderstandings. . . .
Apart from this, nothing; now and again, a few opportunities for for-
getting, a few pleasures, that come and go away poisoned."]

The Stein of this quotation is Brausen's friend and immediate superior in the publicity agency. He helps Brausen negotiate a better severance
payoff than Macleod, the old American in charge, is at first willing to
grant; he suggests going into partnership with Brausen in an independent
agency; he chivvies Brausen into rethinking his life; and he gives him the
idea of writing a film script that would distance him from poverty "as if
from an aged lover" (441). Brausen turns himself into a tough who,
assuming the name Arce, starts an affair with a cheap prostitute who has
moved into the adjoining apartment and whom he brutalizes and even
thinks of murdering. In fact, a gangster called Ernesto does this last deed
and Brausen eventually moves into the fictitious world of his script,
which has been taking shape in his head. The novel ends in a confused
carnival atmosphere where Brausen and his characters, dressed in outlandish costumes, are being pursued by the police for possession of drugs.

Both Conrad's and Onetti's Stein perform the same function in their
respective novels, and in themselves are important characters occupying
considerable space in the latter. Their function is that of dispenser of
paternal, friendly, trustworthy, and wise support and advice to a protagonist who is in a state of existential disarray. Of course, there are
superficial differences in their relationship with this beleaguered protagonist: Conrad's Stein is a whole generation older than Jim, whereas
Brausen and Stein in *La vida breve* are of the same age; and the philosophy of life of Conrad's Stein is conveyed to the reader via the ears and
voice of the narrator Marlow, while Onetti's Stein dispenses his knowledge and counsel mainly to Brausen himself.

The coincidence of name and function must strike the reader of
Lord Jim and *La vida breve* as at least curious, and the more one looks
into *Lord Jim*, and other works of Conrad also, the more one comes to

suspect a direct influence. The quotes that preface this essay point to a common way of tackling life insofar as they both advise accommodation to it, letting oneself go with the tide, finding one's natural niche, being (in the existentialist manner) "what one is." Moreover, there are other clues that suggest that Onetti was a reader of Conrad.

In the recent critical biography of Onetti by María Esther Gilio and Carlos M. Domínguez, *Construcción de la noche*, there is a photograph, inserted between pages 288 and 289, of an older Onetti reading a work by Conrad whose title is hidden. The same photograph provides the cover to the present volume. In addition, there occurs in the very late *Cuando ya no importe* [*Past Caring?*] (1993) a cryptic reference to Almayer (of *Almayer's Folly*, Conrad's first novel). Almayer is a Dutch merchant in the East who goes to the dogs, taking opium and dying prematurely after his youthful hopes have foundered on financial ruin, his wife's turning out to be a harridan, and (the last straw) his daughter's elopement with a Malay trader.

Of course, failure is the pattern of the overwhelming majority of Onetti's novels and short stories, as it is of Conrad's best work. And Conrad's favorite narrative devices (the narration filtered through various mental prisms in a story that is not delivered in strict chronological sequence; an ultimate uncertainty about human personality, motive, or even events themselves; irony, ambivalence, paradox and oxymoron, etc.) all become hallmarks of the mature Onettian technique. Maybe these devices were acquired by Onetti from Faulkner, who himself had picked them up from Conrad and Joyce, and Onetti only read Conrad after writing *La vida breve*. Be this as it may, in the best work of Conrad and Onetti these same devices are subtly employed to convey a philosophy of life that is essentially Schopenhauerian, centering around the idea that man's destiny is inimical to him and is the plaything of forces largely outside his control.

Let us examine our initial quote from *Lord Jim* and compare it to the passage immediately below, taken from *La vida breve*, in the context of what happens in the two novels. The Conradian sequence begins: "A man that is born falls into a dream. . . ." In a highly perceptive commentary of this passage, Cedric Watts begins by stating a common critical response to this enigmatic passage: "You should pursue at all costs the goal suggested by your idealism"; he then moves on to provide a subtler interpretation, which bears in mind the famous fragment on "The horror! The horror!" from *Heart of Darkness*, Conrad's earlier and similarly mysterious work about another ambiguous figure, Kurtz:

On the one hand, such words as "In the destructive element immerse. . . . To follow the dream . . . *ewig—usque ad finem*" sound like a rallying call to all romantic crusaders. Be a Quixote—charge on—don't count the cost—risk your life. And this notion is encouraged by our recollection that *usque ad finem* was the proud family motto that Bobrowski urged on his nephew, Konrad Korzeniowski. But on the other hand, if we follow Stein's speech closely, this contrasting meaning also emerges: When we are born, we fall into the dream of life as if we are falling into a sea. So we should resemble good swimmers. An inexperienced person, finding himself in the sea, tries to climb up out of it in his panic—and for snatching at the sky, he pays the penalty of drowning in the sea. The sensible person cooperates with the water instead of fighting it; he exploits buoyancy, and lets the water carry him while he swims steadily. Thus he survives. In other words, we should be practical realists, ready to adapt to life and make the most of what it offers; we shouldn't be idealists who try to climb up out of ordinary life towards some transcendental goal.[2]

Just as it prefers paradoxes and oxymorons, Watts concludes, Conrad's text fails to provide a definite answer to the moral issues involved; instead, its achievement is having highlighted "the problems of human nature that the work has been exploring." Watts' analysis indicates with acuteness the subtleties of the Conradian text at its best. I would merely enlarge on these points by saying that Stein also appears to be talking about the need (in a person with a sense of right and wrong) for faith, in the sense that faith is the only thing that will enable this person to "keep right on to the end of the road." Stein has most cruelly lost his beloved wife and daughter through fever, and takes refuge in his formidable collection of beetles and butterflies. *Some* faith is necessary (*some* perception of order behind an outwardly chaotic and unjust universe), otherwise you will, like Almayer and other Conradian protagonists who are still decent human beings, "go to the dogs."[3] Of course, the Gentleman Browns of this world come into a different category. Stein does not relinquish his instincts of generosity and decency in the face of his personal tragedy. He lives out his life to the end (there is no thought of suicide), despite the additional burden of Jim's death. But the novel ends on a note of practically total disillusionment: "Stein has aged greatly of late. He feels it himself, and says often that he is 'preparing to leave all this; preparing to leave . . .' while he waves his hand sadly at his butterflies" (352).

If we turn to the quote from *La vida breve* that prefaces this essay (starting "Toda la ciencia de vivir . . . está en la sencilla blandura de acomodarse en los huecos de los sucesos" ["The whole science of living . . . is in the simple suppleness of fitting yourself into the spaces left by the events"]), we will see that Brausen's thoughts are more in line with Cedric Watts' second possible interpretation of Stein's words, pointing to a rather passive acceptance of the vagaries of the human predicament. This is somewhat curious, since Brausen has already transformed himself (at least for certain scenarios of his life) into the thug Arce, a kind of anti-Brausen. It is true that very soon afterwards he is engulfed in the world of his own film script, where he acts out a rather colorless existence among his own fictitious characters. It seems evident that Onetti has had some difficulty with the evolution of his protagonist and even with his conception. Why should a man who is "incapaz, no ya de ser otro, *sino de la misma voluntad de ser otro*" ["incapable, not only of being someone else, *but even of the will to be someone else*"] ever change (476, my italics)? A man of such abjection would never find within himself the qualities necessary for turning into a tough such as Arce. This matter of unconvincing psychology is at the heart of a major flaw in the construction of *La vida breve*.

Conrad, on the other hand, has seen Jim from the start and put his finger on the weakness that will lead to his death, despite his apparent redemption from the *Patna* scandal. Jim is "Janus-faced," to use a term employed by Cedric Watts both about Jim and his creator (*A Preface to Conrad*, 7). Jim is both strong and weak, in a convincing way. Despite his success in Patusan, he still retains a romantic, and thus partly false, image of himself, and this means he is "ready to surrender himself faithfully to the claim of his own world of shades" and in the process to sacrifice Jewel to a false sense of honor (351–52). Onetti, on the other hand, has imagined Brausen and his problems (with, perhaps, the psychological discrepancy I have noted) and has merely forged an anti-Brausen who might just as well be another person altogether, as his new name indicates. For Conrad, "Lord Jim" ("Tuan Jim" in Malay) is still Jim, beneath all his well-won trappings of authority, but where are the seeds of Arce in Brausen? Arce is not a mature Brausen, he is not Brausen at all, and into the bargain Brausen-Arce tapers off into the anonymous "yo" ["I"] of the final chapters. It is not by chance that Onetti cannot finish *La vida breve* convincingly. He has in fact ruined a very promising realist psychological novel by tacking onto it an ending that is altogether on another aesthetic plane. To end this type of novel by a shift into a kind of delirious fantasy world is to admit that you have no resolution for the problematic confronting the protagonist.

The fact is that Onetti knows very well how to make his protagonists fail (that is what the immense majority of them do, because the common script of Onetti's work is man's life as failure). But in *La vida breve* he has desired another ending, and this he has not been able to supply convincingly. Onetti's paradigmatic man is Larsen in *El astillero* [*The Shipyard*], his first really mature novel (and, arguably, his best). The reader will be aware, however, that in the short story—for exam-

ple, "Esbjerg, en la costa" [*Esbjerg by the Sea*], "El infierno tan temido"
[*Hell Most Feared*], and "La cara de la desgracia" [*The Image of Misfortune*]—he has already achieved a mastery of Conradian proportions.
La vida breve may well be a shadowing of Onetti's own feelings about
leaving behind the idea of transforming the world via political or para-
political activity to dedicate himself to his writing, but as a vehicle for
the credible metamorphosis of the character Juan María Brausen it is a
failure.

Let us now return to the two Steins and by further investigation of
them try to illuminate the aims and achievements of the two authors.
Both Steins are disillusioned romantics who try to preserve some idealism about life. The wisdom they possess and dispense is necessarily
rather tentative and hedged with ambiguity because, although they have
considerably more insight into life than Jim or Brausen, they have not by
any means resolved their own problems, simply because life is a complicated and nasty business. According to Conrad, life resembled "a forest
in which nobody knows the way,"[4] and his friend Bertrand Russell
"felt . . . that he thought of civilized and morally tolerable human life as
a dangerous walk on a thin crust of barely cooled lava which at any
moment might break and let the unwary sink into its fiery depths."[5]
Onetti, for his part, once stated: "Onetti es nihilista y es pesimista.
Onetti ha leído a Schopenhauer, y además, leyó el Eclesiastés en algún
momento de distracción. . . . Ahora, si usted puede rebatir el Eclesiastés,
yo lo oiría con mucho gusto" ["Onetti is a nihilist and a pessimist.
Onetti has read Schopenhauer, and moreover, he read Ecclesiastes at
some distracted moment. . . . Now, if you can refute Ecclesiastes, I
would listen to you with some pleasure"].[6] Both Steins show humor and
generosity, as bulwarks against life's cruel surprises and against despair.
Both are major figures in their respective novels, although Onetti's Stein
disappears before the end of the novel, prior, in fact, to Brausen's flight
into his fantasy world.

THE ORIGINS OF THE TWO STEINS

According to Cedric Watts,

> Norman Sherry suggests that this character is based partly on the
> naturalist A. R. Wallace (author of *Malay Archipelago*, one of the
> source books for the Patusan sequence); partly on the German natu-
> ralist Dr. Bernstein, who was known to Wallace; partly on Charles
> Allen, Wallace's assistant; and partly on William Lingard, who
> established a trading post at Berau in Borneo and was friendly with
> the sultan of that area.[7]

My own readings of Conrad's slightly younger contemporary Rudyard Kipling suggest a likely influence of one of Kipling's characters, the comic figure of Hans Breitmann, "the big-beamed German," humorous and wise, who appears in *Life's Handicap* (1891). Like Stein, only exaggeratedly so, Breitmann speaks a Germanicized English; more to the point, he owns "stores of experience as vast as the sea itself; for his business in life was to wander up and down in the world, collecting orchids and wild beasts and ethological specimens for German and American dealers."[8] Breitmann at one point in this story ("Bertram and Bimi") says to the rebellious captive orangutan Bimi "You haf too much ego in your Cosmos" (235), which brings to mind Stein's "This is Nature, the balance of colossal forces. Every star is so—and every blade of grass stands so—and the mighty Kosmos in perfect equilibrium produces—this. This wonder; this masterpiece of Nature—the great artist" (195).[9] Stein is referring here to a beautiful butterfly in his collection. In fact, Breitmann was not Kipling's invention, since he found the character in a book called *Hans Breitmann's Ballads*, comic Germanicized English verses by the American writer Charles Godfred Leland, a favorite of Kipling. Although Conrad's Stein is not a comic character, he does have a sense of humor, and, because of Kipling's tremendous popularity at the turn of the century when Conrad was writing *Lord Jim*, it seems likely that Breitmann was in Conrad's mind during his creation of Stein. According to Conrad's biographer Jocelyn Baines, Conrad had certainly read Kipling by the time he wrote *Lord Jim*.[10]

According to the Gilio and Domínguez biography of Onetti, Julio Stein in *La vida breve* was modeled on a great friend, a drinking and womanizing companion of Onetti called Julio Adín, a typesetter of Russian Jewish origin whom Onetti met in Buenos Aires in 1943. Adín had arrived in Uruguay in 1931 and, already a communist, joined the Uruguayan Communist Party. He subsequently left for Buenos Aires in 1938 and found work as a journalist on a Jewish newspaper. Adín was some four years younger than Onetti and admired him profoundly. A mutual friend remarked: "Julio era como la novia de Onetti" ["Julio was like Onetti's fiancée"], and it appears that on their first meeting they talked about Walt Whitman, a quotation from whom prefaces the text of *La vida breve*. At this time, Onetti, "Sin ser militante, asumía claras posiciones de izquierda" ["Without being a party member, he took clear left-wing positions"], according to Adín, and enthused about the outcome of the battle of Stalingrad (*Construcción de la noche*, 87). Onetti, for his part states: "Era una época terrífica, de garufas todas las noches, junto con otro que era Julio Stein en *La vida breve*. Y eso duró años de años, años de whisky, porque entonces yo trabajaba en Reuter y allí el trabajo empezaba en la madrugada" ["It was a terrific time, with booze-ups every night, alongside another man who was Julio Stein in *La vida breve*. And that lasted for years and years, years of whisky, because at the time I was working for Reuters and there the job started in the early hours of the morning"] (ibid., 91).

Had Onetti already read *Lord Jim*? Perhaps; the above-mentioned biography records the following: "Una noche Julio Adín atendió el teléfono de su casa y oyó la voz de Onetti que le decía: 'Escuchá, no digas nada. . . . Stein, ¿te parece bien? Julio Stein,' repitió. 'Sí,' le dijo Julio, 'me parece bien.'" ["One night Julio Adín picked up the telephone in his house and heard Onetti's voice saying to him: 'Listen, don't say anything. . . . Stein, do you like it? Julio Stein,' he repeated. 'Yes,' said Julio, 'I like it'"] (ibid., 109). Whatever the reality behind the suggestion that Julio Stein may be partly drawn from a Conradian source, his other provenance is more certain, according to Onetti's own words. Onetti and Julio Adín fell out much later, partly over Adín's Zionism (Onetti was strongly pro-Palestinian) and partly over what Onetti construed as Adín's attentions to Dolly, Onetti's fourth wife. Adín also remembers his former friend being very jealous when he danced with La Boya, Onetti's previous wife, Elizabeth María Pekelharing. Readers of *La vida breve* will recall Brausen's reference to Stein having slept with Gertrudis, the former's wife. It was Onetti who broke with Adín, and he does not seem to have emerged very well from this affair. In a comment to the Montevideo weekly *Brecha* he wrote: "Veo que el corresponsal de la nonata *Brecha* en Tel Aviv es un tal Julio Adín. (Su verdadero apellido es Stein y nunca escuché chistes tan graciosos sobre el sionismo como los que me contó entre una mujer y otra)" ["I see that the correspondent of the as yet unborn *Brecha* in Tel Aviv is one Julio Adín. (His real surname is Stein and I never heard such funny jokes about Zionism as those that he told me between one woman and another)"] (ibid., 229). Onetti was obviously trying to damage Adín in the eyes of the Israelis, and surlily rebuffed all Adín's attempts to patch up the quarrel. Adín commented sadly: "Allí terminó mi relación con uno de los hombres más inteligentes y cabales que conocí en mi vida. Es difícil sospechar qué puede herir la susceptibilidad onettiana." ["There finished my relationship with one of the most intelligent and real men I have known in my life. It is difficult to suspect what can wound Onetti's susceptibility"] (ibid., 230).

THE HISTORY AND PSYCHOLOGY OF THE TWO STEINS

Both have a revolutionary past which they are compelled to give up. Conrad's Stein, a German born around 1826, has taken part in the Bavarian Revolution of 1848 and has been forced to flee after its failure.

Onetti's Stein spends one year and a half in Montevideo as a member of the local Communist Party and then leaves for Buenos Aires. He is an Austrian Jew haunted, surmises Brausen, by the memories of relatives buried in an Austrian cemetery (presumably during the Hitler period). Conrad's Stein is a whole generation older than Lord Jim, whom he first meets in the 1880s; Julio Stein plays father-figure to a man of his own age who is his subordinate in a publicity agency. The events of *La vida breve* take place in the 1940s, with nostalgic flashbacks to the thirties (militancy in the Communist Party and life in Paris with Mami). Stein is thirty-five during the main events of the novel.

When the reader first encounters Conrad's Stein, the latter is a rich merchant adventurer, sometime adviser to a Malay sultan and a passionate butterfly and beetle collector. After his escape from Bavaria, he has taken refuge with a poor republican watchmaker in Trieste and later hawked watches in Tripoli, where he meets a Dutch traveler who engages him as his assistant and takes him East:

> They traveled the [Malay] Archipelago together and separately, collecting insects and birds, for four years or more. Then the naturalist went home, and Stein, having no home to go to, remained with an old trader he had come across in his journeys in the interior of Celebes— if Celebes may be said to have an interior. (193)

This old trader, a Scotsman, introduces Stein to the native aristocracy of Celebes and "By means of this simple formality Stein inherited the Scotsman's privileged position and all his stock-in-trade, together with a fortified house on the banks of the only navigable river in the country" (194). After years of turmoil (mainly wars with native enemies), and after becoming well known in Europe as an entomologist, Stein leaves Celebes when his best friend Mohammed Bonso is assassinated. He also loses his native wife and their daughter through fever. "He left the country, which his cruel loss had made unbearable to him. Thus ended the first and adventurous part of his existence. What followed was so different that, but for the reality of sorrow which remained with him, this strange part must have resembled a dream" (194). He eventually sets up business in Samarang (Java), seemingly around the age of forty.

> He drove his buggy every morning to town, where he had an office with white and Chinese clerks. He owned a small fleet of schooners and native craft, and dealt in island produce on a large scale. For the rest he lived solitary, but not misanthropic, with his books and his collection, classing and arranging specimens, corresponding with entomologists in Europe, writing up a descriptive catalogue of his treasures. (195)

It is in Samarang that he meets Jim and launches him into his life in Patusan.

The biography Onetti gives of Julio Stein is much sketchier and, as noted, the character disappears well before the end of *La vida breve*. He becomes second-in-command of the Buenos Aires publicity agency run by "old Macleod," and spends the rest of his time drinking, womanizing, and looking after his aging ex-lover Mami, ironizing constantly about everything, including the values of capitalist society, which he has had to accept, and himself. Conrad's Stein, once in the East, seems to have had no scruples about becoming rich (Marlow is sardonic on this point), having lost his taste for revolutionary politics, and he concentrates on building up his business interests and his collection of beetles and butterflies, behaving at the same time with exemplary individual virtue. Marlow says of him that he was "one of the most trustworthy men I had ever known," possessing the "gentle light of a simple, unwearied, as it were, and intelligent good nature" (191). In this the reader will find a parallel with Julio Stein's unremittingly generous conduct toward Brausen and the rather ridiculous Mami.

Conrad's Stein retains much of his idealism, even after his wife's and daughter's deaths, mainly through "His collection of *Buprestidae* and *Longicorns*—beetles all—horrible miniature monsters, looking malevolent in death and immobility, and his cabinet of butterflies, beautiful and hovering under the glass of cases on lifeless wings" (192). Marlow remarks on the

> intense, almost passionate, absorption with which he looked at a butterfly, as though on the bronze sheen of these frail wings, in the white tracings, in the gorgeous markings, he would see other things, an image of something as perishable and defying destruction as these delicate and lifeless tissues, displaying a splendor unmarred by death.
>
> "Marvelous!" he repeated, looking up at me. "Look! The beauty—but that is nothing—look at the accuracy, the harmony. And so fragile! And so strong! And so exact! This is Nature—the balance of colossal forces. Every star is so—and every blade of grass stands *so*—and the mighty Kosmos in perfect equilibrium produces—this. This wonder; this masterpiece of Nature—the great artist."
>
> "Never heard an entomologist go on like this," I observed cheerfully. "Masterpiece! And what of man?"
>
> "Man is amazing, but he is not a masterpiece," he said, keeping his eyes fixed on the glass case. "Perhaps the artist was a little mad." (195)

When told by Marlow of Jim's plight, Stein remarks: "I understand very well. He is romantic" (199). After Stein's discourse (previously quoted) beginning "A man that is born falls into a dream," he suggests "'a practical remedy—for the evil [of idealism]—for the great evil—' he repeated, with a humorous and indulgent smile" (201). "'He is romantic—romantic,' he repeated. 'And that is very bad. . . . Very good, too,' he added. . . . 'Perhaps he is,' I admitted . . . 'but I am sure you are.' . . . 'Well—I exist too,' he said" (202). Later on, Marlow stresses Stein's practicality, which somehow coexists with his idealism:

> Stein was the man who knew more about Patusan than anybody else. More than was known in the government circles, I suspect. I have no doubt he had been there, either in his butterfly-hunting days or later on, when he tried in his incorrigible way to season with a pinch of romance the fattening dishes of his commercial kitchen. There were very few places in the Archipelago he had not seen in the original dusk of their being, before light (and even electric light) had been carried into them for the sake of better morality and—and—well—the greater profit, too. (204)

Thus Stein, prior to Jim's death. Between twenty and sixty he scarcely ages, but after that death Marlow notices that "there were deep furrows on his pale cheeks" (298). Conrad renders with a subtle pathos and beauty Stein's final disillusionment:

> "Come and see the girl . . . ," he said with a half-hearted show of activity. . . . "An old man like me, a stranger—sehen Sie—cannot do much. . . . Come this way. . . . Young hearts are unforgiving. . . ." I could see that he was in utmost distress. . . . "The strength of life in them, the cruel strength of life. . . ." . . . "He loved her very much," he said interrogatively. . . . "Very frightful," he murmured. "She can't understand me. I am only a strange old man." (299)

He tries in vain to convince Jewel that Jim was true, and not false, as she bitterly asserts:

> Who knows? He is gone, inscrutable at heart, and the poor girl is leading a sort of soundless, inert life in Stein's house. Stein has aged greatly of late. He feels it himself, and says often that he is "preparing to leave all this; preparing to leave . . ." while he waves his hand sadly at his butterflies. (352)

Stein is obviously a Conradian hero, and his defeat makes Conrad's novel all the more tragic, conveying the message that whatever his psychological resources the individual in the end always faces defeat. (There is no trace of a belief in the afterlife; in this Conrad resembles Onetti).[11]

Onetti's Stein ironizes about everything: being a Jew; religion in general; the human race; the Communist Party; "ese año y medio que perdimos absurdamente en Montevideo" ["that year and a half that we wasted absurdly in Montevideo"] (470); Brausen's "puritanism";

Mami; the publicity agency; capitalism, and so on. But his criticisms are usually shot through with ambivalence and humor. For instance, if his communist militancy in Montevideo was "absurd," it remains something he views with nostalgia and a certain respect:

> Es que no puedo, por ahora, aceptar la idea de tener empleados, de explotar gente. Fui sincero todo el tiempo que viví en Montevideo, y lo sigo siendo, aunque trate de olvidar mi fe. Plusvalía sigue siendo mucho más que una palabra. Es tolerable ser sólo una ruedita de la máquina, puedo tranquilizar mi conciencia cuando el viejo Macleod me estafa una comisión. Entonces le cuento la anécdota a Mami, la única persona sobre la tierra capaz de creerme. "¿Ves cómo me explotan?," le digo. "¿No te das cuenta de que toda esta organización social es monstruosa?" (531–32)

> [I just can't, at the present time, accept the idea of having people work for me, of exploiting people. I was sincere for all the time that I lived in Montevideo, and I am still sincere now, even though I may be trying to forget my faith. Surplus value is still much more than just a word. It is tolerable to be only a cog in the machine, I can calm my conscience when old Macleod cheats me out of a commission. When that happens I tell the story to Mami, the only person on earth who can believe me. "Can you see how they are exploiting me?," I say to her. "Don't you realize that the way the whole of society is organized is monstrous?"]

Stein admits he earns good money with Macleod and even enjoys good relations with him, at the same time as he shows his scorn for capitalist values in general and the aims and methods of the publicity agency in particular. The point is that one's ideals founder and one has to dig deep within oneself to find values worth staying alive for until the inevitable day comes to "mandarlo todo al diablo" ["send it all to the devil"] (532).

Although capitalism is constantly attacked throughout *La vida breve*, both by Stein and Brausen, the other system is seen to rest too clearly on false premises: "Esa es mi raza—dijo Stein—, el material que se me ha confiado para construir el mundo del mañana" ["'That is my own race,' said Stein, 'the material that has been handed over to me to build the world of tomorrow'"] (469), in an aside about a fairly ordinary group of men and women coming out of theaters and cinemas and into the cafés of central Buenos Aires. Stein's combination of communist militancy and skirt-chasing among the young girls of the Montevideo party is seen to come to grief in the face of the old story of the brutal way in which the young elbow their elders to one side. There is a particularly entertaining passage where Stein lays bare the false consciousness of the communist youth, male and female, which begins:

Yo también era el pasado para aquellas Santa Juana; me reducían a símbolo de sus pasados ignominiosos y se apartaban de mí, se alejaban siempre con un melenudo de nuez pronunciada, un convicto de la suciedad física, un frenético de veintipocos años que se desprendía del servicio militar como un abrojo y caía, siempre, ¡maldita sea mi alma!, a tierra de Buenos Aires, Capital Federal. Y apenas repuesto del golpe, descubría que Dios lo señalaba con el dedo, lo perseguía con el ojo encerrado en un triángulo para que hiciera la revolución mundial. Tarea que, como es sabido, no puede ser cumplida sin el apoyo, inspiración y proximidad de una muchacha deseable y capaz de ganarse la vida. (658–59)

[I also was the past for those Saint Joans; they would cut me down to a symbol of their ignominious pasts and detach themselves from me, move away always with a long-haired fellow with a prominent Adam's apple, somebody you could condemn for his body dirt, a frenzied twenty-five year old who was pulling himself away from military service as if it were a burr and landing, always, for God's sake!, in the vicinity of Buenos Aires, the Federal Capital. And hardly had he recovered from the shock, he would discover that God was singling him out, pursuing him to make the world revolution. A task which, as is well known, cannot be carried out without the support, inspiration and nearness of a girl who is also desirable and able to earn her own living.]

So what is left worth living for? There is nostalgia (for lost political illusions about making the world a better place; for the adventure in Paris with Mami, fifteen years previously). There is good humor, perpetual irony, drinking, a constant Quixotic defense of the now fifty-year-old Mami, there is generosity toward Brausen, who, by the way, is a considerably nastier personality than Stein. (Stein's advice to Brausen to write the film script as a way of distancing himself from poverty as if from an aged lover is taken by Brausen, whereas Stein never abandons *his* aged lover and chivalrously continues to foster her absurd illusions about her attractiveness to men.) Julio Stein, in fact, lives by a kind of moral imperative, a refusal to be corrupted beyond a certain point by an immoral and unjust world and universe. So does Conrad's Stein, whose admired collection of beetles and butterflies is also a metaphor for a world where evil lives side by side with good.[12]

Both Steins are heroic in their own way, but both await an inevitable defeat, even Julio Stein, who knows that the moment will come when he will "send everything to the devil." He drinks excessively and is not well (we read of his spitting into his handkerchief and of Mami's concern about his health). Both Steins are brilliantly successful portraits, but, as far as their respective protégés go, it seems to me that Conrad's achievement with Jim is not matched by Onetti's depiction of

Brausen. Although Jim is always something of an enigma—Marlow calls him inscrutable at heart (351)—, Conrad makes him credible to the reader. He has in him too much of the beetle to be entirely the butterfly he imagines himself to be in essence. The reader, from the comfort of his armchair, can pinpoint his weaknesses and understand how these can coexist with great strengths. Brausen is another matter, and must be deemed a failure as a convincing character.

He proceeds from weakness to sadism and ends in virtual anonymity. The final paragraph of *La vida breve* reads like the end of many a film whose director has not had the ingenuity to imagine something better; Brausen walks off into the distance with his woman: "Puedo alejarme tranquilo; cruzo la plazoleta y usted camina a mi lado" ["I can go away with no problems; I cross the little square and you are walking at my side"] (712). My own intuition tells me that Brausen is too closely modeled on Onetti himself, at a time when the latter was coming only to some tentative resolution of his problems of identity. It is no coincidence that it is precisely in *La vida breve* that the world of Santa María is born, in the head of Brausen-Onetti. This is why Brausen takes refuge in the world of his film script. Onetti has found himself as a writer and, moreover, he now knows that this is what he is, essentially; sociopolitical optimism is a thing of the past, associated with the inexperience and hubris of youth. As far as the Arce component in Onetti goes, this is sublimated in the cruelty of some of his writing (often directed at women) and manifests itself now and again in off-the-cuff remarks about life in general (and women) that evidence a considerable cynicism and misanthropy. One remembers his character Gálvez (in *El astillero*), who takes to his bed (as a prelude to suicide) in conjunction with Onetti's habits over the last few years of *his* life.

Conrad, on the other hand, has distanced himself from Jim and his Stein (who, of course, bears traces of Conrad's own feelings and psychology) in a way that Onetti has not managed to do with Brausen. In *La vida breve*, significantly, Brausen is the narrator; later on, in Onetti's first really successful novel—perhaps his *most* successful novel—*El astillero*, the main narrator is an anonymous member of the community of Santa María. Thus a distance is inserted between Onetti and the protagonist Larsen. Already by *Heart of Darkness*, published a mere four years after his first novel, *Almayer's Folly* (1895), Conrad has learnt how to distance himself in this way. In fact, in *Heart of Darkness* the anonymous narrator (one of "us") soon gives way to Marlow, who takes over for the rest of the book and provides yet another screen between author and protagonist. It is Marlow who will be the main narrator of *Lord Jim* (1900) and *Youth* (1902), which together with *Heart of Darkness* (1899) form a thematic triptych.

La vida breve, then, is not a work of Onetti's maturity, brilliant though it may be over most of its length. The fact is that Onetti does not know what to do with Brausen and has to burst the confines of a magnificent realist psychological novel to accommodate Brausen's final metamorphosis, in a way that is aesthetically unacceptable. In *Lord Jim*, Conrad operates at a level of much greater technicothematic prowess, which Onetti will only attain (at least in his novels) from *El astillero* onward. In these later works (and in some of the rather earlier short stories), what Onetti has learnt from Conrad (if it is from Conrad that he has learnt, directly or indirectly) may be more satisfactorily examined. There the technical and thematic affinities between these two writers are abundantly clear. But that must be the subject of another essay.

NOTES

1. Epigraph from pp. 200–201. This Penguin edition contains an excellent introduction and critical apparatus by Cedric Watts.

2. Cedric Watts, *A Preface to Conrad*, 129–30.

3. In *Lord Jim*, a case in point is the sudden suicide of Captain Brierly, successful and respected, who through an acute crisis of faith jumps overboard from the stern of his ship, weighted down with two belaying pins. Much of Onetti's work is concerned with the search for meaning in life after youth's ideals have turned out to be hollow. To take just one novel, perhaps his most successful, *El astillero* has the suicide of Gálvez, the "administrative manager" of the shipyard, who at first refuses to go to work and then, like Brierly, drowns himself (after betraying Larsen by revealing the false bond issued by Petrus). Other characters manage to survive by manufacturing a faith, e.g., Kunz with his stamp album and design for a drill or Díaz Grey with his alcohol, drugs, and religious music. In this novel, Larsen's death really commences when he loses faith in everything and "gives up the ghost."

4. Quoted by Cedric Watts in his introduction to *Lord Jim*, 28.

5. *The Autobiography of Bertrand Russell*, 216. Conrad has an even more frightening (and entirely Schopenhauerian) view of man's place in the universe. In a letter to Cunninghame Graham, he wrote: "There is a—let us say—a machine. It evolved itself (I am severely scientific) out of a chaos of scraps of iron and behold!—it knits. I am horrified at the horrible work and stand appalled. I feel it ought to embroider—but it goes on knitting. . . . And the most withering thought is that the infamous thing has made itself; made itself without thought, without conscience, without foresight, without eyes, without heart. It is a tragic accident—and it has happened. You can't interfere with it. The last drop of bitterness is in the suspicion that you can't even smash it. . . . It knits us in and it knits us out. It has knitted time, space, pain, death, corruption, despair, and all the illusions—and nothing matters. I'll admit however that to look at the remorseless process is sometimes amusing." Quoted in Cedric Watts, *A Preface to Conrad*, 68.

6. "Asedio colectivo a Onetti," in Jorge Ruffinelli, ed., *Onetti*, 33.

7. Cedric Watts, in his notes to *Lord Jim*, 359.

8. "Bertram and Bimi," in Rudyard Kipling, *Life's Handicap*, 236.

9. Breitmann also figures in another story in *Life's Handicap*, "Reingelder and the German Flag," which takes place in a steamship sailing to Singapore. He drinks beer before breakfast, and when another passenger warns him, "You will die if you drink beer before breakfast. . . . Beer is the worst thing in the world for—," he replies, "Ya, I know—der liver. I haf no liver, und I shall not die" (241).

10. See Jocelyn Baines, *Joseph Conrad: A Critical Biography*, 180.

11. Despite having his son Borys baptized a Roman Catholic and sending him to a Roman Catholic preparatory school, Conrad was a thoroughgoing skeptic with regard to religion. To his fellow skeptic Edward Garnett he wrote: "Christianity . . . is distasteful to me. I am not blind to its services but the absurd oriental fable from which it starts irritates me." Quoted from Cedric Watts, *A Preface to Conrad*, 52.

12. See especially Tony Tanner, *Lord Jim*.

WORKS CITED

Baines, Jocelyn. *Joseph Conrad: A Critical Biography*. Harmondsworth, U.K.: Penguin, 1986.

Conrad, Joseph. *Lord Jim*. Harmondsworth, U.K.: Penguin, 1989.

Gilio, María Esther, and Carlos M. Domínguez. *Construcción de la noche. La vida de Juan Carlos Onetti*. Buenos Aires: Planeta, 1993.

Kipling, Rudyard. *Life's Handicap*. Harmondsworth, U.K.: Penguin, 1987.

Ruffinelli, Jorge, ed. *Onetti*. Montevideo: Biblioteca de Marcha, 1973.

Russell, Bertrand. *The Autobiography of Bertrand Russell*. London: Unwin, 1975.

Tanner, Tony. *Lord Jim*. London: Edward Arnold, 1963.

Watts, Cedric. *A Preface to Conrad*. London: Longman, 1982.

11

"I have seen all the things that are done under the sun; all of them are meangingless, a chasing after the wind": Onetti and Ecclesiastes

Sabine Giersberg

When asked to describe the curious atmosphere of his novel *El astillero* [*The Shipyard*], Onetti replied: "Es como un día de lluvia en que me traen un abrigo empapado, para ponérmelo" ["It's like being given a soaking overcoat to wear on a rainy day"].[1] This response, which may at first appear to be nothing more than the *boutade* of a reclusive author who scorned the literati, nonetheless evokes in a most potent manner the chilling sensation experienced by the reader on first entering Onetti's world. It is a nihilist world, often described as defeatist, in which an irredeemable pessimism reigns. Eladio Linacero, the protagonist of *El pozo* [*The Pit*], summarizes a recurrent perspective in the works of Onetti when he observes laconically: "Todo es inútil y hay que tener por lo menos el valor de no usar pretextos" ["Everything is futile and one must at least have the courage to avoid making excuses"] (OC 76).

Perhaps Junta Larsen is the best representative of such an attitude. This character makes his first appearance, as a minor figure, in *Tierra de nadie* [*No Man's Land*]. Later, as a protagonist in *Juntacadáveres* [*Body Snatcher*] and *El astillero*, Larsen displays his idiosyncratic nature by immersing himself in two absurd ventures, the establishment of a brothel and the management of a derelict shipyard, to then reappear as a ghost in *Dejemos hablar al viento* [*Let the Wind Speak*]. In *Juntacadáveres*, he is thus described: "Estaba viejo, incrédulo, sentimental; fundar el prostíbulo era ahora, esencialmente, como casarse *in articulo mortis*, como creer en fantasmas, como actuar para Dios" ["He was old, skeptical and sentimental; to establish the brothel now was like getting married *in articulo mortis*, like believing in ghosts, like acting for God"] (831). This portrayal of Larsen clearly evinces the belief that all human activity lacks significance. In other words, activity is meaningless, displaying neither *telos* nor *pathos*. In Larsen's description there is an allusion to God, but how can we visualize Him? Is He dead, absent, existing only in superstition, or simply dozing?[2] The text leaves this question unanswered.

The reader of Onetti embarks upon a profound existential voyage to the very essence of being, a quest that reveals the cruel reality of "el fracaso esencial de todo vínculo" ["the fundamental breakdown of every bond"].[3] It seems that there is something that always evades the reader, as if the author makes us experience in the flesh the "sentido de naufragio" ["sense of total failure"] that Junta Larsen in *Juntacadáveres* "veía cumplirse independiente de cualquier circunstancia imaginable" ["saw being realized independent of any imaginable circumstance"], that "condenación biológica al desengaño" ["biological condemnation to disillusionment"] (923).

A continual subversion of values is a feature of Onetti's texts. There is a strong trait to invert Christian myths—let us recall, for example, the almost omnipresent figure of the Virgin—and whilst the poetic act is exalted, the myth of the romantic genius is simultaneously overturned. The collapse of value systems is total, leading not to a new Nietzschean fervor, but to the feeling of total isolation that seems to characterize human existence.[4] Onetti's radical skepticism extends to the communicative function of language, with the result that the postulated absence of meaning is present at the level of both content and form. The intrinsic mechanisms of fiction come to be questioned as a way of constructing meaning. Onetti's works offer strong resistance to the hermeneutic processes applied to them by critics striving to expose layers of underlying meaning.[5]

With reference to his somber vision of the world, Onetti recalled on various occasions the profound impression left by his reading of Ecclesiastes, whose "Utterly meaningless! Everything is meaningless" (1.2) has found a particular place in the Western cultural canon. The fact that this encounter with Ecclesiastes was far from a passing footnote to Onetti's life is demonstrated by his repeated references to the theme. On one occasion, he revealed that his beliefs were still the same as those he had held during his youth, issuing the following challenge to the Uruguayan critic Jorge Ruffinelli: "Ahora, si usted puede rebatir el Eclesiastés, yo lo oiría con mucho gusto" ["Now, if you can refute Ecclesiastes, I would listen with much pleasure"].[6]

Ecclesiastes, or The Preacher, occupies a special place in the Old Testament. On account of its density and enigmatic character, features accentuated rather than diminished by the evolution of the text, it continues to pose a challenge to modern exegetists. Without doubt, there are affinities between Ecclesiastes and Onetti's fiction, but such similarities have not inspired critics to ponder deeply. Bearing in mind Borges' dictum that every author to some degree creates his precursors, it is my intention to re-examine the existential question and its aesthetic transposition to Onetti through the multiple and complex links with Ecclesiastes, an historically remote text (it dates from around the third century B.C.), but one with which Onetti had a relation of "symphilosophie."[7]

The name "Ecclesiastes" evokes a specific social function; *ekklesiastes* in Greek or *Qohelet* in Hebrew, translates as "one who speaks to the assembly." The text is dominated by the voice of an anonymous king, later identified as Solomon. This is a potent rhetorical device that endows the voice with the authority to express a subjective, individual experience, while losing none of its collective relevance.

This voice attempts to weigh up the meaning of human life, questioning traditional values such as social position and received wisdom, along with certain religious practices, all of which tend to veil the ever-present threat of death. The central role in this process of interrogation is occupied by the Hebrew word *hebel*, which appears some thirty-eight times in the text and thus becomes a leitmotif. This word is difficult to translate on account of its polysemic character, but is probably of onomatopoeic origin; its sound suggests some sort of air current, giving rise to meanings such as "breath," "transitoriness," "nothingness," "lack of substance," "vanity," and so on.[8]

It is important to highlight that the discourse of Ecclesiastes is non-conceptual, a characteristic it shares with Onetti's work. The ideas of the biblical text are developed around popular sayings, proverbs, and Eastern beliefs, weaving a dense web of frequently hermetic symbols. The complex semantic nature and emotional charge of the word *hebel* attribute it with great evocative power, impeding simple definition. Its repetition in the form of a leitmotif endows the text with a particular tone and intensity, as well as producing a purposefully circular movement in the sequence of ideas. At the center of Ecclesiastes lies individual human experience; the word *hebel*, in all its assorted meanings, corresponds exclusively to the human dimension, not that of the universe. The latter is characterized by the eternal return, the perpetual cyclical motion of the elements (sun, wind, water), while man's destiny is determined by the corrosive effect of time.

Man is incapable of escaping his inevitable death, so all attempts to attain transcendence are doomed to failure. Death is the final, definitive point; not even the apparent domination of the world through knowledge, nor the possibility of constituting a public identity—especially as social relations are continually undermined by corruption—can stand in the way of eventual destruction, as revealed in all its raw reality by Ecclesiastes.

Although the foundation stone of Ecclesiastes continues to be the belief in a single God—in this respect, the text is deeply influenced by Hebrew tradition—its perspective is shot through with a radical skepticism, allowing no room for comfort.[9] There is no "memory": "There is no remembrance of men of old, / and even those who are yet to come / will not be remembered by those who follow" (Eccles. 1.11). Neither will there be any recompense in the afterlife: "Who knows if the spirit of man rises upward and if the spirit of the animal goes down into the earth?" (3.21).

But while Ecclesiastes still posits the question of human happiness, Onetti postulates the certainty of failure, from which he develops his own existential philosophy. This is not based upon concepts, but rather emerges from a distinctive fusion of the existential and the aesthetic. As we will see presently, the idea of *carpe diem*—central in the thought of Ecclesiastes (see, for example, 9.1–10 and 11.7–10)—is limited for Onetti to the Dionysiac experience of the poetic act.

The fact that man exists within time and is exposed to the vagaries of fate has given rise to many reflections in both philosophy and literature. It evokes, for instance, the idea of *Sein zum Tode* (the Being-toward-death), the central axis of Martin Heidegger's thought, which removes from death any metaphysical dimension (the term *metaphysical* is employed here in the sense of "existing outside time").

In the writings of Onetti, death is almost omnipresent and indicates a reflection upon the nature of time. Already in the title of one of his first works, *Tiempo de abrazar* ["Time to Embrace"], there is an echo of the eloquent verses on time from Ecclesiastes: "There is a time for everything, and a season for every activity under heaven" (3.1–15). However, the overstatement of reflections upon time in much modern literature is sharply parodied in *La muerte y la niña* ["Death and the Girl"]: "Que el tiempo no existe por sí mismo es demostrable; es hijo del movimiento y si éste dejara de moverse no tendríamos ni desgaste ni principios ni finales. En literatura tiempo se escribe siempre con mayúscula" ["The fact that time in itself does not exist is demonstrable; it is the child of movement, and should the latter cease, we would have neither erosion, nor beginnings, nor ends. In literature, time is always written with a capital T"] (CC 369). Here Onetti indulges in one of his favorite games, that of picking up a common idea, at the same time as alluding to his own keenness to escape temporality through the poetic act, a theme encapsulated in one of the most expressive images he ever created, from *El pozo*: "clavar la noche en el papel como a una gran mariposa nocturna" ["to pin the night onto a sheet of paper, like a great nocturnal butterfly"] (OC 76).

A preoccupation with time in its existential and narrative dimensions is reflected in Onetti's fiction by the figures of the line and the circle. His continual effort to break from the linearity of narration, by means of multiple versions and recurrent characters in a shut-off world, is crystallized in Santa María. Aesthetic regulations, which are superimposed upon the narrative itself, mold the perception of form, shaping the plot and characters to reveal a tendency toward depersonalization. Naturally, this has certain consequences for the production of mimesis within the text. Several instances of this will be observed presently.

The enigmatic short story "La casa en la arena" [*The House on the Sand*], which has often been overlooked by critics, is highly enlightening in this respect. At the center of the story is Díaz Grey's recollection of his meeting with Molly in the eponymous house. This memory is dispersed throughout different versions, a technique that radically subverts any endeavor to relate the events themselves. The awareness that every insertion in the temporal sequence represents a movement toward the point of closure leads to attempts to suspend this progression or to absorb it into the cycle of repetition. The "preferred ending," that is to say, the inferno that consumes everything, suggesting the fire of the Apocalypse, takes us back again to the beginning. In some measure, this anticipates the ending of *Dejemos hablar al viento*. A sort of suspended time is reflected through the fiction-within-a-fiction of "La casa en la arena":

> Here is that sleeping place,
> Long resting place
> No stretching place,
> That never-get-up-no-more
> Place
> Is here. (1245)

A point of neutrality is evoked, where beginning and end come together ("here is—is here"). This verse has virtually no meaning, but a certain magical resonance is produced, heightened by the employment of a foreign language, a tool which Onetti also uses in "Esbjerg, en la costa" [*Esbjerg by the Sea*].

This tendency to suspend all progressive movement is also present on the level of action. Given the certainty of failure, the principal aim of human activity is not to reach happiness, but to avoid falling into the web of misfortune. The following paragraph from *El astillero*, in which Larsen reflects upon mischance, is illustrative in this respect:

> —Esta es la desgracia—pensó—, no la mala suerte que llega, insiste, infiel y se va, sino la desgracia, vieja, fría, verdosa. No es que venga y se quede, es una cosa distinta, nada tiene que ver con los sucesos, aunque los use para mostrarse. . . . Lo único que queda para hacer es precisamente eso: cualquier cosa, hacer una cosa detrás de otra, *sin interés, sin sentido*, como si otro . . . le pagara a uno para hacerlas y uno se limitara a cumplir en la mejor forma posible, *despreocupado del resultado final* de lo que hace. . . . Siempre fue así; es mejor que tocar madera o hacerse bendecir; cuando la desgracia se entera de que es inútil, empieza a secarse, *se desprende y cae*. (1096–97, my italics)

> ["'This is misfortune,' he thought, 'not bad luck that arrives, persists, is unfaithful, and then departs, but true misfortune, old, cold, and of a greenish blue. It's not that it comes to stay, it's something different, it has nothing to do with events, although it exploits them to reveal itself. . . . The only thing left to do is precisely this: anything, do one thing under the cover of another, *without interest, without feeling*, as if some other person . . . were paying you to do so and you were merely complying in the best fashion possible, *disinterested in the final result* of what is being done. It was always like this; it is better than touching wood or having yourself blessed; when misfortune realizes that it is useless, it begins to shrivel, *to come loose, to fall*.'"]

The inversion of perspective stands out, as does the play on words: the expression "to fall into misfortune" is reflected in the "fall" of misfortune itself. The image of a kind of trap is also found in Ecclesiastes: "Moreover, no man knows when his hour will come: / As fish are caught in a cruel net, / or birds are taken in a snare, / so men are trapped by evil times / that fall unexpectedly upon them" (9.12).

Misfortune, in itself abstract, though usually enacted through human experience, is personified, while a depersonalization of the subject is sought. Misfortune is portrayed as a parasite which feeds on every hope of man, ensuring that his endeavors are useless, given that, as is said in *El astillero*, "un *ciego movimiento perpetuo* puede fatigar a la desgracia" ["a *blind incessant movement* can wear down misfortune"] (1106, my italics). Linearity dissolves in perpetual motion, which is represented as being blind, that is to say, with neither end nor *telos*. Moreover, if we bear in mind that eyes and light are linked to man's cognitive capacity, we now engage a central topic in Onetti's work: his radical skepticism regarding such faculties. Reading Onetti always means exposing oneself to a continuous assault upon reason, an attack to which the literary critic is not immune.

For the moment, I wish to return to the issue of depersonalization, a profound influence upon Onetti's aesthetic perspective. If characters cease to be the masters of their own actions, if action itself lacks external *telos*, then the concept of a narrative centered upon a series of actions is broken down. "Como si fuera cierto que todo acto humano nace antes de ser cometido, preexiste a su encuentro con un ejecutor *variable*" ["As if it were true that every human act is born before its execution, that I already exists prior to its encounter with a *variable* agent"] states Larsen in *El astillero*, playing with virtuality, referring to his situation as a created being within a universe "imagined" by a creator-deity (1172, my italics).

Similarly, in *Juntacadáveres* the definition of the subject through the Cartesian formula "Cogito, ergo sum" is subverted:

descubriendo que los pensamientos no nacen de nosotros, que están ahí, en cualquier parte fuera de nuestras cabezas, libres y duros, y que se introducen en nosotros para ser pensados y nos abandonan cuando tienen bastante, *caprichosos* e *invariados*. (928, my italics)

[discovering that we do not give birth to thoughts, that they are all around, outside our heads, free and hard, and that they introduce themselves into us in order to be thought, and abandon us when they have had enough, *capricious* and *unchanging*.]

Reduced to "un ejecutor variable" ["a variable agent"] of deeds, to a consciousness converted into a mere stopping-off point for preexistent thoughts, described as "invariados" ["unchanging"], the subject anticipates his own death. This idea of the repetition of unchanging thoughts, which can also be observed in Borges, figures in Ecclesiastes, echoing the belief in temporal circularity prevalent in ancient times: "What has been will be again, / what has been done will be done again; / there is nothing new under the sun" (1.9).

In the case of Díaz Grey, a privileged character in Onetti's fiction, whose function varies according to the contextual interaction of character, reflective consciousness and narrative moment, the presentation of memory is revealing, given that it is described as impersonal. In "La casa en la arena," where memory is explored on a personal level, the central recollection dissolves in multiple variations: "Su vida, él mismo, no era ya más que aquel recuerdo, el único digno de evocación y de correcciones, de que fuera falsificado, una y otra vez, su sentido" ["His life, he himself, were no longer any more than that memory, the only one worthy of evocation and of revision, from which his meaning was falsified, time and time again"] (1237). There is no essence, only variations, mediations. Given his unknown past and solitude, there is no system of relations with fixed coordinates to underwrite the identity of Díaz Grey as a person. Transferred to the level of consciousness in its function as mediating moment, the implications of depersonalization for the aesthetic experience are revealed: "Desde hacía muchos años su memoria era *impersonal*; evocaba seres y circunstancias, *significados transparentes para su intuición*, antiguos errores y premoniciones, con el puro *placer* de *entregarse a sueños* elegidos por *absurdos*" ["For many years his memory had been *impersonal*; it evoked beings and circumstances, *transparent messages for his intuition*, old errors and premonitions, with the pure *pleasure* of *handing oneself over to dreams* chosen for their *absurdity*"] (*Juntacadáveres*, 796, my italics).

As soon as order and discourse lose their leading role, *logos* is displaced in favor of an experience based mainly upon intuition and pleasure. The existential voyage, therefore, does not begin from the concept of Being as the agent of intentional deeds, but rather turns inward toward *las intensidades de existencia* [the intensities of existence][10] until reaching "el ciego movimiento perpetuo" ["the blind incessant movement"] within the psyche. As Díaz Grey suggests in *Juntacadáveres*, this process is "packaged" in particular forms:

> No es una persona; es, como todos los habitantes de esta franja del río, una determinada intensidad de existencia que ocupa, se envasa en la forma de su particular manía, su particular idiotez. (792)

> [He is not a person; he is, like all the inhabitants of this strip of the river, a certain intensity of existence wrapped in the form of his particular mania, or which occupies his particular idiocy.]

This desire to transcend purely rational connections, to attain a type of ecstasy, that is to say a Dionysiac experience, is a constant in Onetti's fiction, as is revealed by the following paragraph from *La vida breve*:

> Es fácil; moverme mirando y oliendo, tocando y murmurando, egoísta hasta la pureza, ayudándome, obligándome *a ser*, sin idiotas propósitos de comunión; tocar y ver en este cíclico, disponible principio del mundo hasta *sentirme una, ésta, incomprensible y no significante manifestación de la vida*, capricho engendrado por un capricho, tímido inventor de un Brausen, manipulador de la inmortalidad cuando el impuesto ejercido del amor, cuando la circunstancia personal de la pasión. *Saberme a mí mismo una vez definitiva y olvidarme de inmediato*. (562–63, my italics)

> [It's easy; to move, watching and smelling, touching and murmuring, egotistical in the extreme, helping myself, obliging myself *to be*, without idiotic intentions of communion; to touch and see in this available, cyclical beginning of the world until *feeling myself one, this, incomprehensible and insignificant manifestation of life*, a whim engendered by a whim, timid inventor of a certain Brausen, manipulator of immor-

tality when the imposed act of love and the personal circumstance of passion took place. *To know myself definitively for once and to forget myself immediately.*]

The problem of Being is posed from a clearly existential angle; the possibility of its comprehension by means of the intellect is totally ruled out. Instead, a transgressive experience is sought, one which might somehow resolve the enigma. Lying at the center is feeling. At this point, we should note Onetti's insistence on the value of feelings, as opposed to that of events. Let us recall two frequently cited passages (from *El pozo* and "Matías el telegrafista" [Matias the Telegraphist] respectively) which are particularly relevant in this aspect:

> Porque los hechos son siempre vacíos, son *recipientes* que tomarán la *forma del sentimiento* que los llene. (64, my italics)
>
> [Because deeds are always empty, they are *receptacles* that take the *form of the feeling* that fills them.]
>
> Para mí . . . los hechos desnudos no significan nada. Lo que importa es lo que *contienen* o lo que *cargan*. (CC 343, my italics)
>
> [For me . . . bare deeds mean nothing. The important thing is what *they contain* or what *they carry with them*.]

In many of his works, Onetti repeats the idea of the deed as something meaningless, something that exists only on the level of form. This produces a subversion of mimesis, a fact that has certain consequences for the reception of his texts. We are no longer speaking of simple realism, a possibility that we have already discounted, nor of an allegory of a certain human condition, but instead of an aesthetic concept based upon the abstraction of the categories of character and action. These are forms whose value lies not in the construction of a narrative plot with a determinate meaning, but in creating aesthetic orders, peddlers of *intensidades*.

With this we return to our initial supposition. The insubstantiality of the Being, always threatened by awareness of death and by the consequent unease, as set out in the poetical-philosophical text of Ecclesiastes, forms the basis of the aesthetic experience itself. Onetti obliges his readers to move in a universe of floating meaning. Even intertextual allusions (in both the literary and biblical cases) fail to offer us a coherent vision. On the contrary, the gestalt, that is the whole picture, is never revealed; any attempt to imagine it would be simply "meaningless, a chasing after the wind." The aesthetic effect is based precisely upon our inability to plumb the depths, upon the feeling of complete isolation. That said, the continual suspension of meaning is not the end in itself; rather, the aim is absolute displacement, including that of *logos*, which permits access to the total Being.

At this point, we will turn back to Heidegger, since he insists in *Being and Time* that "Understanding always has its mood" (182), that is to say, comprehension depends upon the state of mind in which one may be found (*Befindlichkeit*).[11] For Heidegger, the radical experience of nothingness, which permits no relief from the awareness of death, is angst. It is by dint of isolation that the *Dasein* (the Being-there) comes to understand itself from within. In Onetti, where death is present on all sides, the transgressive experience is based on another, equally isolating, way of finding oneself: upon the sadness which comes to be as much an existential as an aesthetic category.[12] So that this assertion does not appear abstract, I cite the following illustrative paragraph from *Dejemos hablar al viento*:

> Miré mi *tristeza*, todavía saludable y amiga. Los primeros toques de la tristeza, el fracaso nuevo y la distinta soledad me habían llegado . . . *con un ruido de polilla, de fogata en la llovizna, de cachorro arañando una puerta*. . . . *Ningún rastro: el polvillo invisible*. (119–20, my italics)

> [I observed my *sadness*, still wholesome and friendly. The first touches of sadness, the new failure and a different sort of solitude had reached me . . . *with the noise of a moth, of a bonfire in the drizzle of a puppy scratching a door*. . . . *Without trace: a fine, invisible dust*.]

In the background of the gradual decay which invisibly threatens every Being, lies sadness with its gloomy atmosphere of rain and weeping. The reference to the silent labor of the moth evokes a verse from the Psalms, closely related to the ideas of Ecclesiastes: "You rebuke and discipline men for their sin; / you consume their wealth like a moth— / each man is but a breath" (Psalm 39.11). A similar image also occurs in Job: "So man wastes away like something rotten, / like a garment eaten by moths" (13.28).

From the preceding argument, one can begin to comprehend the distinctive interaction of Onetti's fiction with the existential question originally posed with unrivaled clarity in Ecclesiastes. Previous attempts to link Onetti to existentialist thought, such as the aforementioned study by Frankenthaler, have led only to conclusions of the following order: "La resignación, la pasividad, y la falta de acción describen una postura que equivale a un suicidio existencial" ["Resignation, passivity, and lack of action denote a stance equivalent to existential suicide"] (Frankenthaler, 127).

If, however, we lay aside the notion that inertia militates against the attainment of understanding, a less negative interpretation of Onetti's enterprise becomes possible. Instead of engaging in a systematic analysis, Onetti proposes action in the form of introspection, suggesting that the nature of being can be captured through its *intensidades* rather than by means of purposeful speculation, a position more in keeping with the experiential philosophy of Ecclesiastes than with Heidegger's conceptual existentialism. Obviously, such a stance affects communication with the readership, who come to share the sense of isolation that is encapsulated within his aesthetic. To summarize, it is precisely through desisting from a conscious effort to determine the essence of being that its comprehension can be achieved. This elusive understanding is facilitated by poetic language, entailing, of course, a transcendence of the mundane level of communication.

To some degree, the metaphor of wind can express the idea that perception comes to the introspective individual (an example is Pound's epigraph, the source for the title of Onetti's 1979 novel: "Do not move / Let the wind speak / That is paradise"). Perhaps we should note that even the name Brausen bears some relation to this argument, as the German verb "brausen" means to roar, and is employed as much to describe passions in the realm of the psyche as to capture the intensity of the wind.

Translated by Iain A. D. Stewart

NOTES

Quote in chapter title from Ecclesiastes 1.14, in *The Holy Bible*.

1. Luis Harss, "Onetti o las sombras en la pared," 243.
2. Onetti parodies the creative dream in *Dejemos hablar al viento*: "Brausen. Se estiró como para dormir la siesta y estuvo inventando Santa María y todas las historias" ["Brausen. He stretched as if to take his siesta and he was inventing Santa María and all its stories"] (*Dejemos hablar al viento*, 142).
3. Mario Benedetti, "Juan Carlos Onetti y la aventura del hombre," 52.
4. Marilyn Frankenthaler has studied the works of Onetti from the perspective of existentialist philosophy, reaching the following conclusion: "Ni la ética, ni la religión, ni la verdad existen como valores superiores en cuyo seno el hombre pudiera descansar seguro, encontrar alguna estabilidad. Esa actitud inicial de coincidencia entre Onetti y algunos existencialistas consistirá en una diferencia primordial pues el hombre onettiano no crea sus propios valores. La muerte no es el último acto absurdo ni el encuentro con la esencia. Lo mismo podría decirse respecto a la relación con otro ser humano donde la comunicación para Onetti es siempre una negación extrema" ["Neither ethics, nor religion, nor truth exist as higher values in whose bosom man can rest securely or find some stability. The initial coincidence of outlook between Onetti and some existentialists actually involves a fundamental difference, for the Onettian man does not create his own values. Death is not the final absurd act nor the discov-

ery of essence. The same could be said with regard to relationships with other human beings, where communication is, for Onetti, always an extreme form of negation"] (158).

5. This aspect is expanded in the perceptive studies of Josefina Ludmer and Mark Millington. See also D. L. Shaw, "Which Was the First Novel of the Boom?" and his essay for this volume, where he underlines Onetti's contribution to a fresh concept of mimesis and its importance for the Latin American new novel.

6. Jorge Ruffinelli, "Asedio colectivo a Onetti," in Ruffinelli, ed., *Onetti*, 33.

7. "Symphilosophie" is the term employed by German Romantic authors to refer to spiritual affinities of thought.

8. In "The Meaning of *Hebel* for Quohelet," Michael Fox provides an array of possible meanings, such as "vapor," "futile," "empty," "nothing," "ridiculous," "incongruous," "transitory," "illusory," "insignificant," "vain," "incomprehensible," noting, however, that "we cannot say that the meaning of *hebel* is a bundle of all the qualities denoted by these renderings. *Hebel* does not include all of these senses in each application" (411). Fox submits all the options to a critical examination and proposes "absurd" as a possible translation, establishing a direct link with the thought of Camus. However suggestive Fox's proposal might be—the resemblance between Ecclesiastes and Camus is irrefutable—the validity of restricting a multifaceted image to a single, fixed concept may be questioned, especially as it could undermine the non-conceptual character of the discourse of Ecclesiastes.

9. We should note that the production of the biblical text took place in an era during which Hellenism was steadily infiltrating traditional Hebrew thought, provoking a crisis of values.

10. Onetti himself used this phrase. See Harss, *Los nuestros*, 223.

11. We should note that the mood "comes neither from 'outside' nor from 'inside,' but arises out of Being-in-the-world, as a way of such Being" (Heidegger, 176).

12. Heidegger himself noted: "In 'poetical' discourse, the communication of the existential possibilities of one's state-of-mind can become an aim in itself, and this amounts to a disclosing of existence" (Heidegger, 205).

WORKS CITED

Benedetti, Mario. "Juan Carlos Onetti y la aventura del hombre." *Juan Carlos Onetti*. Ed. Hugo Verani. Madrid: Taurus, 1987. 52–74.

Bible, The Holy. New International Version. London: Hodder and Stoughton, 1982.

Fox, Michael. "The Meaning of *Hebel* for Quohelet." *Journal of Biblical Literature* 105.3 (1986): 409–27.

Frankenthaler, Marilyn. *Juan Carlos Onetti: La salvación por la forma*. New York: Ediciones Abra, 1977.

Harss, Luis. "Onetti o las sombras en la pared." *Los nuestros* (Buenos Aires: Sudamericana, 1971): 214–51.

Heidegger, Martin. *Being and Time*. Trans. John Macquarrie and Edward Robinson. Oxford: Blackwell, 1962.

Ludmer, Josefina. *Onetti: Los procesos de construcción del relato*. Buenos Aires: Sudamericana, 1977.

Millington, Mark. *An Analysis of the Short Stories of J. C. Onetti: Fictions of Desire*. Lewiston, N.Y.: Edwin Mellen Press, 1993.

Onetti, Juan Carlos. *Dejemos hablar al viento*. Barcelona: Bruguera, 1985.

Ruffinelli, Jorge, ed. *Onetti*. Montevideo: Biblioteca de Marcha, 1973.

Shaw, Donald L. "Which Was the First Novel of the Boom?" *Modern Language Review* 89 (1994): 360–71.

12

Translating Juan Carlos Onetti for Anglo-Saxon Others

Peter Bush

Anglo-Saxon culture continues to think of itself as dominant and to wield power over the many layers of educational and publishing practice as the decisive arbiter in questions of language and consciousness. You can speak, write, think as you like. Your speech can be as individual and complex as the whorls making up your fingerprints. But tone, rhythm, allusions, personal mythologies, the fascinating personal worlds we all think we inhabit count for very little in the marketplace of good taste where the subjective and the awkward, the radical and the foreign are silenced by the pulsating, finely tuned antennae of our well-bred and in-bred normalizers. Ask any literary translator or publisher trying to break through the blandness of the acceptable vanguard, of the standard talk that fucks us up! How much academic writing is equally an apprentice-ship in the death of thought, a straitjacketing of the personal for the pleasures of inquisitional assessment exercises and vapid quality con-trol? Articles to accompany the burial of an author under a welter of peer-group and career-focused restraints. We will make you invisible. We won't be unsettled from our watchtowers. Even Juan Carlos Onetti (Who he? they mutter) in death was sanctified by the British quality press in obituaries, generous column inches that were never devoted to reviews of his books when he was alive. Blessèd be the dead and diffi-cult foreign author we have never read in translation.

Take issue after issue of the book-reviewing press in the United Kingdom and with the odd exception, translation is usually invisible, only allowed visibility to be shot down. Just take the review section of a recent *Observer* (2 July 1995). Sorry if this seems circumstantial—it was conveniently at hand. U.K. literary translation culture is inevitably filtered through the press in a weekly trickle. I first encountered a page promotion for Susanna Tamaro's *Follow Your Heart*, based on an interview via an interpreter. We learn lots about the writer's ruffled hair, pretty smile, dog, and Kate Kellaway even branches out into comfortable Sunday-morning assertions like "Italy is a country of unpredictable tastes where popular does not necessarily mean lowbrow." However, no mention of the translator or the fact the words of the narrative are someone else's (Avril Bardoni's), apart from a typically snide aside putting down the translation of the title—"In Italian, this is an unfamiliar saying; in English, it translates with stale ease as *Follow Your Heart*."

Flick a page and Maureen Freely is reviewing Orhan Pamuk's *The Black Book*, again no credit to translator, Guneli Gun, no mention the novel was originally written in Turkish. It is in truth a rave review concluding that "it is up there with the best of Calvino, Borges and Márquez," it's "dizzyingly complex without ever losing its seductive power." No specific examples of the language of the mouth-watering invisible others. Eyes wander to the poem "Missing You" by Carole Satyamurti, nestling under Maureen Freely and, yes, another cliché about translation slips easily in at the end of verse two:

> Your box lies
> trestled at the altar
> and already you're mist
> missing in translation.

On to the short notices of paperbacks: García Márquez's *The General in His Labyrinth* and "its suitably oracular tone" has also been magicked into English by some unrecognized remote control, rather than by Edith Grossman. Turn another page and Kate Kellaway is back this time pronouncing her verdict on the first performance in English of Genet's *Splendide*. At last, Neil Bartlett the translator is named but only to be damned. "The play has been *justly* neglected. It's densely written to the point of atrophy." But then, "if only it had an ounce of the eloquence or life of Bartlett's defence of it in the programme. . . ." But isn't the dense and atrophied English also Bartlett's? What is a translator in this literary vision? A struggling dictionary? A poor sod hacking out prose on Grub Street, the hack image from George Orwell to Germaine Greer, not to mention Kingsley Amis's proud boast about never reading a work in translation? Kellaway prefers to be immured in a romantic theatrical experience in St. Pancras or to relax in the undemanding joys of a sexily berserk Tango on the Strand, no need to understand the words, wallow in the soul of Buenos Aires, dream of Evita and Che Guevara.

In fact, not that circumstantial. These examples fall within traditions that Suzanne Jill Levine and Lawrence Venuti have written about in their discussions of literary translation within the Anglo-Saxon tradition. On the one hand, language is praised for clarity, simplicity, readability. Any trace of the foreign must be removed, any upsetting of conventional literary mores eliminated. A good translation assimilates the original to the needs of a politely literate society. It is untroubling and domesticated. The translation and the translator must be truly invisible, slave to the master text and undemanding scribe and servant to the publisher. Fidelity to the original was and is a favorite line of praise exalting the faithful reproduction of literary conventionality, a safe reading of an uncouth original. Translators who use their translations to challenge cultural authority and to rupture the target language will deserve the ignominy of their bad reviews. And so went the reviews of the various translations of Homer and Catullus in the late eighteenth and early nineteenth century, and so Robert Graves excised the homosexual act from his translations of the *Lives* of Suetonius. When the voice of the features editor rings sternly at the end of the line, "sounds a bit way out for us," it echoes this tradition.

There have been translators who went out of their way to preserve the foreign in their translation, thinking that if the original was creating a new source language, then the translation must also renew the target language. Suzanne Jill Levine has described her translations of work by Guillermo Cabrera Infante, Manuel Puig, and Severo Sarduy in collaboration with the authors: recreations that can turn out thirty pages longer that the original text. Translation is original and not original, an act of writing as hybrid and impure as you can get. It is not surprising that the main feature in that same *Observer* review section was a jolly report on a literary festival in St. Malo run by a Sartrean 68er reconstructed into travel-writing, against "those arrogant avant-garde writers reviling storytellers like me, who called our view of life 'simplistic'" (2). His inspiration was an edition of *Granta* devoted to travel writing, and Grantability is, as we know, all about readability: sentences smooth if long, or dirty when short, nothing demanding to be read twice. *Etonnant Voyageurs* with "restlessness in our blood." Fascinated by the foreign under our controlling regard. Not that we translators should complain too loudly: some Sundays or dailies won't even review translations, let alone acknowledge the translator.

Well, I can say my interest in learning languages and reading foreign literatures came from a feeling of dislocation with English. When I entered the state school system at the age of five, I found that the public language known as English was not the language spoken at home in the rural working-class neighborhood where I was brought up in Lincolnshire. Like a great many people I was to be made to feel a stranger to what was my own way of expressing myself. Words and accent were improper, should be silenced along with—as I would soon discover in the Oxbridge scholarship-boy routine—the culture, the way of life from which they sprang. Suppress, don't translate was the ill-concealed message of dons refurbishing army contact with the lower orders through occasional conversations with college servants who cooked their breakfast, made their beds, polished their shoes. No way was Raymond Williams the norm.

Such dislocation led to my first published translations in the late '60s of political reports and analyses from the French, Spanish, and Portuguese. It was ten years later when living in a small town in Murcia that I began to read Juan Carlos Onetti and Juan Goytisolo in cheerful bars where veteran anarchists and communists were breaking their prolonged public silence in the wake of Franco's death. What attracted me to both was the strangeness and honesty, language that was abrupt, elliptical, or elongated and uncomfortable to live with. Fictions that are permeated with politics and history, ironical not triumphalist, nonlinear narrators in love with loose ends. Writers who are jarring and awkward; exiles glowering on the margins of literary society.

I think Juan Goytisolo has not read Onetti. Onetti read Goytisolo's articles in *El País*. They have completely different styles and approaches to writing: one rewriting little, the other drafting and redrafting. Yet for me they have coexisted. After translating the Spaniard's autobiography, *Forbidden Territory* and *Realms of Strife*, I suggested Onetti to the publishers Quartet and was delighted when editor-in-chief Stephen Pickles signed up six of his titles. When over the last two years I translated *No Man's Land* and *Quarantine* I moved constantly from one to the other: from a work written in the wake of the Hitler-Stalin pact to a text developed in the shadows from the Gulf War. I'm not talking about Onetti and Goytisolo but the subjectivity of the translator working on draft after draft where words, plots, ideas come together with day-to-day living, dying mothers, aging, adolescent and adult sexualities, Nintendo and John Major.

With the exception of *The Pit* and *Tonight*, I have worked on the translations with the Onetti household in Madrid. I followed the system of sending a near-to-final draft to Madrid. I would then receive back from Dolly Onetti a series of notes and suggestions that was the product of her working over the translations and consulting with the writer. I would then produce a draft to discuss with Dolly over a weekend in Madrid. Onetti would be in bed, and ready to join in as a last resort.

As a literary translator, I am glad to have collaboration with a writer. While recognizing a work is open to limitless readings, there's no harm in a response from the writer who has a right to his reading. Ignoring the author would seem an act of arrogance, a way of cutting yourself off from the life that has created the text, and all that accumulated knowledge and sensibility, or in the case of Onetti, from Dolly, who was, in every way, his life support system. I also spent time in Uruguay talking to old friends and lovers of Onetti, pacing the streets of Montevideo, reading Uruguayan history, buying dictionaries of *lunfardo* (River Plate Cockney), rereading all Onetti's work, rereading novels by Faulkner, Céline, and others that Onetti had read in translation or not. The sort of thing hick hacks get up to.

However, the proof of the pudding. . . . Let's look at a chapter from *No Man's Land* as a point of entry into one individual's practice of literary translation. First published in 1941, it is a highly disrupted, fragmentary narrative of people living on the edge of the abyss, Benjaminly resurrected we hope by the translation, not that it is even a text many Spanish readers are familiar with. (Translations are written for non-readers of the source language although traditionally many review editors hand translations over to reviewers with a specialist knowledge of that language who then review with their narrow peer group in mind. It's a sad fact that many foreign literature specialists in universities are still very wary of translations that threaten their hallowed enclosures.) Here are two extracts from chapter 35.

> She looked at herself in the grimy glass of the door. Her hair was the faded yellow of dry fields and old books. She again counted the small change in the palm of her hand. Bared a shoulder against the glass and smiled as she looked at her own profile. The children's voices had gone quiet in the yard downstairs. You couldn't just ditch yourself out of the window. The clothes hung on the still air between the dry plants in tins. She felt Sunday on the closed doors, on the becalmed light over the flagstones.
>
> She walked to her bed and stretched out. Imagined the scenes that had been reflected in the wardrobe mirror. Now here she was on a Sunday afternoon, a woman, rotten to the core.

> She fell on the bed, her eyes shut. She could see a big yellow deserted field. Nobody else would walk on the tinder-dry pastures, whether they be men or animals. There was a wooden hut in the middle of the field, right in the middle, against a blurry backdrop of mountains. Suddenly her head started sobbing. She lit a cigarette and started sipping her coffee, always alone in her wooden hut, surrounded by an unbridgeable loneliness. It was the silence of animals sleeping. Sometimes she listened to the sobbing head. It was a soothing lament, on a strange, repeated note, like a child rehearsing over and over again the pronunciation of a vowel in a foreign tongue.

A woman is working her way toward suicide. Unnamed, and without personal pronouns as is possible in Spanish. Onetti makes the reader struggle for connections, introduces a note of strangeness, a vague lack of control, emphasizes the aloneness, lack of persona, of solid identity. The previous chapter was elsewhere, other people. Yet his texts are highly physical, contain closely observed bodies, hats tilted backward over napes of necks, the everyday movement that is automatic, semiconscious, quickly forgotten. Onetti writes about bodily presence, sometimes a cinematic take, sometimes a spirit rapidly becoming alienated from its body, which is what predominates here. A translator has to make choices: not always to use the English pronoun "she," not to write "kill oneself" out of the window that would be the literal translation of *matarse por la ventana*, not to use the obvious "throw oneself," to transform the literal "rotten woman" (*una mujer podrida*) into a "woman, rotten to the core" highlighting the self-loathing. Waves of disgust in an atmosphere of stillness of a Sunday afternoon, unrelieved by glossy supplement, *tranquila* and *tranquilizó*—calm and calmed— reinforcing this calm before the storm by also translating *luz inmóvil* in the first paragraph as "becalmed light."

The anonymous protagonist of this episode goes into an hallucinating dream present in the detail of her hair, "the faded yellow of dry fields." The strangeness of self-loathing, estrangement from self, of being unable to touch her naked body in which two sentences stand out, a separation from her body, foreshadowing the suicide in which she is split in two, as if killing or being killed by her other self: *De pronto su cabeza empezó a llorar*—literally "Suddenly her head began to cry"; *A veces escuchaba el lloro de la cabeza*—literally "she sometimes listened to the crying of her head." A translator has to resist the weight of conventional English pressing down on the brain and reject such versions as "the tears began to stream down," or "she heard herself crying."

To translate of such prose is to confront not only the challenge of interpreting the original but of creating an English that in turn disturbs expected patterns on the page. It is a very subjective struggle in which the translator must allow every strand in her/his linguistic repertoire to play and avoid the influence of commonsense commonplaces of the sort "that sounds like English," "it should read as if it were originally written in English," even "that sounds like translatorese." And he must realize that it is a never-ending process—all that pressure, cajoling, persuading, indeed collaboration when the manuscript reaches the end of the line of copyeditor and house style and then final proofs are away to the printer. In writing about the process, one should be wary about excessive rationalism. Many psycholinguists now investigating translation are obsessed with what they call "Talk Aloud Protocols," with wiring up the translator in order to codify the process, and, at the other extreme, the more materialist approaches overdetermine the translator as a domesticator, ethnocentrically violent in the manipulation of the original. The act of translation is a very particular act of creative, imaginative reading and writing that can never be totally conscious. A translator's reading is not, for example, the reading of a literary critic or reviewer because translation is not description, analysis, taste-forming sound-bite, or whatever, but stands in the stead of the original for readers. Although translators' research will encompass many readings, the writing process will be as varied from one translator to another, as from one writer to another.

Finally, to examine part of the process of translating the first paragraphs of *Past Caring?* via the changes made to the first printout, the suggestions made by Dolly Onetti and the final version. This is only part of a whole work and the tone of the whole is as important as any detail. The first big step for me upon beginning the translation proper is the conclusion of the first draft. I always work at that very intensively and while I am continually changing and altering before the first printout, the first working through is dangerously decisive, the movement into the nooks and crannies while scaling the mountain-face. In prose narrative, you never have the whole on a single page as in much translation of poetry; you have to try to inscribe that length of narrative into the writing process.

My first reaction on reading the Spanish original, *Cuando ya no importe* was of familiarity, the presence of death and the filth of life, the irony and underlying tenderness, and of the distinctive voice of Onetti bidding real farewell to friends and enemies, fictional or nonfictional, a writer in his early eighties finishing on a high, sparring with Yeats on the sexuality of old age, Beckett's poetic bleakness or the disturbing matter-of-factness of Camus's Meursault on the way to his mother's funeral.

Spanish original:
Hace una quincena o un mes que mi mujer de ahora eligió vivir en otro país. No hubo reproches ni quejas. Ella es dueña de su estómago y de su vagina. Cómo no comprenderla si ambos compartimos, casi exclusivamente, el hambre. Nos consolábamos a veces con comidas a las que buenos amigos nos invitaban, chismes, discusiones sobre Sartre, el estructuralismo y esa broma que las derechas quieren universal, saben pagar bien a sus creyentes y la bautizan posmodernismo. Participábamos, reñíamos y adornábamos con nuestras risas las frases ingeniosas. (11)

First printout:
A fortnight or a month ago my present wife took the decision to live in another country. There were no reproaches or complaints. She is the

mistress of her stomach and vagina. I quite understand her position: hunger was in the end about all we shared. Sometimes we found consolation in meals close friends invited us to, when we gossiped, argued over Sartre, structuralism and the scam the right wishes were universal, whose faithful they reward so well and which they've baptized post-modernism. We joined in, defended our corner, laughed effusively at the witty exchanges.

Published translation:
A fortnight or a month ago my present wife decided to live in another country. There were no reproaches or complaints. She's mistress of her own stomach and vagina. I quite understand her: in the end hunger was about all we had in common. Sometimes we found consolation in meals close friends invited us to, when we gossiped, argued over Sartre, structuralism and the scam the right wishes was universal, whose faithful they reward so well and which they've baptized post-modernism. We joined in, defended our corner, laced the witty exchanges with our laughs.

Dolly Onetti's comments:
1. I quite understood her since we both shared hunger almost exclusively.
2. Sometimes we felt consoled when close friends invited us to meals, and we gossiped, discussed Sartre, structuralism and that joke the Right wish were universal.
3. We participated, quarreled and adorned with our laughter.

In the first sentence "took the decision" for *eligió*, literally "she chose." Such padding is frequent and needs to be kept well under control, hence "decided" rather than the literal "chose" because it sounds more decisive. "She's" rather than the more formal "She is" because this is a diary narrative and therefore more informal, and that shortening is an informal flexibility not on offer in Spanish. (Some editorial house-styles still oppose the use of this informality at least at the level of first knee-jerk response. Not, I should say, at Quartet where my editor Georgia de Chamberet has specialized in editing translations of fiction that is stylistically adventurous.) "Mistress" came to me immediately for *dueña* and the later addition of "own" seemed to bring out the strong irony and shock value of the sentence with the repeated *de su*. "Position": remove somewhat laughable padding. There is a choice to be made over tenses where Onetti moves from the preterit of *hubo* and *eligió* to the present of *es* only to end on the conversational infinitive *¿Cómo no comprenderla?*—literally "How not to understand her?" which could be present or past. The present seemed to make for the immediacy of the narrator writing his diary in the here and now. The reshaping of the sentence ends on a false note of togetherness since they only share the emptiness of hunger: the "in common" is an ironically emphatic conclusion to the first paragraph. Although in this case I have opted for a translation that is lengthier than the typically elliptical Onetti, I tried to capture what I read as a rather sad admission of defeat in the relationship after the previous more aggressive turn of phrase. In the next paragraph, "good friends" became "close ones" because "good friend" was needed in a later sentence for *muy amigo*. I chose "scam" rather than "joke" for *broma*. Onetti's word is plainer and the Spanish can imply the sense of a practical joke rather than just joke: "scam" is jauntier, and I wanted a word to carry the reader through the long sentence, a strong word in keeping with the context of the conversation.

Dolly Onetti commented on the translation after the author's death, but she had been very much involved in discussions of the original, and anecdotes flowed about almost every hyphen and comma, let alone particular textual reference. She is a fully bilingual Argentinean and, as can be seen from her three comments, tends to want to draw back the English to a more literal version. Here I've responded by restoring the idea of consolation for *Nos consolábamos*, and that particular emotional appeal rather than the less warm "refuge." However, I retained "laced" for *adornábamos* rather than the literal "adorned," wanting to add to the sense of a well-watered occasion!

Dolly's involvement in the translations has been invaluable on many other counts: for regular consultation with the ailing author, for giving me her version of a literal reading, for her detailed knowledge of Onettian mythology, and, most importantly, of River Plate usage of Spanish. The written notes are a pale reflection of her enthusiastic collaboration in conversation over a long weekend in Madrid. This involvement from the source culture complemented the editing by my non–Spanish reading editor at Quartet, who happily accepted these opening sentences though she too made an impact on the translation.

To conclude, literary translation is not a willful distortion or manipulation or, indeed, the hack activity of a writer *manqué*, but a recreation, a new writing in which the translator makes a unique reading, creating a chosen set of words that are published on the printed page and read as the original. That process is the result of complex forces working together across cultures, through individuals, conventions and institutions. It is an experience at the very least of the bilingualism and biculturalism that distinguishes the lives of so many in the proclaimed monolingualism, monoculturalism of Anglo-Saxon worlds that have never been anything of the sort. It is collaborative, not the straightforwardly solitary activity of the Romantic stereotype of writing, that comes at you with a pitying smile and condescending "I don't know how you stick at it." Translators work at the frontiers between cultures and, language being such a key element of identity and consciousness, at a crucial point for individual and society between communication and noncommunication. And who is to say that a reader of *Cuando ya no importe* in Montevideo wouldn't have the basis for a meaningful conversation with a reader of *Past Caring?* in Edinburgh? Unless you are a cultural solipsist. That is why translating should be central to teaching programs in languages and the humanities, and is being rescued from the mire of the unseen and prose and the bare functionalism of its communicative successor. Why the Anglo-Saxon literary establishment should take it more seriously, cease to be half-hearted or cursorily dismissive. Where would Shakespeare have been without translation? Where, without it, would British critical/cultural theorists, historians, journalists, philosophers, sociologists, or television documentary-makers be today? We translators enjoy licking up the sweat of the other exuding from every canonical pore of our dearly beloved national cultures. Enjoy stoking up the otherness. Positively wallow in it.

WORKS CITED

Goytisolo, Juan. *Forbidden Territory: The Memoirs of Juan Goytisolo 1931–1956* [*Coto vedado*]. Trans. Peter Bush. London: Quartet, 1989.

Goytisolo, Juan. *Realms of Strife: The Memoirs of Juan Goytisolo 1957–1982* [*En los reinos de taifa*]. Trans. Peter Bush. London: Quartet, 1990.

Goytisolo, Juan. *Quarantine* [*Cuarentena*]. Trans. Peter Bush. London: Quartet, 1994.

Levine, Suzanne Jill. *The Subversive Scribe.* Saint Paul, Minnesota: Graywolf Press, 1991.

Onetti, Juan Carlos. *The Pit* and *Tonight* [*El pozo* and *Para esta noche*]. Trans. Peter Bush. London: Quartet, 1991.

Onetti, Juan Carlos. *Cuando ya no importe.* Madrid: Alfaguara, 1993.

Onetti, Juan Carlos. *No Man's Land* [*Tierra de nadie*]. Trans. Peter Bush. London: Quartet, 1994.

Onetti, Juan Carlos. *Past Caring?* [*Cuando ya no importe*]. Trans. Peter Bush. London: Quartet, 1995.

Venuti, Lawrence. *The Translator's Invisibility.* London: Routledge, 1995.

INDEX